The Critical Thinking Companion

For Introductory Psychology
Second Edition

Jane Halonen
James Madison University

Cynthia Gray
Alverno College

WORTH PUBLISHERS

The Critical Thinking Companion for Introductory Psychology, Second Edition
Copyright © 2001, 1995 by Worth Publishers

All rights reserved. No part of this book may be reproduced by any mechanical, photographic, or electronic process, or in the form of a phonographic recording, nor may it be stored in a retrieval system, transmitted, or otherwise copied for publication or private use, except as described in the Preface, without written permission from the publisher.

Printed in the United States of America.

ISBN: 1-57259-882-4 (EAN: 9781572598829)

Third printing

Editor: Craig Donini
Senior Marketing Manager: Renee Altier
Associate Managing Editor: Tracey Kuehn
Production Manager: Sarah Segal
Art Director: Barbara Reingold
Composition: Progressive Information Technologies
Printing and Binding: R. R. Donnelley and Sons

Worth Publishers
41 Madison Avenue
New York, New York 10010
www.worthpublishers.com

Contents

Preface ix

Introducing Critical Thinking 1

CHAPTER 1
Thinking Critically with Psychological Science 6
Exercise 1.1   The Case for Interference, Pattern Recognition   7
Exercise 1.2   You Need an Operation, Practical Problem Solving   9
Exercise 1.3   The Limits of Nursery Rhyme Reasoning, Creative Problem Solving   11
Exercise 1.4   Designing Carefully Controlled Research, Scientific Problem Solving   12
Exercise 1.5   Consumer Safety, Psychological Reasoning   15
Exercise 1.6   Psychology's Perspectives, Perspective Taking   17

CHAPTER 2
Neuroscience and Behavior 20
Exercise 2.1   How Do You Do That? Pattern Recognition   20
Exercise 2.2   The Split-Brain Problem, Practical Problem Solving   21
Exercise 2.3   The New Superheroes, Creative Problem Solving   22
Exercise 2.4   The Addicted Brain, Scientific Problem Solving   24
Exercise 2.5   Phantom Pain, Psychological Reasoning   24
Exercise 2.6   Caring for Phineas, Perspective Taking   25

CHAPTER 3
The Nature and Nurture of Behavior 27
Exercise 3.1   Nature or Nurture? Pattern Recognition   27
Exercise 3.2   Keep on Truckin', Practical Problem Solving   28
Exercise 3.3   Character Building, Creative Problem Solving   29
Exercise 3.4   Seeing Double, Scientific Problem Solving   30
Exercise 3.5   Who's to Blame? Psychological Reasoning   31
Exercise 3.6   It's All in the Genes, Perspective Taking   32

CHAPTER 4
The Developing Person 33
Exercise 4.1   When Bad Children Aren't Bad, Pattern Recognition   33
Exercise 4.2   The Sitter's Dilemma, Practical Problem Solving   34
Exercise 4.3   Developmental Delights, Creative Problem Solving   35
Exercise 4.4   On Death and Dying, Scientific Problem Solving   36
Exercise 4.5   Understanding Teen Pregnancy, Psychological Reasoning   37
Exercise 4.6   Piaget Meets Santa Claus, Perspective Taking   38

CHAPTER 5
Sensation 40

Exercise 5.1	Crossing the Threshold, Pattern Recognition	40
Exercise 5.2	Occupational Design, Practical Problem Solving	41
Exercise 5.3	Reach Out and Touch Someone, Creative Problem Solving	43
Exercise 5.4	It's a Matter of Taste, Scientific Problem Solving	44
Exercise 5.5	Parts Is Parts, Psychological Reasoning	45
Exercise 5.6	The Eyes Have It, Perspective Taking	46

CHAPTER 6
Perception 48

Exercise 6.1	The Big Picture, Pattern Recognition	48
Exercise 6.2	Assessing the Assembly Line, Practical Problem Solving	49
Exercise 6.3	Chaos Control, Creative Problem Solving	50
Exercise 6.4	Cliff Hangers, Scientific Problem Solving	51
Exercise 6.5	The Case Against ESP, Psychological Reasoning	51
Exercise 6.6	Context Cues, Perspective Taking	53

CHAPTER 7
States of Consciousness 54

Exercise 7.1	Conscious Control, Pattern Recognition	54
Exercise 7.2	Professional Project Dare, Practical Problem Solving	55
Exercise 7.3	Rock-a-Bye Baby, Creative Problem Solving	55
Exercise 7.4	Remedies for Jet Lag, Scientific Problem Solving	56
Exercise 7.5	A Midsummer Night's Dream, Psychological Reasoning	57
Exercise 7.6	The Light at the End of the Tunnel, Perspective Taking	57

CHAPTER 8
Learning 59

Exercise 8.1	The Classical Connection, Pattern Recognition	59
Exercise 8.2	Powerful Consequences, Practical Problem Solving	61
Exercise 8.3	Reinforcing Rhymes, Creative Problem Solving	64
Exercise 8.4	A Working Hypothesis, Scientific Problem Solving	64
Exercise 8.5	Little Albert Revisited, Psychological Reasoning	65
Exercise 8.6	The Discriminating Dachshund, Perspective Taking	66

CHAPTER 9
Memory 67

Exercise 9.1	The Magnificent Seven, Pattern Recognition	67
Exercise 9.2	Thanks for the Memory, Practical Problem Solving	68
Exercise 9.3	Story Time, Creative Problem Solving	70
Exercise 9.4	Creating Context, Scientific Problem Solving	71
Exercise 9.5	Roseanne's Dilemma, Psychological Reasoning	71
Exercise 9.6	Making Memories, Perspective Taking	72

CHAPTER 10
Thinking and Language 74

Exercise 10.1	There's Good News and There's Bad News, Pattern Recognition	74
Exercise 10.2	If We Could Talk to the Animals, Perspective Taking	75
Exercise 10.3	Alex the Accountant, Scientific Problem Solving	76
Exercise 10.4	Money in the Bank? Practical Problem Solving	77
Exercise 10.5	Seeing Is Believing, Psychological Reasoning	78
Exercise 10.6	Poor John and Mary, Creative Problem Solving	79

CHAPTER 11
Intelligence 81

Exercise 11.1	"Character"istics of Intelligence, Pattern Recognition	81
Exercise 11.2	Challenging Questions, Perspective Taking	82
Exercise 11.3	To Retest Or Not to Retest? Scientific Problem Solving	83

Exercise 11.4 When to Test, Practical Problem Solving 84
Exercise 11.5 Brave New World, Psychological Reasoning 85
Exercise 11.6 Just Too Cool, Creative Problem Solving 87

CHAPTER 12
Motivation 88

Exercise 12.1 Theories of Motivation, Pattern Recognition 88
Exercise 12.2 Humanistic History, Perspective Taking 89
Exercise 12.3 Chicken or Egg? Scientific Problem Solving 90
Exercise 12.4 The Diet Riot, Practical Problem Solving 91
Exercise 12.5 The Weight-Loss Counselor, Psychological Reasoning 92
Exercise 12.6 The Creative Consultant, Creative Problem Solving 93

CHAPTER 13
Emotions 95

Exercise 13.1 Tourist Trap, Pattern Recognition 95
Exercise 13.2 Forget Your Troubles, Practical Problem Solving 98
Exercise 13.3 Pinocchio's Legacy, Creative Problem Solving 99
Exercise 13.4 What Is This Thing Called Love? Scientific Problem Solving 99
Exercise 13.5 Express Yourself! Psychological Reasoning 100
Exercise 13.6 Honest Is the Best Policy, Perspective Taking 100

CHAPTER 14
Personality 102

Exercise 14.1 Freud Meets Mother Goose, Pattern Recognition 102
Exercise 14.2 Matchmaker, Matchmaker, Practical Problem Solving 105
Exercise 14.3 Pseudoscientific Personality, Creative Problem Solving 106
Exercise 14.4 You Can't Cheat an Honest Man, Scientific Problem Solving 107
Exercise 14.5 Rorschach's Fate, Psychological Reasoning 107
Exercise 14.6 Is It Hopeless—Or Not? Psychological Perspective Taking 108

CHAPTER 15
Psychological Disorders 109

Exercise 15.1 And the Winner Is . . . , Pattern Recognition 109
Exercise 15.2 All I Need Is an Agent! Creative Problem Solving 110
Exercise 15.3 The End, Practical Problem Solving 110
Exercise 15.4 I'm Just Not Myself Today, Scientific Problem Solving 112
Exercise 15.5 The Labeling Controversy, Psychological Reasoning 113
Exercise 15.6 Why Y2K? Psychological Perspective Taking 114

CHAPTER 16
Therapy 115

Exercise 16.1 How Does That Make You Feel? Pattern Recognition 115
Exercise 16.2 Even Domestic Engineers Get the Blues, Practical Problem Solving 116
Exercise 16.3 There Must Be 50 Ways to Leave Your Shrink, Creative Problem Solving 119
Exercise 16.4 Out, Damned Spot, Scientific Problem Solving 119
Exercise 16.5 Not-So-Clever Hans, Psychological Reasoning 120
Exercise 16.6 Who's Got the Check? Perspective Taking 121

CHAPTER 17
Stress and Health 122

Exercise 17.1 Between a Rock and a Hard Place, Pattern Recognition 122
Exercise 17.2 Healthy Living, Perspective Taking 124
Exercise 17.3 Enhancing Immune Function, Scientific Problem Solving 126
Exercise 17.4 Healthy Executives, Practical Problem Solving 127
Exercise 17.5 Step on the Gas, Psychological Reasoning 129
Exercise 17.6 The Game of Life, Creative Problem Solving 130

CHAPTER 18
Social Psychology 132
  Exercise 18.1 Pride and Prejudices, Pattern Recognition 132
  Exercise 18.2 Dear Abby, Practical Problem Solving 135
  Exercise 18.3 But My Teacher *Made* Me Do It, Creative Problem Solving 136
  Exercise 18.4 How Can I Help? Scientific Problem Solving 137
  Exercise 18.5 For the Sake of the Children, Psychological Reasoning 138
  Exercise 18.6 People Were Stupid Back Then, Perspective Taking 139

Answer Key 143

Preface

Ralph Waldo Emerson once said, "A friend is one before whom I may think aloud." It is in that spirit that the original *Critical Thinking Companion* was written. We have strived to maintain that spirit in this new edition. Although the term "companion" may sound a bit old-fashioned, we use it to convey an attitude of friendly support to students embarking on their first adventure in the formal study of psychology. We also want teachers to experience friendly support in their attempts to make the introductory psychology classroom a stimulating and welcoming place to be.

Many students begin their first psychology course with some degree of overconfidence that they already understand the nature of psychology. They are frequently surprised—and sometimes disappointed—to find that the science of psychology is not what they had in mind. Teachers must challenge these erroneous notions to get to the heart of the discipline they know and love.

The best teachers not only help students to understand and apply psychology's basic principles and concepts; they also help to instill or reawaken a sense of wonder and appreciation for the puzzle that is human behavior. Encouraging active learning and critical thinking is the optimum strategy by which to accomplish both of these things. Critical thinking activities that encourage discovery are much more likely to lead to meaningful learning than dutiful reading and memorization. Meaningful learning—thoughtful, involved reading with active attempts to draw connections to life—takes effort but is far more likely to have enduring effects on knowledge and thinking skills. Although teachers who invest class time in active learning and critical thinking may not cover as much content as those who practice more content-oriented methods, they often provide students with a better orientation to the discipline, a better foundation for using psychology in their lives, and better developed thinking skills.

As *The Critical Thinking Companion* moves into its second edition, we have made a few changes. The addition of a co-author, Cynthia Gray, represents a way to reinvigorate the model originally proposed in the first edition. Although we retained the exercises that made the first edition such a popular ancillary, we have added some new examples to provide more options for the classroom. We also have designed some improved feedback mechanisms for student performance. We think that the teachers who were fans of the first edition should be pleased about the fresh ideas presented in this volume.

Good companions make life richer. We hope that your experience as students using *The Critical Thinking Companion* will enrich your understanding and appreciation of psychology as well as enhance your ability to think critically about human behavior. For an introduction to the definition of critical thinking and the skills that comprise it, the categories of critical thinking that you will learn about in this book, and how this book is structured to help you learn and practice these skills, see Introducing Critical Thinking (page 1).

Jane's Acknowledgments

Many individuals have contributed to the evolution of this book. Ludy Benjamin inspired the first edition. He knew that there was a vague concept of a critical thinking book rattling about in my head before I did. Austin Doherty of Alverno College and Bill McKeachie have also been extremely supportive of my development as a teacher. The encouragement and advocacy of these leaders have always been very important to me.

I am also fortunate to have been blessed with the company of extraordinary teaching colleagues, first in the innovative Psychology Department at Alverno College and later in the impressive School of Psychology at James Madison University. I know few faculty members who view department meetings as sources of intellectual stimulation, but I have been lucky enough to find that in two settings. I treasure my colleagues' commitment and companionship.

The psychology teaching community in all its permutations (regional and national teaching conferences, CTUP, Society for Teaching of Psychology, TOPSS) continually reinforces my enthusiasm about this profession.

Fans of the first edition of *The Critical Thinking Companion* have been delightful in their response to the original work. I am particularly pleased when users share with me the exercises that seem to be most effective with their students ("Piaget Meets Santa Claus" was the hands-down favorite of the last edition). Their enthusiasm for the *Companion* is in large part responsible for this new treatment.

It has been a delight for me to share production of the new edition with one of the most talented teachers I know. It was my pleasure to be a teaching mentor to Cynthia Gray in her first year of teaching at Alverno College. I quickly discovered that I was learning more from her in the mentoring deal than I was providing. She is just that good. And she was a natural to join the second edition in figuring out new and fresh ways to promote the critical thinking model. As an intellectual companion, she is unbeatable. I am grateful to Doug, Morgan, and Hannah for giving her the space to create and collaborate.

Finally, I continue to have unflagging support at home for a ridiculously overcrowded professional life. Brian Halonen's willingness to stay grounded so I can keep flying is a miracle. As my favorite companion, he has my admiration and my heart.

Jane Halonen
July 14, 2000

Cynthia's Acknowledgments

To be able to "think aloud" in the presence of others truly is one of the great gifts in this life. I have been blessed to have this opportunity with both my students and colleagues at Alverno College. To have student companions in the classroom—individuals who are willing to take a risk, to try something new, to tolerate a teacher who brings to class some rather wacky activities, and to provide honest feedback about the success of those activities—gives me energy and enthusiasm and reaffirms my commitment to learning every day. In a similar fashion, my colleagues in the department of psychology have listened to my ideas, supported my growth, and helped me curtail some of my wilder notions. These professional companions have helped ensure that I never allow my approach to teaching to become mechanical and have encouraged me to stretch myself with every class that I teach. In short, they have given me the confidence and space to tackle this enterprise and to see it as the exciting challenge that it is. For this they have my undying gratitude.

Gratitude is not nearly enough for the companion who has served as my mentor, and more importantly, as a friend. Jane Halonen is one of those rare individuals who is both magnificently gifted and delightfully exuberant about life. In everything that she does, she demonstrates an excitement about learning and teaching and I am thrilled and honored to have been able to share in that enthusiasm by working with her on this project.

In our home, thinking aloud is the rule. My daughters Morgan and Hannah are a never-ending source of joy as they show me daily that true learning is constant, exciting, and, most of all, delightfully messy. As the person with whom I have chosen to walk a lifelong path of mutual learning, my husband, Doug, provides the encouragement and support that enable me to accomplish dreams and experience hope. As the companions of my heart, soul, and life, my family deserves more thanks and recognition than are possible to give.

Cynthia Gray
July 15, 2000

Introducing Critical Thinking

What is "critical thinking"? Long before you picked up this text you probably heard the term and may have wondered what it meant. Although experts disagree about exactly what critical thinking entails, in this text it means *the special kind of thinking skills that promote conscious, purposeful, and active involvement of the thinker with new ideas.* Observing carefully, inferring accurately, building connections among ideas, asking questions, making decisions, generating new ideas, and analyzing arguments are all skills that comprise aspects of critical thinking.

Critical thinking includes a variety of thinking skills, but it excludes dreaming because dreaming is not a conscious activity. Similarly, daydreaming does not qualify—the fun of daydreaming is that it *is* directionless, not purposeful. Also excluded are behaviors such as signing your name, which have become so automatic that the underlying thinking requires minimal attention and concentration. Finally, memorizing—rehearsal until the desired content is stored—is not critical thinking. Simple memorization, although it is hard work and a valuable process that builds a strong knowledge base, tends to be a one-way process with minimal involvement or engagement of what the thinker has already learned or believes. Although we may use critical thinking skills to reorganize the elements of something to be memorized, critical thinking is not an essential step in successful memorization.

All of us manage to do critical thinking of a practical nature on a regular basis. You engage in a simple form of critical thinking when you decide which cereal to open for breakfast. Your choice of college was probably the result of a longer, more complex chain of critical thought. When you have an argument with a close friend, you use critical thinking skills to try to determine what went wrong and how to fix it. So rest assured—you already have had a great deal of practice in certain kinds of critical thinking.

In contrast to the practical critical thinking you do each day, studying a particular discipline offers an opportunity to develop your critical thinking skills systematically in a specialized area. This text will help you refine your critical thinking skills as you focus them on psychology as a scientific discipline. You will practice the critical thinking skills that have to do with understanding behavior.

Psychology, like all sciences, strives to explain how things work. The science of psychology attempts to understand how human beings and other organisms behave, although the focus of a particular study may be neuron activity in the brain, motivation in overeating patterns, attachment styles of infants, the migration patterns of birds, and so on. The goals of psychology usually include describing, explaining, predicting, and controlling behavior. Critical thinking skills in psychology promote these goals.

You already have spent a great deal of time developing your unique perspective on the world. You have discovered by observation and direct experience how humans function. You have become very skilled at establishing meaningful explanations for why things happen the way they do. You develop good guesses about how behavior patterns fit together to assist you in navigating the challenges of your life. Sometimes your guesses are right; at other times, behaviors don't fit your expectations quite so neatly. You may discover big differences between how you expect the world to operate and how it truly does. These discrepancies are likely to leave you feeling confused or uncomfortable until you can develop new sets of expectations that fit with and explain them.

Once you can explain what you encounter, you no longer need to think critically about that circumstance. Your knowledge base grows as does your ability to adapt to a complicated world. Let's examine how you activate critical thinking processes when confronted with a stimulus that just doesn't make sense according to how you have come to expect the world to operate.

What Happened Here? An Example of Critical Thinking

Suppose that some morning as you are hurrying to a final examination you find a man lying on the sidewalk, blocking your path. This discrepancy from your normal routine will surely prompt you to consider possible explanations for this unusual event. Perhaps you will quickly consider the following questions in your search for additional clues that will help you to decide what to do.

- Is he breathing?
- Does he appear to be conscious?
- Is he bruised or bleeding?
- Does he smell of anything?
- How is his hygiene?
- What is his general age?
- How is he dressed?
- Was he carrying any objects? Are these neatly stacked next to him or strewn about?

With careful observation, you will assemble enough information to begin to interpret the meaning of this unusual event. Was the man attacked? Was he drinking? Could he be sick? Was he done in by the stress of a final exam? Is he a student participating in a psychology experiment? As you put all the clues together, you might relate your observations and interpretations, concluding that he is an assault victim in need of medical attention, an alcoholic who has passed out as the result of a drinking binge, a person who is ill and in need of medical attention, or a student with a melodramatic flair expressing despair over impending failure. Each conclusion suggests a different potential resolution for the event. In this case, it is likely that only one conclusion will produce the most satisfying or accurate explanation. However, not all forms of critical thinking reduce to one simple conclusion.

This example illustrates the basic role that critical thinking processes play in psychology. An event captures your attention because it differs from what you would normally expect in a given set of circumstances. This unusual event represents a *discrepancy* from your normal expectations or *personal theory* about how the world operates. If the discrepant behavior is compelling, you will observe it; interpret its significance; relate these ideas, sometimes using formal concepts in psychology; and come to a conclusion that is satisfying because it enables you to understand the discrepancy.

Personal theories vary. For example, if you live in a neighborhood where street people take refuge, finding a human form lying on the sidewalk might not be particularly discrepant with your experience. You would not regard this occurrence as very unusual from the events you expect to encounter under normal circumstances. If you live where you rarely see a street person, however, this would be an extremely discrepant and probably quite disturbing event.

Some resolutions of discrepancy require action. In the above example, if you conclude the man is an assault victim, you probably will call an ambulance or at least notify the campus police. Alternatively, you may merely construct some less compelling meaning to the discrepancy so that the event will make sense. *"This person is snoring loudly and is surrounded by books and papers. I guess finals really can do you in."* In effect, you modify your personal theory to take into account the unusual event. In future, you won't be surprised to see other human forms on the sidewalk at final exam time.

Categories of Critical Thinking

The man-on-the-sidewalk scenario serves as an example of **pattern recognition,** one of six categories of critical thinking you will learn about in this book. For example, someone used to such encounters may identify the pattern of behavior without perceiving it as a problem. Some might conclude that the fallen figure is a student in serious need of a nap; some might decide that the man is making an unsuccessful bid for attention. Neither conclusion calls for action on the part of the observer. Pattern recognition serves as the foundation for all other forms of critical thinking in psychology. This category includes the use of concepts of psychology to describe and explain behavior patterns and discrepancies.

Pattern recognition includes five types of critical thinking skills:

- *Observing*—We carefully observe behavior, especially discrepancies from expected behavior.
- *Inferring*—We interpret possible meanings of the observed behavior, distinguishing between the actual observed behavior and our inferences about its meaning or cause.

- *Relating*—We make connections among the observations and inferences, sometimes linking these ideas to psychological concepts.
- *Explaining*—We select the most appropriate relationships derived from our observation of behavior, and we use them to understand and explain the behavior, resolve the discrepancy, and modify our personal theory.
- *Describing*—We use behavioral concepts in psychology to label behavior for efficient communication.

Psychological concepts provide a kind of shorthand that enables us to describe familiar behavior patterns and processes efficiently.

Problems represent a discrepancy from an orderly, workable world. When a pattern of behavior constitutes a problem, critical thinking involves **practical problem solving,** the second category addressed in this book. Using our prior example, some people might encounter a prostrate form on the sidewalk and decide, "This is not *my* problem." In contrast, those who see it as a problem may employ psychological concepts and theories to develop a solution and a plan of action. For example, concluding that the man on the sidewalk is in need of medical attention may prompt an emergency intervention.

Creative problem solving, the third category of critical thinking, involves being able to make a novel connection between previously unrelated or disconnected ideas. In creative problem solving we may create new realities or reorganize assumptions in the process of developing a unique insight.

There are four components to successful creative problem solving:

- *Defining creative opportunity*—We actively seek discrepancies in behavior as opportunities to develop new connections among ideas.
- *Preparing the problem*—We analyze assumptions for possible shifts in perception that may assist us in identifying novel relationships among the elements of the problem. We may attempt to form as many creative connections as possible, often refraining from negative evaluation until the process nears completion.
- *Developing insight*—We identify satisfying novel connections.
- *Evaluating success*—We determine whether the new insight meets appropriate criteria: originality, breadth, playfulness, usefulness, etc.

New developments in psychological theory often are the result of creative problem solving. A willingness to be playful with ideas promotes this type of critical thinking. When we allow ourselves to entertain different kinds of life stories that might lead to the circumstances of the fallen man, we are tapping into the same kinds of creative problem-solving skills that novelists and storytellers employ.

As we discussed earlier, psychological concepts help us to describe and explain behavior. However, psychology as a science has loftier goals. Scientists seek to explain behavior more comprehensively and more precisely by identifying the factors, or *variables,* that influence or produce the behavior. They strive to determine the most systematic explanations for the relationships among variables. This complex activity is **scientific problem solving.** Psychologists construct scientific *theory* about behavior to develop explanations that are more comprehensive, rich, and intricate than the simpler relationships we are likely to develop in our personal theories.

Scientific problem solving has four components:

- *Forming hypotheses*—We develop tentative predictions about the causes of behavior; hypotheses represent an attempt to resolve a discrepancy in our formal knowledge about the causes of behavior.
- *Defining variables operationally*—We define research components in terms of operations in order to promote objectivity in observation and precision in measurement.
- *Conducting systematic or controlled investigations*—We strive to reduce cause-effect explanations to their simplest possible forms. We often emphasize experimental comparisons as a preferred method for developing the sturdiest and most truthful cause-effect explanations. We carefully use control procedures to eliminate alternative explanations for any obtained results.
- *Interpreting results statistically*—We use statistical analysis to help determine whether we have isolated the most important variables.

You will encounter some more complex and objective theoretical explanations in later chapters of your psychology textbook. In fact, we could adapt the fallen-man example to serve as an appropriate stimulus for research in social psychology in trying to isolate the factors that may encourage people to help others.

Psychological reasoning, the fifth category of critical thinking, consists of applying the principles of psychology in creating, defending, or challenging arguments about behavior. Many interesting, compelling claims about behavior confront us in the course of nearly every day. Each occurrence provides an opportunity for exercising our critical thinking abilities. With each opportunity, we may actively examine, evaluate, and accept or reject some argument about behavior. For example, the fallen man could be a homeless person. People view the causes of homelessness from many perspectives, and each new argument requires a fresh evaluation. The primary outcome of psychology-based critical thinking is to prompt us to ask, "What is your evidence?" for any particular position. Then we must determine if that evidence is sufficiently strong to influence us to maintain, revise, or reject our original ideas and beliefs.

The final category of critical thinking is **perspective taking,** a process of increasing importance to psychologists. Our *inferences*—the interpretations or simple meanings we assign to what we see—and the relationships we draw among our inferences depend on our own experience and values. For example, if you just "pulled an all-nighter" to prepare for an examination, you might be more inclined to infer that scholastic despair is the reason for the fallen man's distress. You might conclude that his "crashing on the sidewalk" is a justifiable, understandable aftermath of a challenging experience. Your developmental history might shape a quite different judgment if alcohol caused a great deal of unhappiness in your own family history. The course of action you choose will depend on other factors besides your decisions about whether the man needs help. The value you place on being someone who *should* help will also help determine your actions. Your unique experiences have shaped your system of values and critical thinking biases. Effective critical thinking skills involve being able to identify the values that influence any given course of action. Education in psychology should help you develop:

- *Respect for differing realities*—Psychological thinkers recognize that individuals' perceptions (reality) are shaped by their genetic endowment, their culture, and their personal experience. As a result, no two people have exactly the same reality.
- *Appreciation for individual differences*—We maintain a humanistic regard for the uniqueness of each individual and use psychological methods and theories as ways of exploring and explaining differences.
- *Objectivity*—We tend to prefer scientific evidence (especially controlled comparisons) to subjective experience as support for our beliefs about behavior. Psychological thinkers place great value on being able to distance themselves from their own thoughts, beliefs, and feelings in order to be as unbiased as possible in comprehending behavior and increasing their accessibility to different viewpoints.
- *Flexibility*—Because we can't ever reach complete objectivity, psychological thinking encourages the ability to shift viewpoints and to try out other points of view to gain a more complete picture of that which we wish to understand.
- *Tolerance of ambiguity*—Many puzzles about human behavior may never be completely understood because so many variables (and perspectives) are involved. Our cause-effect conclusions are therefore usually tentative or temporary as we continue to increase our understanding of behavior.
- *Nonjudgmental attitude*—Because we cannot fully account for all motivating forces, psychological thinkers are inclined to uphold an ideal of reserving judgment on the actions of others.

Perspective taking is a particularly important aspect of critical thinking in psychology. Our capacity to set aside or minimize our personal biases enhances our ability to understand human behavior. We can learn to understand what motivates behavior as we identify how people think and feel. We recognize that each individual's perspective is unique; our beliefs and value systems may not match those held by someone else.

How This Book Will Help You Develop Critical Thinking Skills in Psychology

As you learn the discipline of psychology, your knowledge of psychological concepts and theories will grow, and your ability to think critically about psychological issues and concerns will also increase. Your descriptions of behavior will become more specific and more efficient as you accurately apply psychological concepts, principles, and theories. You may discover that you pay more attention to behavior systems and variations and that you interpret them more carefully. You will become more efficient and effective in solving problems related to behavior. You may recognize new possibilities with practice in creative thinking. You'll be more inclined to ask for evidence before you accept a new position. You may be more attuned to the values and assumptions that undergird your own and others' actions. However, all of these outcomes will take some time and some practice.

This book will help you expand your abilities

to think critically as you actively learn about the discipline of psychology. Each chapter includes two or more exercises that correspond to topics discussed in your psychology textbook. Each exercise emphasizes a particular category of skills designed to assist your overall development of critical thinking abilities throughout your studies. Exercises conclude with a list of critical thinking skills you will refine as you complete the exercise and learn the relevant psychological concepts. As you work your way through the exercises, you'll find some expanded descriptions of the categories of critical thinking in later sections of the book. These descriptions will help you polish your understanding and your ability to use critical thinking skills in psychology.

1

Thinking Critically with Psychological Science

The primary difference between personal and scientific explanations of behavior rests in the nature of acceptable evidence. Psychologists have learned to question observations based only on personal experience because they know how biased or subjective human judgment is. This knowledge comes from their own research in perception, cognition, information processing, and social psychology. Psychology as a science promotes the belief that the sturdiest kind of evidence comes from *systematic* and *controlled* observation. This reliance on well-designed research leads to the most credible conclusions about behavior. Scientific critical thinkers try to support their ideas with evidence from controlled comparisons whenever possible, whether they design their own experiments or rely on the controlled observations of others.

Designing meaningful research that will increase our understanding of human behavior is a challenging but exhilarating enterprise. This enterprise relies on some key ideas and procedures. When researchers link concepts or variables to speculate about causes of behavior, they create *hypotheses*. Hypotheses are inferences that predict cause-effect relationships between behavioral variables. There are two kinds of variables in psychological research. *Independent variables* are factors that promote changes in behavior; researchers typically manipulate independent variables (causes) to produce a desired effect in experiments. The desired effect is called the *dependent variable* because the effect *depends* on the various causes.

Suppose that we wanted to find out whether drinking coffee promotes anxiety. In our experiment we could establish three different groups: one group would get no coffee, another group would get two cups, and the final group would get four. In this example, the amount of coffee (none, 2 cups, or 4 cups) constitutes the levels of the independent variable that we think will lead to different intensities of anxiety. Our hypothesis could be that drinking coffee increases anxiety: The independent variable (coffee drinking) causes the dependent variable (anxiety). Or stated conversely, the level of anxiety (dependent variable) depends on coffee intake (independent variable).

Another important aspect of scientific critical thinking in psychology is defining and measuring behavior. Psychologists like to be as precise and as unbiased or objective as possible when exploring the meaning of a behavior. We often define the behaviors we wish to understand by describing the "operations" we go through to produce the behavior. These *operational definitions* promote objectivity in observation.

For example, how will we measure anxiety in our coffee-drinking subjects? We might measure each subject's anxiety response by counting nervous gestures, measuring blood pressure elevations, or requesting a self-rating of anxiety on a scale of 1 to 10. Each approach would give us a different way to quantify anxiety. Operational definitions provide the opportunity to measure behavior as precisely as possible. Researchers evaluate the precise measurements statistically to determine whether the experiment (or other research method) produces meaningful comparisons or patterns.

Competently designed experiments must have clear definitions of the variables in the research and acceptable methods of measuring behavioral responses. But effective *control procedures* are also essential to rule out alternative explanations. We want to make sure that we control all aspects of the experiment so that we can be certain a cause-effect statement is valid or truthful. Control procedures allow us to rule out all cause-effect explanations other than the one we intend to explore in the experiment.

In our coffee-drinking study, we would try to control other factors that might contribute to anxiety. For example, we might want to limit our subject population to people of a certain age. We would avoid conducting our experiment during a period in which those people might be expected to be anxious for some other reason (for example, during final exam time). We would need to make sure that our subjects drank only the amount of coffee specified in their research assignment. And we would have to decide what to do with subjects who hate coffee. All these conditions represent threats to the valid construction of an experiment on the anxiety-producing effects of coffee. As psychologists, we would strive to produce an experiment in which any findings we obtain would be as free as possible from alternative explanations.

The exercises in Chapter 1 emphasize the importance of understanding and applying the principles of experimental design in scientific research and in consumer contexts.

Exercise 1.1

THE CASE FOR INTERFERENCE — *Pattern Recognition*

One of the first decisions that psychology researchers must make is *how* to study their target behavior. *Correlational methods* involve studying behaviors as they are. These approaches involve careful observation, measurement, and interpretation of behaviors to uncover relationships among the factors that influence behavior. Correlational methods can be employed in case studies, surveys, and field work.

In contrast, *experimental methods* involve procedures that manipulate the conditions surrounding the behavior being studied. In effect, the experimenter interferes with normal behavior to narrow down the causes of behavior. By establishing equivalent conditions and systematically varying a specific factor, the experimenter determines the impact of that factor. This is the chief advantage of experimentation; experimental methods allow us to determine cause-effect relationships in a way that correlational methods cannot. Experiments can be conducted using a single subject or many participants. The key to determining cause-effect conclusions is providing good controlled conditions and making accurate comparisons across conditions.

Read the following examples and judge whether the procedure described would be considered a correlational (non-interfering) approach or an experimental (interfering) approach.

The Problem of Child Abuse

Social scientists study the backgrounds of children who have been assigned to foster care. They discover that the majority of children who receive foster care have experienced physical punishment methods in their prior homes that would be severe enough to qualify as abusive.

Would this conclusion be derived from a correlational study or an experiment? Why?

_____

_____

Charlie's Weight Loss

Charlie is trying hard to lose his "spare tire" before his wedding. He has two months to get ready for the event. He decides to go about his weight loss systematically. The first week, Charlie exercises vigorously. The second week, he gives up meat. The third week, he drinks large amounts of water. The fourth week, he eats just bananas. He continues to vary his approach each week. At the end of his eight-week experiment, he concludes that his best weight loss comes from exercise.

Would Charlie's conclusion be derived from a correlational study or an experiment? Why? _____
_____
_____

The Curious Teacher

Ms. Tucker decides that she wants to evaluate which of her teaching methods might make the biggest impact on her students. For the first half of the semester, she teaches using a lecture format. She evaluates what students have learned using a 50-point multiple choice test. For the second half of the semester, she teaches using demonstrations and active learning exercises. She evaluates the second half using a 50-point multiple choice test. She discovers that her students have better test scores when using active learning strategies.

Would Ms. Tucker's conclusion be derived from a correlational study or an experiment? Why? _____
_____
_____

The Lucky Pen

Peter noticed that every time he used his special pen with green ink, something wonderful would happen to him. First, he got an A on his history exam. When he loaned his pen to Amy, she later agreed to go out on a date with him. While he was carrying his pen, he bought a lottery ticket that later won $2,000. He decided that his pen truly had lucky powers and he put it away so he wouldn't lose it.

Would this conclusion be derived from a correlational study or an experiment? Why?
_____
_____

The Best Neighborhood

The local newspaper publishes the results of a finding that produce a significant impact on the real estate market. Their researchers identify various neighborhoods in the city and compare the SAT scores of students who live in different regions of the city. Based on these comparisons, they decide that the suburb of Suffolk has the best education. As a consequence, the real estate market in Suffolk booms.

Would this conclusion be derived from a correlational study or an experiment? Why?
_____
_____

Copycat Crime

A new popular movie depicts a grisly scene of teen violence against senior citizens. Although the criminals in the movie are caught and punished, city officials are dismayed to discover that similar acts of violence increase across the city shortly after the movie opens. A reporter decides to compare crime rates before and after the movie to determine if the movie has stimulated teen violence.

Would the reporter's conclusion be derived from a correlational study or an experiment? Why? _____
_____
_____

Doctor's Choice

A physician is intrigued by a new medication that has been developed for sleep disturbance, but he is concerned about its expense relative to the medication he usually prescribes. He decides to evaluate the success of the medication. He determines that the next 20 patients who complain of sleep problems will help him establish the effectiveness of the medication. Once he identifies the complaint, the physician slips out of the room and tosses a coin. If it comes up "heads," he prescribes the new medication. If it comes up "tails," he prescribes the medication he previously prescribed. At the end of a three-month period, he asks his patients to report the degree of improvement on a ten-point scale. He discovers that the new medication provides no real advantage over the older, less expensive medication.

Would the physician's conclusion be derived from a correlational study or an experiment? Why? _____
_____
_____

After completing this exercise, you should be able to
- describe the key features of correlational research.
- explain why correlational studies cannot confirm cause-effect conclusions.
- discuss the key characteristics of experimental research.
- distinguish between scientific and nonscientific explanations.
- identify how correlational studies differ from experimental studies.

Exercise 1.2

YOU NEED AN OPERATION *Practical Problem Solving*

One of the distinguishing features of people who are trained in psychology is their concern for precision when confronting problems. Psychologists believe that you need to define behaviors in precise and measurable ways if you are going to make progress toward a solution. They routinely refine vague explanations in order to develop **operational definitions.** When an operational definition is successful, it sets the stage for more effective problem solving. Let's look at an example to clarify. Suppose a teacher tells her struggling student, "Your work is awful!" That criticism is not only broad, it is potentially very damaging. What could be some operational definitions that would help the student embark on a more effective strategy?

- Your grade point average declined over the last six-week period.
- You seem to be on-task in class about 30% of the time.
- You have submitted only one of the last six assignments.

Notice that each of these operational approaches to the teacher's concern gets at the heart of the problem and gives the student an opportunity to focus on concrete ways of improvement.

Look at the following three problems in which behaviors are discussed in a vague manner. Try to imagine at least two possible ways to operationalize the behavior, in order to set the stage for more effective problem solving.

The Sloppy Roommate

Jack and Ed are roommates. Jack is tidy and Ed is not. After coming home from a hard afternoon at the library, Jack finds the living room in its usual shambles; Ed's clothes are strewn over the couch, floor, and tables. When Ed emerges from the messy kitchen, where he has been eating nachos next to a pile of dirty dishes, Jack explodes, "I can't stand living this way!" and runs from the room.

What are two ways we could operationalize the problem ("living this way") to help the roommates get back on track? Remember to address observable behavior, precision, and measurement where you can. _____

_____

_____

The Surly Boss

Joe was having problems with his supervisor at work. Although he was doing his work on time and seemed to get along with everyone, the supervisor rarely gave him feedback of any kind. The supervisor seemed to look at him funny at times. Sometimes Joe thought the supervisor might be talking about him and laughing behind his back. Joe asked for an appointment and then challenged the supervisor, "Why don't you like me?"

What are two ways we could operationalize Joe's concerns to help him have a more productive relationship with his supervisor? Remember to address observable behavior, precision, and measurement where you can.

_____

_____

Bonnie's Worry

Bonnie had been working at the day-care center for three months. All of the children were a lot of fun, but Bonnie was starting to develop some concerns about Emily. Emily preferred solitary play. She occasionally stayed focused on one or two objects for a long time. She also regularly talked to herself. Sometimes she would grab the other children inappropriately and would steal toys from others. When Emily's parents reported for a conference at the day-care center, Bonnie told the parents that she thought Emily was "slow."

In what two ways could "slow" be operationalized to help the parents better understand the nature of the difficulties that Bonnie was noticing? _____
_____
_____

After completing this exercise, you should be able to
- identify the impact of vague behavior concepts.
- formulate operational definitions to improve problem definition.
- reflect precision and measurement as important characteristics in operational definitions.

Exercise 1.3

THE LIMITS OF NURSERY RHYME REASONING — *Creative Problem Solving*

One of the issues we emphasize in this chapter is the limit to which we can rely on common sense and intuition in the practice of psychology. Many times, what we think we know just isn't so. We tend to overestimate both our knowledge and our abilities. When evaluating past events, we assume that we would have foreseen the outcome (hindsight bias), and when evaluating potential events, we assume that we will know or perform better than we probably will (overconfidence). Demonstrate your understanding of how these phenomena occur by rewriting nursery rhymes as if the author were suffering from either hindsight bias or overconfidence.

Example for hindsight bias:

Little Miss Muffet
Sat on a tuffet,
Eating her curds and whey.
She should have expected
A big black arachnid
At a picnic on such a fine day.

Example for overconfidence:

Humpty Dumpty sat on a wall.
Humpty Dumpty had a great fall.
After watching him die,
His friend said, "Not I:
For I'm a coordinated guy."

If you are having trouble thinking of rhymes, here are some suggestions:
- Little Boy Blue
- Little Bo Peep
- Jack Horner
- Hey, Diddle Diddle
- Old Mother Hubbard
- Three Little Kittens

For each of your revised rhymes, answer the following questions:
1. How successful were you in describing hindsight bias and overconfidence within this context?
2. How playful were you with this exercise?

After completing this exercise, you should be able to

- define hindsight bias and overconfidence.
- use the novel context of nursery rhymes to demonstrate how hindsight bias and overconfidence operate in everyday life.
- appropriately evaluate the success of your creative enterprise.

Exercise 1.4

DESIGNING CAREFULLY CONTROLLED RESEARCH — *Scientific Problem Solving*

Scientific problem solving has four components:

- *Forming hypotheses*—We develop tentative predictions about the causes of behavior; hypotheses represent an attempt to resolve a discrepancy in our formal knowledge about the causes of behavior.
- *Defining variables operationally*—We define research components in terms of operations in order to promote objectivity in observation and precision in measurement.
- *Conducting systematic or controlled investigations*—We strive to reduce cause-effect explanations to their simplest possible forms. We often emphasize experimental comparisons as a preferred method for developing the sturdiest and most truthful cause-effect explanations. We carefully use control procedures to eliminate alternative explanations for any obtained results.
- *Interpreting results statistically*—We use statistical analysis to help determine whether we have isolated the most important variables.

The following three badly designed experiments and the questions accompanying them will help you to recognize research concepts and sharpen your ability to detect flaws in experimental design. After you complete all the questions, compare your answers with those in the Answer Key at the end of the book.

The Colorful Boss

Arlene wanted to increase the productivity of the clerical staff in her plant. She thought painting their cubicles blue (her favorite color) would increase their rate of work completion but that painting the cubicles yellow (a color she thought was harsh) would have no effect or might even slow down the clerical staff's rate of completion. To test this idea she had the work cubicles in the Sales Department painted blue and those in the Public Relations Department painted yellow. Then she kept track of how many projects each department completed in the next three months. For the two-month period following the painting, the sales clerical staff dramatically outperformed the public relations clerical staff in the number of projects completed.

Research Design Elements (See Answer Key.)

What is the *focal behavior* of the study and how is it *defined operationally?* _____

_____

What is the *hypothesis?* _____

_____

_____

What is the *independent variable?* _____

How is the *dependent variable* measured? _____

What variables are controlled? _____

What variables are not controlled? _____

Did the research measure what Arlene thought she measured? Justify your answer:

_____

The Bad Driver

John is intrigued by the relationship between frustration and aggression. He proposes to study whether socioeconomic status is a factor in how drivers express aggression when they are frustrated. John decides to employ a high-status car (a shiny new Mercedes) and a low-status car (a dented, rusty 1983 Volkswagen) as the stimuli in a "field" experiment on the roads near his home during a sunny April afternoon. He plans to drive the high-status car from 1 to 3 P.M. and the low-status car from 3 to 5 P.M. During these periods, he will linger when he has to stop for red lights and will move forward only when the driver behind him honks. His research assistant, riding on the passenger side, will time how long it takes the driver of the car behind the experimental car to honk. John believes drivers will take longer to honk when they are behind the Mercedes than when they are behind the Volkswagen. He thinks frustrated people will suppress their frustration and aggression when the person causing the frustration is of high socioeconomic status.

Research Design Elements (See Answer Key.)

What is the *focal behavior* of the study and how is it *defined operationally*? _____

What is the *hypothesis*? _____

What is the *independent variable*? _____

How is the *dependent variable* measured? _____

What variables are controlled? _____

What variables are not controlled? _____

How can the experiment be improved? _____

Going for the Gold

Rita, a sports psychologist, has applied for a huge grant sponsored by the American Olympiad Organization. She wants to identify variables that will produce more winners in the next international competition. She plans to build a special camp where the athletes can train for two weeks each summer with other athletes. She will fly all the volunteer athletes to the camp and will randomly assign each of them to one of three conditions. Rita will host only one type of group at a time. In Condition 1, which meets during the first two weeks of the experiment, the athletes get no special treatment beyond the opportunity to train in the specially designed camp. Athletes assigned to Condition 1 are control group members. In Condition 2, during the second two weeks, the athletes will receive a well-regulated diet and low-dose steroids. In Condition 3, during the last two-week period, the athletes will sleep with a self-esteem training tape under their pillows. Rita believes that unconscious sleep preparation will be superior to other forms of training in producing winning athletes. She plans to measure her success by contrasting the number of medals the three groups of athletes win in their next outing.

Research Design Elements (See Answer Key.)

What is the *focal behavior* of the study? _____

What is the *hypothesis?* _____

What is the *independent variable?* _____

How is the *dependent variable* measured? _____

What variables are controlled? _____

What variables are not controlled? _____

Would you fund this proposal? If so, give your reason. If not, describe some ways in which the study could be improved: _____

All three experiments have flaws of sufficient magnitude that their findings would be invalid or at least questionable. However, even in well-designed and published research, you may encounter subtle problems in design, control procedures, and variable definitions that will challenge the interpretation of the results described by the researcher. As you continue to read about scientific experimentation, look for flaws. All those who publish their results expect criticism. Effective criticism helps the literature of psychology—and our knowledge about human behavior—to grow.

After completing this exercise, you should be able to

- recognize the experimental design elements (such as hypothesis, independent and dependent variables, and so on) in a description of simple research designs.
- describe how control methods are used to rule out alternative explanations.
- understand the importance of careful operational definition in experimental design.
- make some overall judgments about the quality of an experimental design.

Exercise 1.5

CONSUMER SAFETY *Psychological Reasoning*

One sophisticated form of critical thinking applies the principles of psychology in creating, defending, or challenging arguments about behavior. Without effective critical thinking abilities, we could easily fall prey to questionable claims about the causes of behavior, such as this simulated sampling of headlines from tabloid papers over the last few years:

"Wiggling Your Ears Makes You Smarter"

"Woman's Head Explodes During Psychic Trance"

"Belly Button Shape Reveals Your Character"

"Eating Bananas Increases Your Bust Size"

"Elvis Spotted . . . "

Psychological reasoning is an important intellectual ability, whether we are selecting a product for purchase or exercising our citizens' rights by deciding which candidate will get our vote. The positions we create and defend on important issues will determine the kinds of actions we take. Understanding the principles of critical thinking in psychology should enable us not only to create and defend our opinions more effectively but also to challenge behavioral arguments that are invalid.

The primary emphasis of this type of thinking is one question: "What's your evidence?" Psychological research design teaches us to examine claims about behavior and to consider alternative explanations. What other variables might account for the relationship being claimed? By applying the following experiment-based principles of psychological reasoning, we can protect ourselves against invalid claims.

1. *Don't expect simple cause-effect relationships.* They rarely exist in relation to behavior, so a skeptical or disbelieving stance is generally the safest response to simplistic claims about the causes of behavior.

2. *Don't settle for cause-effect statements without sufficient evidence.* Remember that question: "What's your evidence?" Is the evidence *objective* (derived from systematic, unbiased, and well-controlled observation) or *subjective* (influenced by personal experiences, characteristics, and biases)? Personal testimony is particularly problematic, especially when the enthusiastic advocate is being paid for it.

3. *Don't confuse interpretation of behavior with behavior itself.* People often embellish their observation of behavior with statements about the meaning of the behavior. They then report their conclusions about the behavior instead of describing the behavior they observed. For example, on witnessing a professor's late arrival to class, we might leap to the conclusion that she is *busy* or *disrespectful* or *scatter-brained* rather than sticking to the facts. The observable behavior is arriving late to class. Invalid claims may report interpretations or judgments about a behavior rather than focusing on a description of behavior without interpretation.

4. *Don't mistake correlation for causation.* It is easy to come to the wrong conclusion about what causes behavior. Sometimes what appears to be a strong cause-effect relationship may be an illusion. For example, let's examine the first statement in the roster of tabloid headlines—"Wiggling Your Ears Makes You Smarter." Digging underneath this headline, you may discover that the writer swears by ear wiggling as a method of increasing intelligence. His evidence? He wiggled his ears all the way through his college admission test and his score was in a top percentile. This silly example demonstrates that the occurrence of two variables close together in time (for example, ear wiggling and intelligent performance during test taking) can sometimes be interpreted as causal. (Even smart people make this error!) Clearly, other variables could have led to the writer's performance on his admission test.

5. *Do look for experimental comparisons that involve control conditions.* Controlled comparison is the key to ruling out alternative explanations that make some claims implausible or unbelievable. We may never know the real cause for some effect unless we perform systematic study on the proposed relationship to determine whether there is any other way to account for observed changes in behavior. Psychological research is heavily biased toward experiments in which controlled comparisons can reduce alternative explanations.
6. *Do examine how behaviors are defined or operationalized.* Definitions can be very slippery, as anyone who has gone to a hair stylist and asked for "just a little" hair trimming knows. Precision in definitions is even more important in psychological research. Some cause-effect claims may seem very compelling until you require precise definition of the terms used in the claim.

In the following pages, eight consumer and civic claims are described. Your job is to decide how well each of them stands up to the principles outlined in this chapter. First identify the principle that is involved. Then decide whether the claims should be challenged or accepted, based on the six principles reviewed in this chapter.

Principle(s) Involved

The Tanned Rock Queen

A famous female rock star encourages you to join a new tanning salon and shows you her tan marks to prove the salon's effectiveness.

The Moralizer

A local politician suggests that heavy metal music is responsible for increasing violence among teenagers and proposes that all such music be banned.

The Laundry

A photogenic child wallows in a mud puddle in a TV advertisement. The smiling (and rich) Mom who wants to try out the effectiveness of her new detergent rips the child's shirt in half and launders one half in her old detergent and the other half in the new detergent. The half laundered in the new product is substantially cleaner.

The New Car

A toothsome announcer promises you that your social life will have lots of pizazz if you buy his company's new car—the Pizazz-mobile.

Halloween Wisdom

A psychologist strongly endorses the traditional children's practice of trick-or-treat at Halloween. In a video produced by a leading U.S. candy company, he suggests that trick-or-treat rituals help children overcome common childhood fears. The psychologist also mentions that chocolate candies are probably the most beneficial treats to give because they contain a chemical that promotes the release of neurotransmitters.

	Principle(s) Involved

One Bad Apple

The president of the most successful company in town has developed some strong preferences in her hiring practices. She had a bad experience with a graduate of your college three years ago. As a result, the company will no longer employ anyone graduating from your college, even though the legality of this practice seems questionable.

The Blind Date

Your friend sets you up with a blind date. He describes your date as someone who has strong interests in the environment. At the start of the evening, your date proposes a walk along the beach and during that walk, picks up cans and shoves them into a backpack. You conclude that the rumored interest in environmental issues is valid.

The Burglars

A recent newspaper reporter speculated that a full moon may have an enhancing effect on criminal behavior because crimes, especially breaking and entering, seem to increase dramatically when the moon is full. The reporter cited interviews with several leading mental health specialists who have noted a "full moon effect" in other areas of mental health management. (See Answer Key.)

In most situations in which a compelling cause-effect relationship is presented, your best reaction is to ask, "What's your evidence?" Psychologists believe a skeptical stance (a general attitude of disbelief) may provide the greatest protection until objective, controlled evidence supports a claim.

After completing this exercise, you should be able to
- identify some principles that will help you evaluate claims made in commercials.
- describe why clear definitions are so crucial in making fair claims.
- recognize why psychologists may not accept personal testimony as valid evidence.
- apply principles of experimental design to claims about behavior to judge whether the claims are valid or should be challenged.
- see why it is important to ask, "What's your evidence?" when someone is trying to "sell" you on a cause-effect relationship.

Exercise 1.6

PSYCHOLOGY'S PERSPECTIVES — *Perspective Taking*

The field of psychology is a broad one. Although all psychologists explore issues of behavior and mental processes, researchers in the field can approach these issues from multiple perspectives. The perspectives addressed in your text—neuroscience, evolutionary, behavior genetics, behavioral, cognitive, and social-cultural—are complementary. Each contributes to our understanding of how organisms think, feel, and act. As you work to think critically about psychology, understanding the different perspectives and their respective limits and strengths will help you make accurate judgments about what you are reading and learning.

Below are some of the issues that are of interest to psychologists working from all perspectives. For each of these examples, describe how psychology's six perspectives would approach the area of study. What are questions that psychologists from these perspectives might ask?

Issue: Drug Abuse

Neuroscience: _____
_____
_____

Evolutionary: _____
_____
_____

Behavior Genetics: _____
_____
_____

Behavioral: _____
_____
_____

Cognitive: _____
_____
_____

Social-Cultural: _____
_____
_____

Issue: Love

Neuroscience: _____
_____
_____

Evolutionary: _____
_____
_____

Behavior Genetics: _____
_____
_____

Behavioral: _____

Cognitive: _____

Social-Cultural: _____

Issue: Intelligence

Neuroscience: _____

Evolutionary: _____

Behavior Genetics: _____

Behavioral: _____

Cognitive: _____

Social-Cultural: _____

After completing this exercise, you should be able to
- describe the focus of all six of psychology's current perspectives.
- link appropriate concepts with their corresponding perspectives.
- recognize that any psychological event can be explored from multiple perspectives.
- identify questions that are of particular interest to psychologists working within a specific perspective.

2

Neuroscience and Behavior

Students new to psychology sometimes express surprise at how much psychology resembles biology. From the beginning, psychology has been fascinated with the workings of the brain and the nervous system. Psychologists have made significant progress in identifying brain function. As our technologies improve, we will continue to decode the brain's mysteries. For the time being, the following exercises encourage you to use your critical thinking skills to explore our current understanding of the biological roots of behavior.

Exercise 2.1

HOW DO YOU DO THAT? *Pattern Recognition*

Learning how the brain works is one of introductory psychology's greatest challenges. This three-pound organ is a marvel of complexity as it processes incoming stimulation and governs a variety of simultaneous demands.

In this exercise you will develop a map that describes how the various parts of the brain collaborate to enable you to perform leisure activities. For this exercise, assume that you play cards in your leisure time—perhaps the game of bridge. Using the following table, identify whether the specific brain sites in the list would be involved in the complex skills employed in playing bridge. Begin by identifying the general brain function of the specific site. (Consult your text if you need a quick refresher course.) Then determine whether that part of the brain is directly involved or is not essential in card playing. (See Answer Key.)

Brain Site	**Function?**	**Involvement?**
Hypothalamus		
Occipital lobe		
Reticular formation		

Cerebellum

Parietal lobe

Corpus callosum

Medulla

Temporal lobe

Frontal lobe

Thalamus

Amygdala

Hippocampus

Obviously any leisure activity requires the collaboration of various brain functions. If you ever play cards in the future, you may have a new appreciation of the architecture of the nervous system that enables your behavior.

After completing this exercise, you should be able to
- identify the function of the component parts of the brain.
- distinguish the differing contributions that each component part makes in a complex activity.
- appreciate the complexity of brain function.

Exercise 2.2

THE SPLIT-BRAIN PROBLEM   *Practical Problem Solving*

Early studies in brain function led to the conclusion that the hemispheres of the cerebral cortex specialize in certain kinds of activities. Some reports have exaggerated the difference between the right and left brains' effects on behavior; in reality, most behaviors rely on an integrated functioning that causes both hemispheres to hum with electrical activity. However, we can explore the idea of hemispheric specialization by identifying the side of the brain that might be primarily responsible for certain behaviors. The discussion here assumes a right-handed person with no brain damage.

The left hemisphere is primarily responsible for matters of language, symbols, logic, and mathematics. The right hemisphere, sometimes referred to as the more creative hemisphere, responds to spatial, musical, and emotional kinds of stimuli. Designate each of the following behaviors with an *R* if it is a right-hemisphere specialization and an *L* if it is a left-hemisphere specialization. (See Answer Key.)

Studying concepts from psychology   _____

Drawing a map of your campus   _____

Daydreaming about your next holiday trip   _____

Listening to a piano concert   _____

Listening to rap music   _____

Thinking about your next "night out"   _____

Reading junk mail   _____

$6 \times 4 - 2 + 5 =$ _____

Redecorating your room   _____

Doodling   _____

Completing this form   _____

The split-brain exercise engages us in using the five critical thinking skills of pattern recognition: We must *observe* the target behavior, *infer* the type of cognitive skill represented in the target behavior, and *relate* the inference to the appropriate hemisphere responsible for that type of skill in order to *explain* hemispheric specialization. Then we *describe* our conclusions, emphasizing appropriate behavioral concepts.

After completing this exercise, you should be able to

- differentiate the primary functions of the right and left hemispheres.
- state the kind of brain function implied by each activity.
- classify the targeted brain ability and relate it to the proper hemisphere.
- speculate about the possible losses that might be connected with hemispheric damage.

Exercise 2.3

THE NEW SUPERHEROES   *Creative Problem Solving*

Science fiction writers are always searching for good ideas for plots that will capture the interest of their readers. A common premise during one particular era of science fiction movies was that radiation somehow altered biological processes, transforming normal human beings into superhumans—some good and some evil. One such example is the Incredible Hulk, who, through a laboratory accident, developed superhuman strength that manifested itself when he was angry.

Your task in this exercise is to create your own team of three superheroes by pretending that it is possible to magnify the abilities governed in selective sites in the human brain.

Identify the area of the brain that would have to be altered to accomplish the special skill of each superhero. Then create a simple story line in which the superheroes' special abilities could be useful.

In this exercise, you confront a rather novel discrepancy in thinking about brain functions. You take a familiar concept—superhero figures—and combine the possibilities of science fiction with brain function concepts to develop new heroes. You may find it helpful to begin by listing the component parts of the brain and their functions. Then give your imagination free rein as you explore the kinds of alterations that might fit the demands of a superhero's life. What challenges would allow your superheros to demonstrate their exceptional abilities? Try not to limit your possibilities or to get bogged down by old ways of thinking. Finally, evaluate whether your novel combinations are satisfying. (See Answer Key for some examples.)

Name of superhero 1 _____

What superability does this superhero possess? _____
_____

What brain structure is augmented? _____

What simple plot would encourage this superhero to come to the rescue? _____
_____
_____
_____

How original or playful is your creation? _____
_____

Name of superhero 2 _____

What superability does this superhero possess? _____
_____

What brain structure is augmented? _____

What simple plot would encourage this superhero to come to the rescue?
_____
_____
_____

How original or playful is your creation? _____
_____

Name of superhero 3 _____

What superability does this superhero possess? _____
_____

What brain structure is augmented? _____

What simple plot would encourage this superhero to come to the rescue? _____
_____
_____
_____

How original or playful is your creation? _____
_____

After completing this exercise, you should be able to
- identify certain brain functions with specific sites in the brain.
- loosen your thinking patterns to allow for playful thinking.
- use criteria to evaluate whether a creative product is adequate.

Exercise 2.4

THE ADDICTED BRAIN *Scientific Problem Solving*

A long-term cocaine user is confronted by his former college roommate, who is shocked to observe some significant changes in his old friend. Instead of being outgoing and curious, his friend seems sullen and suspicious. The roommate suggests the addict seek help for his addiction. During the course of the conversation, the addict uncharacteristically becomes very suspicious and aggressive, accusing his friend of wanting him out of the way so that he can take all his money. Later that evening, the addict takes a large amount of cocaine and begins to have difficulty breathing. Although the roommate calls an ambulance, the addict continues in respiratory distress and starts having convulsions. He dies a short time later of cardiac arrest.

Given what you understand about the functions of the brain, list several brain areas that could be involved in the behaviors/experiences of the cocaine addict. Make sure you are explicit about which brain areas are responsible for which behaviors.

_____

_____

Pick one of these relationships and state it as a clearly written hypothesis.

_____

_____

Design and briefly describe a study, using rats as subjects, in which you might be able to test your hypothesis.

_____

_____

Discuss whether evidence from a study with rats could generalize to human behavior.

_____

_____

After completing this exercise, you should be able to
- identify brain areas responsible for specific drug-related behaviors.
- create a clear hypothesis statement.
- design an experiment that would allow you to test your hypothesis.
- discuss the generalization possibilities for animal analogue studies.

Exercise 2.5

PHANTOM PAIN *Psychological Reasoning*

Current explanations of phantom pain focus on the motor and somatosensory cortex. Neurons from adjacent areas of the motor cortex branch and grow to the areas where the neurons have been damaged or have died because they have not received stimulation. Those areas are still connected to the area of the somatosensory cortex related to the missing limb. When the motor neurons that have "taken over" send signals to the somatosensory cortex, they can be experienced as pain in the missing limb. For example, a woman loses her hand in an automobile accident. Motor neurons from the adjacent area controlling the eyebrows and eyes branch out to utilize this space. The stimulation from these new neural branches is perceived by the sensory cortex as pain in the missing hand. Because the eye and brow move almost constantly and unconsciously and uncontrollably, the woman's pain is constant and is not relieved by medication.

A young man loses an arm to a land mine in Kosovo. After several months, he begins to experience unrelieved pain in the missing limb.

How might you explain this pain? _____

_____

Given your understanding of the structure of the somatosensory cortex, from what areas of his body might these signals be coming?

_____

_____

After completing this exercise, you should be able to

- use your understanding of the structure of the somatosensory cortex to identify areas responsible for specific functions.
- describe how neural death and growth might account for instances of phantom pain.
- recognize that explanations of experiences and behaviors are often complex because of the interconnectedness of the central and peripheral nervous systems.

Exercise 2.6

CARING FOR PHINEAS   *Perspective Taking*

Phineas Gage was a young railroad worker who was injured when an iron tamping rod was accidentally propelled up through his left cheek and out the top of his skull. Amazingly, he was able to sit up and speak immediately after the accident, but there was massive damage to his frontal lobes. Although this damage did not interfere with his memory or physical abilities, it did leave him a profoundly changed person. His personality became radically different; this formerly responsible, hardworking, and respectable person became aggressive, verbally abusive, and unpredictable. He ended up losing his job and leaving his family.

Describe how Phineas and his family and friends might have perceived these changes.

_____

_____

If you were a social worker assigned to this family, what types of services might you offer them?

_____

_____

What would be your expectations for the rest of Phineas's life? Why?

_____

_____

Speculate about what other kinds of changes might have occurred in Phineas's recovery if the tamping rod had pierced the brain at a different location.

_____

_____

After completing this exercise, you should be able to
- recognize that specific areas of the brain are responsible for particular functions.
- identify potential consequences of an injury to a specific area of the brain.
- discuss the long-term prognosis of an individual with a particular brain injury.
- speculate about treatments and support services that might aid in recovery.

The Nature and Nurture of Behavior

The exercises in this chapter focus on the ways human behavior is affected by two forces: the developmental processes that unfold in our lives from nature (our biological heritage) and the processes that are constructed in our lives through nurture (the social environment in which we live). The fundamental question inherent in explaining most developmental processes is to what degree biological factors cause behavior patterns and to what degree the environmental and cultural forces that surround us account for these patterns. Psychologists often refer to this issue as the nature versus nurture controversy. This designation is somewhat misleading since both forces are likely to be influential in the development of any human behavior.

Exercise 3.1

NATURE OR NURTURE? *Pattern Recognition*

You can almost trace the history of psychology by looking for changes in the way the field has viewed individuality and differences between peoples and groups of people. At times, psychology has assumed that we are a blank slate; that everything we are and know is a result of our experience. At other times, science works with the assumption that we are a product of our traits and inherited features and that experience makes no significant modification to our personality. Most of the time the truth lies somewhere in between. As these views work their way into the common culture, they influence everything from literature to educational practices. Below are some clichés and popular sayings. Evaluate each one, deciding which represent the assumption that life history determines who we are (nurture) and which assume that we are shaped by our heredity (nature).

> "Sugar and spice and everything nice, that's what little girls are made of . . ."
> "Handsome is as handsome does."
> "Like father, like son."
> "You can't teach an old dog new tricks."
> "Early to bed and early to rise, makes a man healthy, wealthy, and wise."
> "Boys will be boys."
> "You are what you eat."
> "Blood will tell."
> "All men are created equal."

Can you think of your own examples? _____
_____

After completing this exercise, you should be able to

- describe the approaches to understanding human behavior that are characterized by the terms "nature" and "nurture."
- identify assumptions about nature and nurture that underlie common sayings.
- recognize that assumptions about nature and nurture can be found in many unexpected places.

Exercise 3.2

KEEP ON TRUCKIN' *Practical Problem Solving*

You are a consultant asked to work with a company that has suddenly experienced a huge increase in the diversity of its workers. This trucking company has employed almost exclusively males for the last twenty-five years, but over the last five years they have employed increasing numbers of women. In fact, as of their last hiring blitz, 40% of their employees are women. Many of the men who have been there for a while are beginning to grumble. Some are hassling the women about their choice of career. In an effort to ease the transition for both old and new employees, the company's owners want you to help them design a program to make their current employees aware of the biases they bring to the workplace regarding gender roles. After much reflection, you decide that the best way to do this is to teach the employees about how people develop gender-based expectations for behavior. You decide to use social learning theory and gender schema theory to help change attitudes and behavior within the company.

Describe how you would use each theory to explain to the current male truckers how they have formed their notions of appropriate male and female occupations. Give one example for each that is specifically related to their situation. In addition, pick one of these theories and use it to design a program or campaign that the owners can use to help change the male truckers' attitudes about women in their workplace.

Social learning theory: _____
_____
_____
_____

Example: _____
_____

Gender schema theory: _____
_____
_____
_____

Example: _____
_____

What plan would you suggest to the owners? How does it use either social learning theory or gender schema theory? _____

_____

_____

_____

After completing this exercise, you should be able to

- define social learning theory and gender schema theory and describe how each explains gender-typed behavior.
- recognize how these theories would lead to workplace problems as women and men move into occupations that are traditionally associated with the other gender.
- Apply the principles of social learning theory and gender schema theory to a particular workplace situation.

Exercise 3.3

CHARACTER BUILDING *Creative Problem Solving*

You are a novelist writing a mystery. You begin with a marvelous plot and the realization that your detective needs certain traits and abilities to be successful. This person needs to be sensitive enough to deal with witnesses and victims; tough enough to stay alive in the face of bombs, hired killers, and guard dogs; intelligent enough to break secret codes and outwit the criminal mastermind; and witty enough to be interesting and to find the humor in devastating situations. Create a brief biography for this fictional character, in which you outline the heritable traits and life experiences that have allowed your detective to become this person. Which characteristics seem to be primarily "inborn"? Which ones were acquired by experience?

Biography: _____

_____

_____

_____

_____

_____

After completing this exercise, you should be able to

- articulate the interaction of genetic and environmental factors in the development of individual characteristics.
- speculate about the genetic makeup and life experiences that could lead to the development of specific traits in a fictional individual.
- weigh the potential contributions of genes and experiences for specific characteristics.

Exercise 3.4

SEEING DOUBLE — *Scientific Problem Solving*

As psychologists and other scientists grapple with understanding the roles that genetics and environment play in our development as unique individuals, the experiences of twins, particularly monozygotic twins, have been invaluable. Monozygotic twins are genetically identical, yet it is clear that they are unique individuals. Why? The environment must play a large role in these differences, but how? Temperamental differences in identical twins are noted from birth, so environments must be different in utero, even for individuals carried in the womb at the same time. Identical twins are also similar in many ways. Are these similarities the result of their shared genetic makeup? Maybe. It is also possible that they share enough of the same environment—a particular family and all the related social, economic, and educational correlates—to have been shaped by similar life experiences. This outcome is supported by the fact that non-twin siblings are also similar in many ways, even though they are genetically different.

One way in which these ideas can be teased apart is by looking at twins and siblings who have been raised in different environments since birth. Although current adoption practices in the United States do not encourage the placement of twins in separate families, it has happened in the past, both here and in other countries. Sometimes these twins find each other as adults, and scientists are presented with a wonderful opportunity: a chance to study differences in genetically identical (monozygotic) or related (dizygotic) individuals who have been raised in different environments. However, looking at existing situations only allows scientists to find correlations; it doesn't allow them to answer questions about cause and effect.

Imagine that you want to examine the role that environment plays in an individual's level of extraversion. Generate your hypothesis for an "ideal" twin study experiment, in which you can ask and answer some questions of cause and effect. Outline the basic experimental design. What are the ethical issues that prevent you from actually conducting this experiment? Can you think of ethical ways to ask the same questions?

Hypothesis: _____

_____

Brief description of design: _____

_____

_____

Ethical issues: _____

_____

_____

_____

Alternatives? _____

_____

_____

After completing this exercise, you should be able to

- identify the difference between monozygotic and dizygotic twins.
- recognize the ways in which identical twins have different environments.
- describe how studies of twins adopted or raised by different families provide scientists with insight about the role of genetics and environment in an individual's development.
- design an experiment using twins to examine the role that environment plays in extraversion.
- discuss the ethical considerations that make such experiments impossible.
- identify possible ethical alternatives to twin experiments.

Exercise 3.5

WHO'S TO BLAME? *Psychological Reasoning*

Any conversation about the role of genes and environment in the development of an individual seems to flow naturally to a discussion about the responsibility parents have for their children's behavior. Early in 2000, a 6-year-old girl in Michigan was shot and killed by a first-grade classmate. This young boy brought a loaded gun to school and shot her after a petty conflict developed during class. He later claimed that he had only intended to scare her but that the gun "went off." The bullet struck the little girl in the throat and she died a short time later. No one was surprised to discover that the 6-year-old killer was being raised in neglectful and abusive circumstances, complicated by his caretaker's drug abuse. Amid reactions of shock and outrage, one question was repeated over and over: How could it happen? Was there something biologically wrong with the child, so that he didn't understand or couldn't control what he was doing? Did his life experience make him prone to violence?

Using the concepts from this chapter, provide your explanation of how the boy's development—both nature and nurture—might have led to this tragedy. Explicitly discuss issues of genetics and environment, explaining how each factor might, or might not, have contributed to his behavior. You might find it helpful to organize your discussion around specific topics, such as temperament, prenatal environment, peer influence, culture, and gender.

After completing this exercise, you should be able to

- recognize that behaviors and behavior patterns are often the result of environment-gene interactions.
- identify potential environmental and genetic influences on violent behavior in a real-life situation.
- develop opinions about the influence genetic and environmental factors have on violent behavior.

Exercise 3.6

IT'S ALL IN THE GENES *Perspective Taking*

One of the longest-running debates in psychology is the nature-nurture debate: How much of who we are and what we do is genetically based (nature) and how much is a result of our environment (nurture)? Until the late 1950s and early 1960s, the United States based its educational system on the assumption that we inherit intelligence (as measured by success in school and IQ tests). Then, in 1965, the federal government founded the Head Start program. Its purpose was (and is) to provide basic health, social, and educational services to low-income children, in order to facilitate their success in school. Relying heavily on parental and community involvement, Head Start has become one of the nation's most successful preschool programs. Its premise is that by providing a safe and healthy environment, children will be able to respond to intellectual stimulation and demonstrate academic proficiency. This program was in conflict with the view that intellectual ability was primarily inherited and not susceptible to significant environmental enhancement. In part because of the success of this program, our educational system now provides additional support services for those students who need them, in order to ensure that they have a chance to be successful.

How might this preschool program have been different if the creators of the program believed the earlier premise that intelligence was strictly inherited? What would our educational system look like now? What do you believe is the role of genetics in intelligence? (You will be able to explore this in more depth in Chapter 11.)

After completing this exercise, you should be able to

- differentiate between the nature and the nurture perspectives on intelligence.
- describe your understanding of the heritability of intelligence.
- identify the consequences for education of changes in our understanding of the heritability of a specific feature (intelligence).
- understand how public policy can be affected by scientific theory.

The Developing Person

Life is quite miraculous. From the moment of conception to the moment you shed this mortal coil, you undergo continuous changes. Sometimes the changes are quite dramatic, such as the loss of your first tooth or the first appearance of pubic hair. At other times, the changes are subtle, so much so that you may not notice the little differences that suddenly become apparent. Developmental psychologists focus on the nature of those changes, emphasizing physical, social, cognitive, and emotional differences over time. In this chapter, we explore many of the frameworks that psychologists have used to describe, explain, and predict those changes.

Exercise 4.1

WHEN BAD CHILDREN AREN'T BAD — *Pattern Recognition*

No matter how charming the child, eventually parents find themselves exasperated with their child's behavior. Sometimes it is easy for a parent to assume intentional misbehavior when other motives actually may be at work. By watching his own children, Piaget gave us some cognitive concepts to reexamine what bad kids may really be up to. See if you can identify the cognitive concept from Piaget that explains each child's cognition.

- Although the parents spent $300 on holiday toys for their 1-year-old daughter, she spent more time playing peekaboo by sticking her head in and out of a box that one of the toys came in. Why should the parents have kept their money?
- A well-meaning aunt talked with her 9-month-old nephew about meeting her new boyfriend. However, when he saw the young man, the child shrieked inconsolably. "It must be his mustache!" the aunt thought.
- "Stop doing that!" screamed the exasperated mother in response to her infant's irritating habit of throwing his bottle from the high chair to the floor. She must have stooped over at least twenty times during this meal alone and her child just wasn't learning! Why should the child's behavior not be suprising?
- An older brother and younger sister constantly fight when they are playing cards. No matter how many times the brother explains the rules to his sister, the sister spreads hers out in a long line instead of a pile and declares, "I win! I have more cards!" What principle is keeping the sister from learning the rules?
- A 4-year-old girl walks into the kitchen and sees her mother pouring herself a glass of juice. The little girls asks for a glass, too, so the mother reaches into a cabinet and

pulls out a kid-sized cup. Her daughter screams and cries because she wants "a bigger amount of juice." She doesn't stop crying until her mother pours the juice out of the child's cup and into a larger container.

- Two-year-old twins were forever arguing about whose toy belonged to whom. The young father decided to put a stop to the arguing once and for all. He sat them both down and gave them a lecture about understanding the way the other twin felt. Although the twins nodded their heads, they were fighting again almost before the father had left the room. Why should the father have saved his breath?

After completing this exercise, you should be able to

- recognize Piaget's key developmental milestones.
- apply Piaget's ideas to routine child-caretaking situations.
- describe how knowledge of Piaget's principles could increase your patience as a parent.

Exercise 4.2

THE SITTER'S DILEMMA *Practical Problem Solving*

As a college student, you are probably hard up for money. So when a nearby family advertises for a sitter two nights a week, you are very tempted by the thought of what you feel should be easy money. After one night, however, you realize that this money is not going to be so easy. This family has gone through five babysitters in as many weeks because the children—ages 9 months, 2 years, 5 years, and 9 years—are energetic and difficult to manage. You need the money, however, so you decide to put your newly acquired knowledge about child development to use to create a plan to keep the children occupied and out of trouble.

List two activities that would appeal to each of the children, based on their ages. _____
_____
_____
_____

What activities might interest all of the children? _____
_____
_____

Because of the differences in their ages, these children all have different bedtimes. The infant goes to bed at 7:00 P.M., the 2 and 5 year olds at 7:30 and 8:00 P.M. respectively, and the 9 year old retires about 8:30 P.M. How might your plan for the evening change as the younger children go to bed?

After completing this exercise, you should be able to

- identify the cognitive, social and physical abilities of children of these ages.
- use your understanding of these abilities to create appealing activities.
- demonstrate the ability to design differential plans by age.

Exercise 4.3

DEVELOPMENTAL DELIGHTS   *Creative Problem Solving*

Play is an inherent part of human nature and part of the serious work of childhood. Most of us, when allowed to explore our environment and freed from concern with other tasks, play. And, despite what the advertisers would have you believe, one does not need expensive gadgets, bells, whistles, and lights to have fun. Given something as simple as a piece of fabric, an infant will play peekaboo, a preschooler will play dress-up, a school-age child might use it as a prop in a self-written play, and even an adult could have fun, perhaps creating a quilt or using it to help redecorate a bedroom. Below are some lists of everyday objects. Think about what a fun activity would be for children of the given ages, and use the objects to make toys.

Example:

Objects: string, empty thread spools, hanger, markers, paper

Children: 2 months: Using hanger and string, make mobile with shapes from paper, markers, and spool

14 months: Use all of above to make a pull toy

4 years: Use all of above to make a puppet for telling stories

Objects: drinking straws, cardboard, large plastic cups, string
Children: 6 months, 4 years, 7 years

_____
_____
_____

Objects: 4-quart pot, spoon, measuring cups, sink full of water
Children: 9 months, 3 years, 10 years

_____
_____
_____

Objects: 2 chairs, pillows, several books, large blanket
Children: 12 months, 2 years, 9 years

_____
_____
_____

After completing this exercise, you should be able to

- identify the cognitive, physical, and social abilities of children of different ages.
- use an understanding of these abilities to determine appropriate play activities.
- look at everyday objects in new ways to create "toys" that would be fun for children of various ages.

Exercise 4.4

ON DEATH AND DYING *Scientific Problem Solving*

After reading his own premature obituary in the newspaper, Mark Twain was reported to have said, "The news of my death is greatly exaggerated." Although most of us don't have a chance to read our own obituaries, some of us will have an opportunity to contemplate our own deaths when we are diagnosed with a terminal illness.

Surprisingly, death has been a taboo subject in Western culture, and as a result research in understanding the impact of terminal illness is comparatively recent. Elisabeth Kübler-Ross developed a provocative set of observations about the grief processes many people go through in coping with terminal illness. Many demonstrate *denial,* rejecting the bad news and assuming that someone somewhere has made a mistake. *Anger* becomes prominent when resentment brews about why they must struggle with this awful fate. Typically, terminally ill people often begin *bargaining*—either with God or with the attending physicians—for another alternative. *Depression* about impending losses and unpleasant ends can dominate the emotional life of these people. Some people discover *acceptance,* creating a feeling of peace about their fate. Kübler-Ross provides an interesting general description of how people adjust to terminal illnesses. However, her observations can also lead us to new ideas in our own research on death and dying.

In this exercise we are going to practice the characteristic of *variable-mindedness.* As pointed out earlier, we may never be able to isolate—and therefore completely understand—all the variables that contribute to any behavior pattern. Psychologists expect behaviors to be hard to identify and complicated to explain. Being variable-minded means thinking very broadly about all possible factors that might influence some behavior.

Can you identify three factors or variables that might influence the emotional experience of the terminally ill? That will be your task in this exercise. You will be given three general categories—characteristics of the illness, characteristics of the person, and characteristics of the environment. For each category, you will identify one independent variable that might influence the way terminally ill people experience the stages of death and dying. Then you will speculate about the impact of that variable. In effect, you will be creating a hypothesis about the way each of these variables influences the terminally ill person's grieving process.

For example, under "characteristics of illness" rate of decline is an independent variable that might affect the nature of the emotions a terminally ill person experiences. Perhaps abrupt decreases in physical strength will prompt angry responses more quickly than more gradual losses of strength and well-being. A possible hypothesis might then be *"Diseases that produce more rapid deterioration may exaggerate the negative processes of grief."* Can you identify other characteristics of a terminal illness that might influence the ill person's grief processes? (See Answer Key for some examples.)

Characteristics of the illness

Variable: _____

Hypothesis: _____

_____

Characteristic of the person

Variable: _____

Hypothesis: _____

_____

Characteristics of the environment

Variable: _____

Hypothesis: _____

_____

    This task illustrates how difficult it may be to isolate the specific causes of behavior. Even if we were able to identify some hypothesis that we thought might be valid, we would be unable to set up experiments to demonstrate the differences we predict. Experiments require the experimenter to manipulate independent variables in experimental design. It would be unethical to experiment with humans in controlled procedures to answer most of the questions involved in our hypotheses. In such cases, we may instead substitute correlational studies in which we determine the strength of the relationship between two or more variables without directly manipulating them.

After completing this exercise, you should be able to

- identify at least three variables that might influence the grief process.
- generate a simple hypothesis or prediction about each of those variables.
- describe what it means to be "variable minded" as a way of thinking about the behavior of others.

Exercise 4.5

UNDERSTANDING TEEN PREGNANCY — *Psychological Reasoning*

Teen pregnancy has been a popular issue at the forefront of a variety of political and social forums. Many organizations have created programs designed to reduce teen pregnancy, but sometimes the outcome of these programs is uncertain. Some programs use traditional pregnancy statistics, such as "percentage of high-school girls who get pregnant," as a way to document reductions in the overall rate. Some program planners worry that these programs have limited impact on teen pregnancy rates. Your task in this example is two-part:

1. Brainstorm at least two ideas for additional steps that could be taken to reduce teen pregnancy. Be sure to think about the problem from the various dimensions of development (e.g., biological, social, cognitive, etc.) as you generate your suggestions. Given what you understand of adolescent development, what might make such programs unsuccessful? How might you use this knowledge to create a program that has a high rate of success?
2. Identify one pregnancy statistic that you think would be the most persuasive in verifying a reduction in teen pregnancy that was related to the impact of a specific pregnancy prevention program.

After completing this exercise, you should be able to

- explain how the social, cognitive, and emotional abilities of adolescents influence pregnancy teen rates.
- generate some ideas for ways to decrease the pregnancy rate.
- advocate for a valid statistical measure that would reflect a successful intervention program's impact.

Exercise 4.6

| **PIAGET MEETS SANTA CLAUS** | *Perspective Taking* |

Swiss psychologist Jean Piaget was a careful observer of the cognitive patterns of children. Through systematic observation and careful recording he was able to deduce stages of cognitive activity that became apparent as children interacted with their environments over time. One of his most well-established concepts is *conservation,* the ability to recognize that even though the shape of an object changes, its mass does not change. To demonstrate conservation, researchers may form shapes out of equivalent amounts of clay, perhaps rolling one mass of clay into a snakelike configuration and shaping the other into a ball. A child who can conserve recognizes that the physical masses of the two objects are the same despite their different shapes.

Although the conservation demonstrations of Piaget are interesting to watch, we demonstrate our ability to understand physical realities through the life span in other ways as well. An effective comparison contrasts how humans in different phases of development react to cultural symbols, such as Santa Claus.

Your task in this exercise is to develop the point of view of children who are dealing with Santa at various stages of their own cognitive development. As you assume their perspective, try to anticipate the kinds of observations and impressions an encounter with Santa would trigger. How would you react in each stage of development? What features of Santa would be most important? What would you believe about his existence?

To be successful in this task, you must develop an objective or unbiased way of looking at a concept you already know quite well. Chances are good that you are a formal operational thinker in relation to the existence of Santa Clause. But can you set aside what you know (and believe and feel) in order to describe an encounter with Santa from the perspective of a child at the stages targeted in this exercise? The characteristics of the stages as Piaget described them should help you to identify with experience, thoughts, beliefs, and feelings of those whose behavior you are attempting to explain. You may want to review the stages of cognitive development in your text before you predict the experiences of children in the different stages. (See Answer Key.)

What are the general characteristics of the *sensorimotor stage* child?

_____

_____

_____

On encountering Santa, what would the *sensorimotor stage* child

- observe?
- think and feel?
- believe?

What are the general characteristics of the *preoperational stage* child?

_____

_____

_____

On encountering Santa, what would the *preoperational stage* child

- observe?
- think and feel?
- believe?

The breakdown in belief in Santa Claus tends to correspond with a child's transition into the *concrete operations stage.*

What are the general characteristics of the *concrete operational* child?

_____
_____
_____

On encountering Santa, what would the *concrete operational* child

- observe?
- think?
- feel?
- believe?

How do these transitional experiences differ from the characteristics of the formal operational child and adult?_____

_____

After this exercise, you should be able to

- suspend your viewpoint as a formal operational thinker and assume the perspective of someone else at an earlier developmental stage.
- recognize the most probable characteristics and reactions of children in different stages of development.
- observe how the nature of beliefs, feelings, and cognition shift over time.
- identify changes in cognition that lead to changes in belief.
- generalize how children with different traditions change in their cognitive ability to evaluate cultural myths similar to Santa Claus.

5

Sensation

Human beings (and all animals) need certain information to survive and thrive. We need to be able to find the edge of a cliff, feel the temperature of the air, taste the bitterness of a particular poisonous plant, and detect the presence or absence of other creatures. This is the job of our senses: to take the world around us and turn it into neural signals inside our bodies. This process of sensation relies on several physiological systems that translate (or transduce) different kinds of energy. As you apply the concepts in this chapter, you will take the first steps in understanding how these systems prepare us to live in the vast and everchanging world around us.

Exercise 5.1

CROSSING THE THRESHOLD *Pattern Recognition*

Our senses provide the information that enables us to detect the presence of objects and then to distinguish different objects from each other. Each sense organ has the job of detecting the presence of a particular kind of energy (light, chemical, sound) and differentiating among different levels of that type of energy. We call the minimum amount of energy that the sense organ can detect the *detection threshold* or *absolute threshold*. The *difference threshold* or *just noticeable difference (jnd)* is the smallest change in energy that the sense organ can perceive; the amount of change needed to tell that two things are different. We use these abilities constantly as we perform our everyday tasks. There is also debate about how much we rely on information that is below our ability to detect. Energy that cannot be detected by a sense organ is called *subliminal* or *subthreshold*.

For each of the situations below, identify which of the following concepts is necessary to complete the task successfully: absolute threshold, difference threshold, or subthreshold. Then think up your own examples from your daily life, to illustrate each of these concepts.

- A woman preparing for a trip to Mexico tries to learn Spanish using a "Learn While You Sleep" tape.
- A sentry on night duty notices a very soft noise and calls out for the thief to "Halt!"
- A father takes his children to the playground. During the visit, a child starts to cry. Without looking, the father can tell that it is not his child's cry.
- There is a sale on 5-pound prepackaged russet potato bags. In order to make sure that you get the most for your money, you pick up several to see which is the heaviest.

- You help your friend look for her contact lens on her white kitchen floor.
- A music group records the phrase "Buy our tapes" backwards in one of their songs.
- It is late at night and you are trying to go to bed without waking your roommate. You want to find your favorite nightwear without turning on the light. After carefully and quietly opening your dresser drawer, you reach in and try to pick it out of the four other things that are in the drawer.
- You are one of the judges in a chili-tasting contest and are trying to select the winner of the "Hottest Chili" award.
- In that same chili-tasting contest, you are asked to try to identify which of ten chili samples contains cinnamon.

Your examples:

Absolute threshold: _____

Difference threshold: _____

Subthreshold: _____

After completing this exercise, you should be able to

- define and differentiate among absolute threshold, difference threshold, and subthreshold.
- determine which type of threshold is being used to successfully complete some everyday tasks.
- apply threshold concepts to daily activities.

Exercise 5.2

OCCUPATIONAL DESIGN   *Practical Problem Solving*

Humans differ in the quality of their sensory abilities. Whether by variations in genetic endowment or by deficits caused from environmental damage, human sensory abilities differ from person to person. These abilities also vary over time for each individual; when you catch a cold, for example, several of your senses are affected. Your stuffy nose and head cold may prevent you from smelling, may flatten the taste of your food, and may even interfere with your ability to maintain your balance. We also are subject to a decline in some abilities as we age.

This exercise will cause you to think about how the range of sensory abilities could influence a person's choice of career—and your own. For example, think about the unique blend of sensory abilities that would be required for a successful career as a trapeze artist. The ideal combination of sensory abilities that would enable the trapeze artist to soar are reflected in the accompanying Sensory Profile of a Trapeze Artist. The sense of vision, touch, and balance would need to be especially acute. Hearing could be average because trapeze artists rely somewhat less on hearing. To perform their jobs, they really do not rely at all on taste or smell. Finally, a reduced capacity to transmit pain would probably enable longer hours of practice and performance without distraction, although this diminished ability could pose some danger form the artist's not recognizing or attending to serious injury.

Sensory Profile of a Trapeze Artist

	Diminished abilities	Average abilities	Heightened abilities
Vision			X
Hearing		X	
Smell	X		
Touch			X
Taste	X		
Pain	X		
Balance			X

Consider the three occupational choices of garbage collector, dessert chef, and college professor. Construct your version of an ideal sensory profile for each job. Justify your choices. (See Answer Key.)

Sensory Profile of a Garbage Collector

	Diminished abilities	Average abilities	Heightened abilities
Vision			
Hearing			
Smell			
Touch			
Taste			
Pain			
Balance			

Justification: _____
_____
_____
_____

Sensory Profile of a Dessert Chef

	Diminished abilities	Average abilities	Heightened abilities
Vision			
Hearing			
Smell			
Touch			
Taste			
Pain			
Balance			

Justification: _____

_____

_____

_____

Sensory Profile of a College Professor

Vision

Hearing

Smell

Touch

Taste

Pain

Balance

| | *Diminished abilities* | *Average abilities* | *Heightened abilities* |

Justification: _____

_____

_____

_____

Some jobs demand far more obvious abilities than others do. However, this exercise does suggest that our sensory abilities may play a subtle role in shaping our future choices.

After completing this exercise, you should be able to
- use graphic strategies for communicating simple relationships.
- recognize that jobs vary in their sensory requirements.
- identify situations in which sensory deficits may confer performance advantages.
- offer plausible explanations for proposed sensory profiles.
- anticipate the kind of sensory profile that might be involved in your own occupational future.

Exercise 5.3

REACH OUT AND TOUCH SOMEONE *Creative Problem Solving*

Think for a minute about how we communicate. Most of the time we use words, and although we write and read those words, much of our daily communication relies on speaking and hearing them. Talking is fast, easy and, with technology, almost unlimited by distance. About twenty years ago, there was a long-running and very successful ad campaign that encouraged people to use the telephone to "reach out and touch someone," by calling long-distance to talk with friends and family. Although the ad talked about touching, talking requires that we detect sound, the sense organ we use is the ear, and the instrument that allows us to do this long-distance is the phone. What would happen, however, if we actually did rely on touch to communicate? Communication would have an entirely different set of behaviors and requirements, because the skin detects a different kind of energy than does the ear. Using what you know about the sense of touch, try to invent a way to communicate using this sense. The following questions will help you think about the issues involved.

What sensations can the skin detect? _____
_____
_____

How might you use the skin's sensory abilities to "talk"? (If you need an idea, think about individuals who have lost the use of either sound or sight; how do they communicate?)_____
_____
_____

What form might long-distance communication take and what kind of instrument might you use? _____
_____
_____

After completing this exercise, you should be able to

- discuss the skin's ability to sense pressure, pain, warmth, and cold.
- recognize the relationship between the energy that a sense organ can detect and the way that sense organ can be used to communicate.
- use your knowledge of touch to create a novel form of long-distance communication.

Exercise 5.4

IT'S A MATTER OF TASTE   *Scientific Problem Solving*

As you learned in Chapter 1, Thinking Critically with Psychological Science, the scientific method is a process. You ask a question, design an experiment to find the answer, and find that often the answer leads to more questions. The result of this process is an everchanging, and more accurate, understanding of the world around us and within us.

One area in which a fairly major shift in our understanding of how a sense organ works has occurred recently is the area of taste. You are probably familiar with the "tongue map" theory of taste. This theory suggests that specific areas of the tongue are sensitive to specific tastes: The back of the tongue senses bitter tastes; the sides and middle, sweet and sour; and the tip, salty. You may have been surprised to find that this "map" was not included in your textbook. Recent studies have demonstrated that this map is not accurate; rather, there are receptors for each taste all over the tongue.

Design an experiment in which you test a component of either the "tongue map" theory of taste or the idea that each of the four basic taste sensations can be detected all over the tongue. You don't need to test the whole theory; rather, decide on a single question that has variables easy to define operationally.

What is your hypothesis? _____

What is/are your independent variable(s)? _____

How would you define it/them operationally? _____

What is/are your dependent variable(s)? _____

How would you define it/them operationally? _____

Briefly describe the design of your experiment: _____

_____

_____

_____

What are some things you will need to be careful to control if you conduct this experiment? (Hint: What about the subjects or variables could change the results of your experiment?) _____

_____

_____

If practical, why not conduct your experiment and bring the results to class? Even better, why not work on this exercise in groups or as a class and conduct the experiment together as a lab. Explore and have fun!

After completing this exercise, you should be able to

- create a specific hypothesis giving a theory of taste.
- identify the independent and dependent variables within that hypothesis.
- operationalize variables.
- design control procedures to eliminate alternative explanations for your findings.

Exercise 5.5

PARTS IS PARTS   *Psychological Reasoning*

Remember the last time you walked by one of those perfume testers in the mall, or opened the container that had been sitting in the back of the fridge for two weeks too long, and were overwhelmed by the smell? What about the time you were trying to study and the music down the hall was so loud you couldn't hear yourself think? How about those psychedelic plaid pants from the 1970s that your Uncle Frank insists on wearing for special occasions; you probably wish you didn't have to see those. And who wants to taste those nasty cough syrups? There are always times in our lives when we would rather our senses didn't transduce signals from the environment quite so successfully. It would be much easier if we didn't have to attend to all those inconvenient or uncomfortable signals. But what would be the negative consequences of turning off each sense's ability to transduce energy from the environment? You might not have to smell the moldy leftovers, but you also wouldn't be able to smell Mormor's Swedish coffee cake. No loud music, but no soft whispers of love.

Using the chart below, list each of the senses, the type of energy from the environment that the sense organ transduces to create the sensation, and three positive and negative consequences of turning off that sense organ. If you had to pick, which one would you turn off and why?

Sense	Energy	Positive consequences	Negative consequences
Vision			
Hearing			
Smell			
Touch			
Taste			

After completing this exercise, you should be able to
- identify the energy detected by each sense organ.
- describe the ways in which such detection is painful or inconvienent.
- articulate the value of the information detected by the various sense organs.

Exercise 5.6

THE EYES HAVE IT *Perspective Taking*

Most of us take vision for granted, going through our lives depending on the accurate transduction of light into form, color, and movement. Imagine how your daily life might be different if something happened to change the way you experience your visual world. How would you adapt and how long would it take?

Select an activity that you can perform safely (with a partner) even with your eyes closed. Maybe you could play catch with something soft, fold laundry, put away the dishes, water the plants, or walk the dog. First, perform the activity with both eyes open. Then try covering one eye with a patch (be careful not to put pressure on the eye) and perform the activity again. After this, try the activity completely blindfolded. If you wear corrective lenses, why not try removing them? Finally, if you have access to upside-down goggles, try your activity while wearing them.

- What differences did you note in your ability to judge the shape, distance, speed, and direction of the objects with which you were working? _____

- How did your attention change or focus differently in each situation? _____

- Which situation was the most difficult for you? Practice doing your activity several times under these most difficult circumstances. Did you adapt? How long did it take? _____

- Compare your answers with your classmates to see if their experience differed from yours. If so, see if you can find patterns to the differences. Are some activities easier to perform completely blindfolded than with one eye patched? _____

Perception

Psychologist William James believed that the world starts out as a "blooming, buzzing confusion" for the newborn. Perception is the process by which we work to make sense of what can be a confusing array of sensations. Using expectations and experiences to help select, organize, and interpret important sensations, we turn the world around us into a meaningful, and meaning-filled, place.

Exercise 6.1

THE BIG PICTURE *Pattern Recognition*

Gestalt psychology offers principles of good form and rules for grouping stimuli. Typically these principles are illustrated using two-dimensional stimuli: lines, dots, images orchestrated to demonstrate specific effects. However, the Gestalt principles can also be seen in operation in three-dimensional, dynamic forms, as this exercise will illustrate.

Let's start with a group performance such as the work that might be performed by a marching band during the half-time activities in a football game. Recall some performance you have seen and try to think of it as a demonstration of Gestalt principles of good form and grouping.

Figure-ground. Marching in front of the band and waving a baton, the drum major stands out from the rest of the band, enhanced by more dramatic costuming and a central position in relation to the other band members.

Proximity. Certain band members may cluster together, particularly when their assignment is to create a visual impact distinct from the rest of the band. The minimal distance maintained within the cluster enhances the crowd's perception that this subgroup is a unit by itself. This principle is apparent when band members must form a particular letter of the alphabet or some other visual design; their proximity helps us to perceive that design as distinct from the activities of the other subgroups on the field.

Similarity. Band uniforms, musical instruments, and choreographed marching enhance our perception of the band as a group or as subdivisions that form meaningful smaller groups.

Closure. When the music and movement stop, we see the performance as a completed experience.

Continuity/connectedness. As band members break into smaller marching groups to develop a distinctive formation, their movements relative to each other and to members of other groups will cause the crowd to perceive them as subgroups. For example, the horn section, moving clockwise in a circle, will be perceived as a whole group because their movements cause them to appear to be connected with one another. In contrast, the drum section, moving counterclockwise, will be perceived as a separate group.

Now it's your turn. Apply the design principles to either a football game or a ballet performance. (See Answer Key.)

Selected performance:

Figure-ground: _____
_____
_____

Proximity: _____
_____

Similarity: _____
_____

Closure: _____
_____

Continuity/connectedness: _____
_____
_____

The principles of good form are readily apparent in virtually every aspect of life. However, we would be distracted if we constantly attended to the components of good design rather than to the overall form itself. Although this exercise generally emphasizes principles applied to visual stimuli, we could illustrate the Gestalt ideas in other sensory modes (such as hearing or taste).

After completing this exercise, you should be able to

- recognize that perceptual images can be analyzed into specific design principles.
- apply Gestalt principles to perceptual stimuli.
- identify other group performances that illustrate Gestalt principles.
- speculate about how the design principles work in sensory modes other than vision.

Exercise 6.2

ASSESSING THE ASSEMBLY LINE   *Practical Problem Solving*

A large manufacturing company is working to ensure that its new gidgit line has the appropriate quality control. (Gidgits are block-like toys with a very complex shape.) They hire inspectors to look at the items as they roll by on a conveyer belt and to pull off the ones that are not made properly. Using what you know about visual perception, how would you set up the situation so that the inspectors' jobs would be easiest? What could you do to facilitate their recognition of the correct shape and/or their comparison among gidgits?

After completing this exercise, you should be able to

- describe the perceptual task involved in a real-life scenario.
- use an understanding of the visual system to identify essential elements necessary for completing the described visual perception task.
- manipulate the physical environment to facilitate successful completion of the given perceptual task.

Exercise 6.3

CHAOS CONTROL *Creative Problem Solving*

Perceptual processes help us to maintain a sense of stability and control in what could be perceived as a chaotic environment. Two processes—habituation and perceptual set—are especially important in promoting our adaptation to complex environments. *Habituation* allows us to disengage from environmental stimuli that don't offer us new information or that become boring. This process frees us to "attend" to changing elements in the environment. *Perceptual set* represents our formulation of expectations about how the physical world and its inhabitants will behave. From each experience we extract a meaningful pattern so we can predict that similar procedures and outcomes will be part of that experience in the future.

In this exercise, imagine that your perceptual skills of habituation and perceptual set are "broken." Identify five probable effects of this malfunction as you go about a regular school day. (Hint: You may find it helpful to remember some of your feelings and experiences while visiting a new place, where your awareness might be heightened and your expectations might be few.)

What kinds of effects could you anticipate if your perceptual skills malfunctioned?

1. _____

2. _____

3. _____

4. _____

5. _____

After completing this exercise, you should be able to

- identify the role that habituation and perceptual set play in organizing chaotic environments.
- revisit routine behaviors to examine why they become routine.
- appreciate the efficiency of perceptual processes in attending to important stimuli and ignoring unimportant ones.
- use your imagination to envision life with perceptual impairments.

Exercise 6.4

CLIFF HANGERS — *Scientific Problem Solving*

Evidence suggests that the ability to perceive depth is at least partly innate. As mentioned in your textbook, human infants less than 1 month old will turn away from objects with trajectories that would hit them, but they will not turn away from objects with trajectories that are angled away from them. In addition, human infants between 6 and 14 months (as well as day-old goats, newly hatched chicks, and young kittens) will stop when approaching a visual cliff (a drop-off covered by a stable, yet transparent, material). Even coaxing from parents is not enough to convince most of them to venture out "into space."

Identify two possible cues that the infants (and goats, chicks, and kittens) might be using to perceive the drop-off. How might you test those hypotheses? Given what you know about infant development, what would improve or increase this ability to detect visual cliffs?

After completing this exercise, you should be able to

- identify the binocular and monocular cues essential for depth perception.
- articulate two hypotheses about how infants might be using monocular or binocular cues to perceive depth.
- create appropriate experimental designs for evaluating these two hypotheses.
- discuss what factors might influence an infant's ability to use cues to depth perception.

Exercise 6.5

THE CASE AGAINST ESP — *Psychological Reasoning*

- You are driving along in your car and find yourself humming a pleasant tune. You turn on the radio and that very song comes on. You smile to yourself and think your ability to predict music on the radio is just a bit uncanny.
- Brenda prides herself on being able to predict the gender of unborn children. Expectant parents eagerly sought her predictions until newer, less fallible medical technologies displaced her skills.
- Eugene is one lucky guy. Almost every month he wins something in the state lottery. His friends believe he must be clairvoyant.
- Pat hates it when she gets those "ooky feelings." Her heart starts to race and she knows something terrible has happened, sometimes to a loved one but most of the time to a stranger whose bad luck is reported on television.
- Bruce hardly studies at all and he gets superb grades. He claims he has a special ability to predict the kinds of questions instructors will include on exams. He brags that this ability saves him hours of study and earns him nearly a 3.5 grade-point average.
- A magician claims he can identify the most pressing concerns among audience members. He asks each person to fill out an identical index card, stating his or her most serious worry of the moment. He collects the cards, raises one index card to his head, and—without reading the card—voices a specific concern. Then he asks, "Whose worry is this!" A shy woman in the middle of the room raises her hand and claims, "It's mine!" He examines the card to verify her claim. One by one, the magi-

cian then accurately identifies at least five more pressing concerns for astonished members of the audience.

Do these examples prove the validity of *extrasensory perception?* The scientific community may not have delivered a final verdict, but most psychologists would say no. Why would scientists who express pride in their open-mindedness seem to have such a closed mind when it comes to such mysteries of the universe? Psychologists believe that the absence of objective evidence weakens the claims that support ESP.

As shown in the chapter exploring brain function, our brains actively make sense of the stimulation from the environment. Sometimes our brains distort incoming sensations to produce more acceptable perceptions. This creativity is just one factor that encourages skeptical psychologists to disbelieve claims of supernatural knowledge. Most psychologists would insist that there is a compelling alternative explanation for events that might be mislabeled extrasensory perceptions.

Try your hand at proposing reasonable *alternative hypotheses* for the behaviors in this exercise. (See Answer Key.)

How else could you explain predicting music on the radio? _____
_____
_____

What other factors might account for Brenda's accurate predictions of gender? _____
_____
_____

How can some people be so lucky at picking lottery numbers and others be terrible?
_____
_____

How might someone be able to predict disaster for others? _____
_____
_____

How could someone know just what to study so that he could excel on an exam?
_____
_____

What other explanations could explain a magician's ability to "read your mind"?
_____
_____

After completing this exercise, you should be able to
- see the importance of objective evidence in challenging claims of ESP.
- identify how illusions can be used to create a powerful subjective argument for extrasensory perception.
- recognize how normal rates of occurrence of behavior influence reported successes of ESP.
- generate some alternative explanations for reported paranormal behaviors.
- understand why psychologists are skeptical of claims that cannot be verified objectively.
- justify saving your money rather than spending it on pseudoscientific claims.

Exercise 6.6

CONTEXT CUES   *Perspective Taking*

One of the many concepts that you have learned in this chapter is that perception involves the interpretation of stimuli and can be influenced by various internal factors (like expectations and beliefs), as well as by external factors (like perspective or environmental context). Predicting how ambiguous stimuli will be interpreted in the real world is tricky business, because the possibilities are almost as varied as the number of interpreters! Nevertheless, it is possible to *design* stimuli in such a way that there are limited, and predictable, interpretations. The reversible figure-ground picture on page 185 of your textbook is a good example. A person could see either the vase, the faces of Prince Philip and Queen Elizabeth II, or alternate between the two. Using what you know about setting context, speculate under what conditions a person would see only the vase, only the faces, or would alternate between the two.

After completing this exercise, you should be able to

- recognize the role of context and expectation in the interpretation of ambiguous stimuli.
- create situations in which the same stimulus would be perceived differently.
- use an understanding of perceptual processes to predict people's response to ambiguous stimuli.

7

States of Consciousness

You are driving down the highway. It is a lovely day for a drive, so you relax, roll the window down, and allow your mind to wander. Suddenly, you realize you are many miles down the road without having paid attention to how you got there. You don't remember passing familiar landmarks, although you obviously did in order to reach the place in which you now find yourself.

Does this process sound familiar? Such trance states are regular occurrences in the course of our daily lives. We are capable of executing well-learned behavior without paying much attention. We are likely to experience many levels of consciousness during a single day. The following exercises explore aspects of conscious and unconscious experience.

Exercise 7.1

CONSCIOUS CONTROL? *Pattern Recognition*

Conscious experience comes in different forms. You may recognize that conscious experience can be ordered along a continuum from "extremely alert and self-aware" to "out of it." Below we list a variety of common and some not-so-common experiences that could be organized along a continuum of alertness and conscious control. Create a rank order of consciousness out of the list below. Then compare your answers to those of your classmates.

a. Nodding off in a boring class _____

b. Preparing to give your first speech in a class _____

c. Studying for an exam _____

d. Feeling the effects of having taken a painkiller _____

e. Meditating _____

f. Quacking like a duck while hypnotized _____

g. Counting backward while being anesthetized _____

h. Having one social drink _____

i. Having one more drink than you should _____

j. Driving down the road but realizing that you are two exits past your stop _____

k. Praying

l. Meeting an attractive person for the first time

m. Daydreaming

After completing this exercise, you should be able to
- recognize different forms of conscious experience.
- articulate conscious experiences as a continuum of awareness and control.
- defend your position in a group discussion about categorizing conscious experience.

Exercise 7.2

PROFESSIONAL PROJECT DARE — *Practical Problem Solving*

You are part of a drug prevention team that is trying to foster a campaign to help reduce illegal drug use in adults, similar to the DARE program that police officers use when working with children. As a starting point, you have decided to create targeted anti-drug campaigns for different groups, based on the risks of impairment of performance inherent in their activities. For each type of specialized occupation or interest below, specify the illicit or illegal drug that would most dangerously impair the user's function and explain the likely effect of using the drug on the individual's preferred activity.

Preferred Activity or Profession	Most Dangerous Drug Substance and Predicted Risk
Bicycle messenger	
Marathon runner	
Artist	
Stay-at-home mom	
Sword swallower	
Teacher	
Tightrope walker	
Accountant	

After completing this exercise, you should be able to
- recognize the impact of illegal drug substances on the performance of professionals' activities and on the preferred leisure activities of adults.
- articulate the impact of specific drugs on aspects of human activity.
- compare degrees of dangerousness among drug substances.
- formulate some reasonable ideas about how one might campaign to persuade a specific individual about the dangers of drug use.

Exercise 7.3

ROCK-A-BYE BABY — *Creative Problem Solving*

How people sleep—and how well they sleep—is an issue for many. In the United States, advertisers present an almost overwhelming array of books, tapes, songs, foods, and drugs guaranteed to put anyone to sleep. The old sleep standby, however, is the lullaby. Adapt or create a lullaby to address some aspect of sleep and sleep schedules. We offer two adapted examples below. Because you won't be able to hear our creative melodies, we will leave crafting an original lullaby to your imagination!

Traditional Examples:	**Sleep Theory Adaptation:**
Rock-a-bye baby, on the tree top,	Rock-a-bye baby, going to sleep,
When the wind blows, the cradle will rock.	Alpha waves cease and delta waves peak.
When the bough breaks, the cradle will fall,	Then comes a dream with stage-one-like REM,
And down will come baby, cradle and all.	And the next night it starts all over again.
Go to sleep,	Go to sleep,
Go to sleep,	Every night,
Go to sleep, little baby.	The same time to bed, you will sleep tight.
When you wake, we shall have cake,	When you wake, refreshed and right,
Go to sleep, little baby.	You will do it every night.

After completing this exercise, you should be able to
- appreciate the essential qualities of lullabies in inducing sleep.
- apply sleep theories in a creative expression.
- put your sleep-starved friends at rest if you perform for them!

Exercise 7.4

REMEDIES FOR JET LAG *Scientific Problem Solving*

If you have ever traveled cross-country, especially from east to west, you have probably experienced the phenomenon of *jet lag*. This confused and overtired feeling supports the speculation that we have a *biological clock* that governs our sense of fatigue. We may experience the same disorientation when our weekend sleep schedules don't match the schedules we maintain on weekdays. For people with these mismatched schedules, Mondays are horrors.

Suppose you have just been given a research grant to identify effective treatments for minimizing jet lag. You have been exploring possible treatments and have come up with three suggestions—(1) preventive doses of vitamin B complex; (2) 10 minutes of meditation; and (3) 15 minutes of aerobic exercise. Each suggestion is complete with a reasonable physiological rationale. How might you discern which, if any, of those treatments would reduce or prevent jet lag?

Your task in this assignment is to design a simple experiment that will determine the relative effectiveness of those treatments. To do this, you will provide the important elements of the study by answering the following questions. (See Answer Key.)

What is your hypothesis? _____
_____
_____

What is the independent variable? _____
_____
_____

How will you measure the dependent variable (jet lag)? _____
_____
_____

What other variables will you need to control? _____
_____
_____

After completing this exercise, you should be able to
- standardize the experience you are studying in an experiment.
- develop some method for making the participants' experience comparable.
- design simple studies that attempt to exclude alternative interpretations.
- recognize that experiments are an expensive and complicated means of gathering evidence.

Exercise 7.5

A MIDSUMMER NIGHT'S DREAM — *Psychological Reasoning*

Peter is a young man who lives in North America. Although normal in most ways, he is quite unable to sleep unless there is natural darkness. This is not generally a problem where he lives, because even though summer days are quite long, there is still enough dark time for him to get sufficient sleep. One December, however, he has the opportunity to go to Antarctica. He is there for four days, during which time the sun never sets. Describe what will happen to Peter's behavior and physiological well-being over the course of the four days. What can he expect when he returns to his home?

After completing this exercise, you should be able to
- identify the role of sleep in recuperation and energy conservation.
- discuss the effects of sleep deprivation on behavior and emotional states.
- anticipate Peter's rapid return of health and normal behavior when he resumes his usual sleep patterns.

Exercise 7.6

THE LIGHT AT THE END OF THE TUNNEL — *Perspective Taking*

One unresolved controversy in the area of consciousness involves the explanation of the near-death experience. Some patients who survive cardiac arrest characterize the near-death experience as a pleasant journey in which lights and tunnels are prominent features. Some report encountering loved ones who have already died. Others report the sensation of being drawn out of their bodies, sometimes being able to look down on those who are administering their care. Many people report that their near-death experience is transformational: They retain a sense of peace and often report that death is no longer something to be feared.

Two conflicting explanations are offered for this experience of altered consciousness. The first, which we will call the *spiritual hypothesis,* proposes that near-death experiences verify that the body and soul are two distinctive components of human experience. According to this view, a near-death experience simply provides a preview of the experience the human soul will encounter after death.

The second explanation we will call the *physiological hypothesis* because it is grounded in physiology. This explanation suggests that the light at the end of the tunnel is simply a hallucination. Physiologists know that challenges to the integrity of the brain (such as suffocation or injury) can produce hallucinations. They argue that many patients who have experienced the near-death experience have also been subject to harrowing medical conditions in which oxygen deprivation has developed. According to this view, the perceived experience of the afterlife is merely a hallucination, not a promise of a life to come.

This particular controversy highlights very different values and belief systems. Your task in this exercise is to identify the values that are the support structure for the spiritual and the physiological hypotheses. Then identify the position that has greater appeal for you, given our current state of knowledge. What do you believe is the source of the near-death experience? What values support your belief? (See Answer Key.)

Summarize the spiritual hypothesis:_____

_____

What values and beliefs support the spiritual hypothesis?_____

_____

_____

Summarize the physiological hypothesis: _____

_____

_____

What values and beliefs support the physiological hypothesis? _____

_____

_____

What position has greater personal appeal to you? Why? _____

_____

_____

Psychological and religious explanations differ in their emphases. Preference for objective evidence derived from empirical research dominates psychological thinking. Religious thinking is primarily subjective; faith does not require objective evidence.

After completing this exercise, you should be able to

- identify at least two values involved in the conflict regarding near-death experiences.
- state your own preference for interpreting the near-death experience.
- trace the way your own belief system has developed from your values.
- distinguish some general differences in the values of science-based versus religious-based thinking.

Learning

The basic ideas in the learning traditions of psychology can be difficult to master if your view of learning is too narrow. It is relatively easy to think of learning as only the kind of "book learning" we do in school. In psychology, learning generally refers to the learning of behaviors that help us survive better in some environment. The "learning" associated with the acquisition of concepts or ideas is more likely to be found in the traditions of memory research, which we will explore in Chapter 9.

There are two dominant traditions of learning theory in psychology. Ivan Pavlov accidentally discovered the principles of classical conditioning when he was examining the digestive processes of dogs. His approach helps us understand how we learn to attach significance to events associated with automatic, reflexive responses. Operant conditioning, attributed to B. F. Skinner, switches the emphasis from reflex-based learning to learning that is shaped by consequences. The exercises in this chapter differentiate the two kinds of learning and clarify some concepts that are especially difficult to master.

Exercise 8.1

THE CLASSICAL CONNECTION *Pattern Recognition*

In most classical conditioning examples, we should be able to identify an *involuntary response* at the core of the learning process. In Pavlov's original conditioning experiment, the dog's salivary reflex was the involuntary response. When food is presented to a hungry dog, the dog will salivate. This connection is natural and unlearned, or unconditioned. It is the brain's way of readying the digestive tract, and it assists in our survival. We might say that this is a "hard-wired" feature of dog design. Food is an *unconditioned stimulus (UCS)* and the salivation is an *unconditioned response (UCR)*—a natural and unlearned one.

If you present a neutral stimulus—one that has no particular meaning, such as a bell—to a dog just prior to presenting the food, and if you present this pair of stimuli often enough, you are likely to see a new learned connection develop. The bell will come to signify that the food is on its way. Since the bell had no effect initially, the meaning of the bell had to be conditioned. Therefore, it is called the *conditioned stimulus (CS)*. When the researcher has successfully conditioned the dog to respond to the bell, the dog will salivate in the absence of food. This salivation is called the *conditioned response (CR)*. Note that the unconditioned response and the conditioned response are virtually the same. They are likely to differ only in intensity. (Even dogs are smart enough to know you shouldn't eat a bell. . . .)

Chapter 8 Learning

Now it's your turn. Four examples of classical conditioning are outlined in the following paragraphs. Each describes a situation in which an unconditioned stimulus, an unconditioned response, a conditioned stimulus, and a conditioned response occur. Can you identify the components in each example? (See Answer Key.)

The Troublesome Shower

Martin likes to take a shower in the men's locker room after working out. During one such shower, he hears someone flushing a nearby toilet. Suddenly, boiling-hot water rushes out of the shower head, causing Martin serious discomfort. As he continues the shower, he hears another toilet flush and immediately jumps out from under the shower head.

What is the unconditioned response (UCR)? (The UCR is the *involuntary, "hard-wired" reaction* that does not need to be learned.) _____

What is the unconditioned stimulus (UCS)? (The UCS is the event that automatically *elicits the involuntary response.*) _____

What is the conditioned response (CR)? (The CR is the new behavior that is *acquired through learning.*) _____

What is the conditioned stimulus (CS)? (The CS is the event *that takes on new meaning through conditioning.*) _____

The Water Show

Jeanette was happy when she heard about her family's plan to go to a water sports show. Then she heard the weather report, which predicted temperatures exceeding 100 degrees. Jeanette suspected that the weather would be hard to bear, but she went to the show. As she watched the water skiers perform taxing routines to the blaring organ music, she got more and more sweaty and uncomfortable. Eventually, she fainted from the heat. After the family outing, Jeanette could never again hear organ music without feeling a little dizzy.

Unconditioned response (UCR): _____

Unconditioned stimulus (UCS): _____

Conditioned response (CR): _____

Conditioned stimulus (CS): _____

The Trouble With Tuna

Brian was really looking forward to lunch. His mother had prepared a tuna salad sandwich. Unfortunately, the mayonnaise she used had been left out too long and was tainted. Not long after eating, Brian felt extremely nauseated and had to rush to the bathroom. Thereafter, the mere mention of a tuna sandwich would send Brian scurrying to the bathroom with a rolling stomach.

UCR: _____

UCS: _____

CR: _____

CS: _____

Captain Hook's Time Problem

Captain Hook had a nasty encounter with a crocodile in Never-Never Land. As a result of the battle, he lost his hand to the croc, which also swallowed an alarm clock. Fortunately for Hook, the loud ticking warned him of the hungry croc's approach. Unfortunately for Hook, any clock's ticking now ushers in a full-blown anxiety attack. (Be careful here.)

UCR: _____

UCS: _____

CR: _____

CS: _____

After completing this exercise, you should be able to

- isolate the behaviors involved in the classical conditioning process.
- relate the appropriate terms to the conditioning examples.
- recognize how classical conditioning procedures produce learned responses.
- use classical conditioning terminology to describe the process of learning.
- identify the involuntary response that is the origin of most classically conditioned responses.
- identify how classical conditioning processes can cause phobic reactions.
- describe how generalization extends the number of scary things that cause phobic reactions.

Exercise 8.2

POWERFUL CONSEQUENCES — *Practical Problem Solving*

In classical conditioning, objects take on new meaning when they are closely associated with some type of involuntary behavior. In operant conditioning, consequences determine behavior. We will tend to repeat things that make us feel good (principles involving *reinforcement*), avoid things that make us feel bad (principle of *punishment*), and disengage from behaviors that have no impact (principle of *extinction*).

Any time consequences *reinforce* a behavior, it will be strengthened. For example, a builder who wants to reinforce a wall to make it stronger may add another stud, and a tailor who needs to reinforce a seam will restitch. Similarly, reinforced behavior is more likely to occur in the future. When you see the term *reinforcement,* expect that the target behavior will get stronger or increase in intensity.

Positive reinforcement is relatively straightforward. When a good consequence follows some performance, you are more likely to repeat that performance in order to capture more of the good consequences that follow it. For instance, if you study hard for a test and receive an *A* for your efforts, you will probably expend the same energies on your next test because you have received this positive reinforcement.

Negative reinforcement is a little trickier. Negative reinforcement is often confused with punishment, but they are not the same. In negative reinforcement situations, the target behavior is the one you can perform to help you escape some bad circumstance. When a behavior is negatively reinforced, the behavior has helped you escape some pain, some embarrassment, or some other negative situation. For example, if you live in a rainy climate, you may routinely carry an umbrella to prevent getting soaked by the rain. Your habit of carrying an umbrella would be negatively reinforced: You escape an unpleasant outcome by remembering to bring the tool that will keep you dry. When you see the term *negative reinforcement*, try to identify what is negative about the target situation. Will a specified behavior allow you to escape or avoid the unfavorable circumstance? If so, that escape behavior will be negatively reinforced. We rarely enjoy being in uncomfortable or painful situations. This explains why negative reinforcement situations are such powerful incentives to strengthen behaviors that will allow us to escape.

Punishment tends to reduce the frequency of the behavior it follows. However, almost any parent can tell you that the effects of punishment vary. To be effective in reducing undesirable behavior, punishment should be swift, consistent, and sufficiently strong. Coordinating punishing consequences to meet those criteria can be a challenge. Even when punishment works, punishing practices may have undesirable side effects. For example, children associate the punisher with pain and may dislike or avoid the punisher.

Extinction is also a process that reduces the occurrence of behavior. When a behavior meets with no consequence, there is no incentive to continue the behavior. Although extinction is effective in reducing behavior, the process may take a very long time.

Here are some clues that should help you determine which of the four principles of operant conditioning are at work.

Positive reinforcement: When a behavior is followed by a favorable outcome (+), the behavior is likely to be strengthened in the future (↑).

Negative reinforcement: When a person is trapped in a bad situation, he or she performs a behavior to escape the bad situation. The escape is a favorable outcome (+); the escape behavior is likely to be strengthened in the future (↑).

Punishment: When a behavior is followed by an unpleasant outcome (−), the behavior *may* decrease in the future (↓). *Note:* Punishment is risky business. To ensure effectiveness, it must be done quickly, consistently, and with the proper intensity.

Extinction: When a behavior has no meaningful consequence (0), the behavior *will* decrease in the future (↓).

The following scenarios describe some behaviors and their consequences. Your task is to apply the principles of operant conditioning to predict whether the targeted behavior (the underlined one) will recur. Read the short scenario, focusing on the underlined behavior, and identify whether the consequence for the person performing the behavior was good (+), bad (−), or none (0). Then specify whether the targeted behavior is likely to increase (↑) or decrease (↓) in the future. (See Answer Key.)

Scenario	Nature of Consequence	Likelihood of Recurrence	Principle
a. A student volunteers to answer a tough question in class, and the teacher comments favorably on the quality of the student's contribution.			
b. A wife brings home flowers to her husband because of the special dinner he had cooked for her.			

Scenario	Nature of Consequence	Likelihood of Recurrence	Principle
c. A child is sent to his room with no supper after presenting a bad report card.			
d. Dad and tot enter the checkout lane of the supermarket. When the child screams for candy, dad pops a sucker in her mouth to quiet her down.			
e. A child spills milk all over the supper table, and Mom (having had a very bad day) swoops the child up from the high chair and spanks him.			
f. A student has a terrible headache after an intense preparation period for a test. He takes two aspirin to make it go away.			
g. Two children, who usually spend most of their time fighting, finally play peaceably over a coloring book. Dad peeks in and sighs, "At last, they are getting along." He returns to work without saying anything to them.			
h. As a spoiled child is being driven by a fast-food restaurant, she begins screaming that she must have french fries or she won't survive. The parents surrender and drive in for a large supply.			
i. A teenager whines about having nothing to do. Dad gives him a lecture about all the stuff in his room and the good old days when he, the father, didn't have all that stuff but still managed to be happy.			
j. A terrorist applies an electric current to the feet of a spy to make her confess. She tells him everything she knows.			

After completing this exercise, you should be able to

- describe the four principles of operant behavior.
- explain how reinforcement processes increase the likelihood of a behavior's recurrence.
- distinguish between negative reinforcement and punishment.
- demonstrate effective problem-solving processes to make accurate predictions.
- see how these principles might make you better at predicting behaviors in your own life.

Exercise 8.3

REINFORCING RHYMES — *Creative Problem Solving*

Learning principles can be serious business. Companies use them to determine effective pay schedules, parents use them to direct the behavior of children, and police officers use them to get you to obey the speed limit.

Learning about learning principles doesn't have to be so serious. These principles can be found (or inserted) in the most unexpected places. Common nursery rhymes can illustrate basic learning concepts. Rewrite a nursery rhyme so that it illustrates one or more of these principles. If no traditional nursery rhyme appeals, write your own. You might even feature your instructor or a classmate as the star of your rhyme.

Revised examples:

Mary Had a Little Lamb
Mary had a little lamb;
She wanted to teach it tricks.
Stay, come, and go
Were easy, you know,
When she gave it a peppermint stick.

There Was an Old Woman Who Lived in a Shoe
There was an old woman who lived in a shoe.
She had so many children she didn't know what to do.
Should she punish the bad or reinforce the good?
Reinforcement works best, if only she would.

Original examples:

Bountiful Bribery
Dr. Jones was a tough nut to crack.
His students felt put on the rack.
They finally agreed
That all would succeed
If they gave him his office key back!

Negative Reinforcement Rag
Tom was a bit of a heel.
His friends all knew he would squeal.
When the police got tough
And threatened rough stuff,
He spilled all he knew to appeal.

After completing this exercise, you should be able to

- recognize how widespread examples of learning principles can be.
- create a plausible, but rhyming example of a learning mechanism.
- have others recognize your learning expertise.

Exercise 8.4

A WORKING HYPOTHESIS — *Scientific Problem Solving*

Corporations often hire industrial-organizational psychologists to help solve management and production problems. Learning principles are often part of the solution that I/O psychologists develop to help the employer.

The owner of ROYAS-R-US decides to employ you (as a budding I/O psychologist) to ensure that its workers make the most royas possible. The employer wants to know whether paying people for piecework or by weekly salary would be more effective in the production of royas. Design an experiment that will address this question and state the hypothesis in terms of reinforcement schedules.

Hypothesis: _____

Independent variable(s): _____

Dependent variables(s): _____

Extraneous variables for which you would control: _____

Basic experimental protocol: _____

Potential ethical concerns: _____

After completing this exercise, you should be able to

- use experimental methodology to propose a solution for a corporation's production concerns.
- apply terminology regarding schedules of reinforcement to production.
- speculate about current ethical controls on research activities.
- explore possible job elements of industrial/organizational psychology.

Exercise 8.5

LITTLE ALBERT REVISITED *Psychological Reasoning*

Do you remember the story of poor Little Albert? Psychologist John B. Watson used the principles of classical conditioning to create Albert's fear response to a white rat (which later generalized to other white furry things). Watson's explanation of this outcome was that pairing the rat (the CS) with the loud noise (the UCS) resulted in a fear response to the rat (CR). The explanation that someone like B. F. Skinner would have, however, is that the experience with the rat was punished by the loud noise and so there was a strong desire to decrease the experience of the rat.

Although the rationale for this phenomenon may not seem very important, both have implications for treatment. How would someone attempting to treat Little Albert's fear of rats do so if she or he believed that classical conditioning provided the best explanation for the cause of the fear? How would it be different from the treatment used by someone who believed that the fear was the result of punishing Little Albert's experience with the rat? Can you use the appropriate terminology to explain what the treatment procedure might be?

No one knows what happened to Little Albert, although historians discuss the possibilities from time to time. What do you think might have happened to Little Albert's level of fear without intervention?

After completing this exercise, you should be able to

- describe the original outcome of Watson's Little Albert conditioning study.
- suggest a treatment strategy that follows logically from a classical conditioning approach to fear.
- propose a treatment strategy that exemplifies operant conditioning logic.
- provide a plausible prediction about what happens to conditioned fear over time without intervention.

Exercise 8.6

THE DISCRIMINATING DACHSHUND — *Perspective Taking*

Mike and Laura's pet dachshund, Greta, loved to play fetch. While playing fetch one afternoon with a tennis ball, she accidently picked up the ball after it had, unfortunately, landed in a fire ant hill. Needless to say, Greta's mouth got many painful bites. From that point on, Greta avoided tennis balls and would only play with soccer balls. She also avoided any ball that was the same size as a tennis ball or smaller. How would Pavlov and Skinner each have explained this outcome?

Pavlov's explanation:_____
_____

Skinner's explanation:_____
_____

After completing this exercise, you should be able to
- use learning theory terminology accurately.
- apply classical conditioning to explain avoidance behavior.
- use operant conditioning to explain avoidance behavior.
- discuss discriminating responses in both frameworks.

Memory

Sometimes it feels like a precision instruction. Sometimes it feels like a dusty, locked file cabinet that has been undisturbed for years. Sometimes it yields up its contents only after we give up the pursuit. The human memory is a remarkable process whose secrets we have yet to understand in its entirety.

Exercise 9.1

THE MAGNIFICENT SEVEN — *Pattern Recognition*

Quickly! Name as many of the Seven Dwarfs as you can in the next minute. Be sure you provide seven names. Guess even if you aren't sure you're right.

_____ _____ _____ _____ _____ _____ _____

This may not be a fair question. The question assumes that you know a particular fairy tale, "Snow White and the Seven Dwarfs," which is popularly told in this culture. Yet, a surprising number of people can dredge up accurate names from their long-term memories. Snow White used to hang out with Dopey, Happy, Sleepy, Grumpy, Sneezy, Bashful, and Doc. If you succeeded in retrieving all of them from storage in long-term memory, congratulations! That's an unusual accomplishment. For you to achieve that result, every element of memory processes had to work efficiently.

If you didn't succeed in retrieving all seven, you are in good company. Most people can't do this task easily. And that's very helpful, because we can use the results to demonstrate some important features of forgetting.

A simplified model of remembering involves a three-stage process: encoding, storage, and retrieval.

- *Encoding:* To become a memory, information must first be registered in sensory memory—it must stand out among the variety of stimuli and be selected for further processing. When stimuli are novel or important, they can be encoded as material available for later short-term memory processing.
- *Storage:* When we rehearse short-term memories sufficiently, we encode them for placement in long-term memory. We make a conscious decision to rehearse information when we think we will need it again for some future challenge.
- *Retrieval:* We seek information from long-term memory storage to assist in some adaptive problem; however, long-term memory storage is huge. Many kinds of processes can hinder effective retrieval, including

—*Interference:* when other items in long-term memory clutter the retrieval of the specific items we are seeking.

—*Insufficient cueing:* when we cannot retrieve specific items because we don't have quite enough information to allow the location of the items we are seeking.

—*Repression:* when the emotional consequences of recalling specific items might be too painful, we may unconsciously lose access to the potentially harmful memories.

The next part of this exercise demonstrates some problems that can crop up in long-term memory when we consciously try hard to dredge up semantic information to solve a problem, similar to the challenge we might experience when taking a multiple-choice test or playing a board game that relies on the quality of our long-term memory processes. (Trivial Pursuit is one such game.) Describe the quality of long-term-memory performance on the Seven Dwarfs task for someone who suffers from the following problems (see Answer Key):

An encoding problem: _____

_____

_____

A storage problem: _____

_____

_____

An interference problem: _____

_____

_____

A repression problem: _____

_____

_____

Now, think about the answers you provided to the original recall problem. If you had trouble recalling all seven names, what explanation seems to apply to your pattern of forgetting?

After completing this exercise, you should be able to
- identify some common patterns in forgetting.
- deduce some explanations for error patterns that are consistent with memory processes.
- identify the explanation that best addresses your own errors.
- recognize the challenges of recalling stories accurately from childhood.
- remember the names of the Magnificent 7 now because of your additional rehearsal.

Exercise 9.2

THANKS FOR THE MEMORY *Practical Problem Solving*

Your psychology instructor probably will use objective testing (multiple-choice, or true-false questions) as one way to determine whether you are learning effectively. You may have recognized that the chapter on memory in your psychology textbook contains information that you could apply to your own learning to become a more efficient learner.

Read through the following strategies and compare them with your own practices for preparing for examinations in this class. For each strategy, circle the number that most closely corresponds to your present learning pattern. This inventory is uniquely your own; there won't be an answer in the back of the book for this exercise, but it may lead to improving your study habits.

overlearning: multiple study sessions

1 _____ 2 _____ 3 _____ 4 _____ 5

not at all characteristic of my learning   very characteristic of my learning

active practicing with the material

1 _____ 2 _____ 3 _____ 4 _____ 5

not at all characteristic of my learning   very characteristic of my learning

personal elaboration of meaning of the material

1 _____ 2 _____ 3 _____ 4 _____ 5

not at all characteristic of my learning   very characteristic of my learning

mnemonic devices

1 _____ 2 _____ 3 _____ 4 _____ 5

not at all characteristic of my learning   very characteristic of my learning

re-creating learning contexts

1 _____ 2 _____ 3 _____ 4 _____ 5

not at all characteristic of my learning   very characteristic of my learning

anticipating test questions

1 _____ 2 _____ 3 _____ 4 _____ 5

not at all characteristic of my learning   very characteristic of my learning

reducing interference

1 _____ 2 _____ 3 _____ 4 _____ 5

not at all characteristic of my learning   very characteristic of my learning

Assuming that the principles of improving memory are accurate, which skills have you already developed reasonably well to support more effective long-term-memory performance? _____

_____

_____

Which would be the most appropriate for you to develop in order to enhance your performance on objective tests? _____

_____

_____

Which skills would be more likely to result in a deeper understanding of the ideas you are trying to memorize? _____

_____

_____

What obstacles would you need to overcome to implement a more efficient system of study? _____

_____

_____

How motivated are you to make the changes that would be required to become a more efficient and effective memorizer? _____

_____

_____

After completing this exercise, you should be able to
- articulate the factors that account for effective long-term-memory performance.
- evaluate your own strengths and weaknesses in long-term-memory challenges.
- assess which memory improvement strategies are likely to produce more effective recall and learning.
- identify whether this issue is serious enough to prompt further problem-solving effort and personal change.

Exercise 9.3

STORY TIME *Creative Problem Solving*

If we could create a magic formula that would ensure that people could remember everything they wanted to, we would be rich. Many people believe that an improved memory would allow us to perform all of our daily tasks better. Although there is no magic formula, there are techniques that can help people effectively remember important events and information. One of the most fun of these techniques involves creating vivid stories that help organize words and ideas that need to be remembered.

Imagine that you are at a party that your significant other's parents have hosted to introduce you to the family. Needless to say, it is important to remember everyone's name. Once you are all seated at the restaurant, your friend introduces you to everyone. Going around the table, clockwise, you meet: Sally and Mike (the parents); Samantha (an aunt); Elaine, Vanessa, and Laura (sisters); Chris (an uncle); Melissa and John (grandparents); Larry (another uncle); and Tisha and Devon (Larry's children). Create a story that you can use to remember this hoard of relatives' names. Test yourself two hours, one day, and five days after you create your story to see how many of the names and relationships you remember. If you didn't remember them all, what factors seemed to contribute to remembering the ones that you did remember?

Exercise 9.4

CREATING CONTEXT — *Scientific Problem Solving*

Godden and Baddeley (1975) concluded that information was better remembered when it was recalled in the same context in which it was learned. You may remember the experiment. They had a group of people listen to a list of words. Half the group listened to the words while sitting on the beach, and the other half listened to the words while they were underwater. When later asked to remember the words in the list, the participants remembered more words correctly when they were in the same setting in which they heard the list. If a person originally heard the list while underwater, that person would remember more of the list if asked while underwater than if asked while sitting on the beach.

This finding has interesting implications for education. For example, a psychology professor interested in improving student performance on tests might choose to conduct her own experiment on the effects of context on recall. The basic hypothesis is that taking a test in a context similar to the learning context will improve performance. What are the specific variables and how might she conduct this experiment in "real life"?

Independent variable: _____

Dependent variable: _____

Extraneous variables for which she should control: _____

Outline of a basic experimental protocol: _____

After completing this exercise, you should be able to

- recount the original findings of the Godden and Baddeley experiment.
- construct an experimental strategy to test a hypothesis.
- describe variables that need to be controlled to eliminate alternative hypotheses.
- speculate about how context-based learning could influence study habits.

Exercise 9.5

ROSEANNE'S DILEMMA — *Psychological Reasoning*

During the last decade or so, an increasing number of court cases have involved recovered memories of childhood abuse. Some famous individuals reporting recovered memory experiences received considerable media attention. For example, comedian and talk show host Roseanne recovered memories of parental sexual abuse that involved episodes she claimed had occurred when she was less than two years old. Roseanne's family was outraged and vehemently denied her public charges. This case was well known because it involved a celebrity; many families in private life experienced trauma when sons and daughters began to recall memories of abuse in therapy. Anecdotal reports suggest that some recovered memories of abuse are real, whereas others are not.

When previously forgotten episodes are suddenly remembered many years after the event has occurred, we can raise many questions about whether these memories are valid. Because dealing with these memories is often devastating to the individuals involved, psychologists can contribute to an understanding of how real memories can suddenly surface, as well as how events that never happened can be remembered when they haven't occurred. Develop your understanding of these issues using the following questions as prompts.

Formulate one hypothesis that might explain how a real, traumatic, and previously forgotten event could suddenly be remembered: _____
_____
_____

Formulate one hypothesis to explain how people could remember something that never really happened: _____
_____
_____

Describe one strategy that might help distinguish between real and false memories:
_____
_____

Share your conclusions with a discussion group. How many different hypotheses and strategies can your group develop? _____

After completing this exercise, you should be able to
- discuss the current controversy of recovered traumatic memories.
- explain how distant memories can be triggered by retrieval cues.
- speculate about how memory fragments might trigger inaccurate recall.
- discuss problem-solving strategies that distinguish between real and false memories.

Exercise 9.6

MAKING MEMORIES *Perspective Taking*

Amnesia is a concept that is portrayed rather romantically in the media, particularly on the daytime soaps. A person, usually a young woman, is injured in an accident or in an attempt on her life, and loses her memory. After undergoing some great trials and tribulations she suddenly recovers her memory and either finds the love of her life or is able to testify against the person who attempted to kill her. This scenario bears little resemblance to real life. Not only is amnesia quite rare, there is also nothing of romance about it.

Imagine the case of Patsy, a young woman who received a head injury in a car accident. When her seat belt came loose in an automobile accident, her head hit the side window and the windshield. The front and side of the skull protect two areas of the brain that store long-term memories—the frontal and temporal lobes. When Patsy awoke several hours after the accident, she remembered nothing—not her name, the date, her nine-year-old daughter, any friends, or even how to walk or talk clearly. After spending much time in recovery, she was sent home, still not possessing any memory of the time before the accident. Although Patsy eventually developed a new and satisfying life, she never remembered anything about the "old" Patsy and is, according to the reports of friends and family, a different person.

Suppose you have been hired as a psychological consultant to help Patsy and her family adjust and adapt to Patsy's condition. Outline some of the physical, emotional, and social challenges they would face. What do you think they could do to help overcome these problems and to survive together as a family?

After completing this exercise, you should be able to

- describe amnesia accurately and discuss why typical daytime soap opera treatments of the disorder are inaccurate.
- explain what happens to the brain to produce amnesia.
- imagine practical impacts on a family in which a member suffers memory loss.
- develop some opinions about whether a career in human services with clients who suffer memory problems would be satisfying.

10

Thinking and Language

The topics discussed in this chapter examine how we adapt to our environments. We are born into cultures with established languages, belief systems for viewing the world, and methods for evaluating our experience. The following exercises give you an opportunity to explore challenging questions about how we learn and use language and specific cognitive abilities, as well as how these abilities are, or are not, unique to the human experience.

Exercise 10.1

THERE'S GOOD NEWS AND THERE'S BAD NEWS — *Pattern Recognition*

How we process our facts influences how we make our decisions, but "facts" can be "framed" in different ways, depending on our purpose and the context. For example, consumers are more likely to buy ground beef that is "80 percent lean" than to purchase the package labeled "20 percent fat." Both descriptions are accurate, and logically they are equivalent. But only one of them is likely to make us reach for our wallets to make a purchase. (The other may launch us on a fat-free self-improvement campaign.)

Framing comes into play in how we present information to others. A common practice when one North American needs to impart mixed news to another is to start with the statement, "There is good news and there is bad news. Which would you like to hear first?" By making this statement, we offer the news recipient an opportunity to influence how we will frame the good and bad details that will follow.

Examine the following situations and speculate about how you could frame the information to produce the intended outcomes.

Have I Got a Deal for You!

You sell used cars. The best car on your lot has 100,000 miles on it. How could you describe this car to a prospective buyer to make the purchase more attractive?

_____
_____
_____

Making the Grade

You're carrying six full classes. You've had a hard semester, and you are about to talk with loved ones at a family gathering about how things have been going. You've excelled in five courses, but you know you won't pass the other course. How do you talk about your experience in this difficult semester?

_____
_____
_____

IRS Blues

You've just started working for the Internal Revenue Service. Tax specialists have developed tax brackets to assist in equitable taxation. Will you work with taxpayers by describing how much tax they will pay or by explaining how much income they will keep?

_____
_____
_____

Rain, Rain, Go Away

As a weather forecaster in an area that depends on the tourist industry, will you state your forecast as the likelihood of sunshine or as the likelihood of rain?

_____
_____
_____

After completing this exercise, you should be able to

- recognize how framing can influence decisions.
- identify two different versions of the "facts" of a situation.
- select the version of the "facts" that is more likely to produce a desirable outcome.
- offer a reasonable justification for your framing choices.

Exercise 10.2

IF WE COULD TALK TO THE ANIMALS   *Perspective Taking*

Few controversies have so divided the scientific community as has the controversy about the apes' capacities for language. Although many scientists have made serious attempts at rearing apes in language-rich environments, the results have not overwhelmingly demonstrated that apes can use language as human beings use it.

At the heart of the argument are the criteria we use to determine true capacity for language. Generally, scientists specializing in the study of language impose the following criteria on the debate.

- Is the language *symbolic:* Can it be used to represent absent objects?
- Does the language have systematic *syntax,* or word order?
- Can the language be used in a creative or *productive* manner?

There are two opposing viewpoints on whether apes can truly learn human language. Some psychologists who believe apes are quite capable of acquiring language have gone to creative lengths to gather support for their position. Other psychologists dispute the idea that apes are capable of learning language.

Before attempting this exercise, review the evidence your psychology textbook presents for the topic of animal language. Find two examples that support the viewpoint of those who believe apes can learn language. Then find two examples that could be used by those who disagree with that position. Finally, identify the side that you believe presents the strong evidence. (See Answer Key.)

Here are two sources of evidence supporting the viewpoint that animals have the capacity for language.

1. _____

2. _____

Here are two sources of evidence challenging the viewpoint that animals have the capacity for language.

1. _____

2. _____

Identify the side you find more convincing and, if possible, explain how you have applied the appropriate language criteria to make your choice.

_____

After completing this exercise, you should be able to
- identify why the scientific community is torn about the apes' potential to use language.
- report the criteria scientists use to make judgments about language capacity.
- support both perspectives with evidence from language research.
- evaluate the two perspectives and judge which is more strongly supported.

Exercise 10.3

ALEX THE ACCOUNTANT *Scientific Problem Solving*

The degree to which humans are the exclusive owners of language is one of the great questions of cognitive and comparative psychology. Researchers have worked with chimps, apes, dolphins, and even an African gray parrot to explore questions about animals' abilities to understand and express abstract concepts and to comprehend the semantic nuances of human language. One series of experiments involves Alex, an African gray parrot trained and tested by Irene Pepperberg and her associates. When given an assortment of different objects, Alex can correctly answer questions of number and color. For example, if asked how many red blocks are on the table, Alex will answer approximately 80 percent of the time. (One of the things that makes Alex such an interesting subject is that he has been trained to talk, so he gives his answers verbally.) Imagine for a moment that you are a researcher working with Alex. Given these findings, what other numerical concepts might Alex understand? How might you test them?

Generate at least one hypothesis about Alex's understanding of abstract numerical concepts and design an experiment to test it. For example, how would you go about establishing that Alex comprehends the terms "more" and "less"?

Hypothesis: _____
_____
_____

Briefly describe the experiment you would use to test this hypothesis, making sure to identify both the independent and dependent variables. _____
_____
_____
_____
_____
_____
_____
_____
_____

If your hypothesis is supported, how might this change our understanding of human language and thinking? _____
_____
_____
_____
_____

After completing this exercise, you should be able to

- describe experiments that explore the capacity of animals to use language.
- use the findings of one animal language experiment to generate a hypothesis about the ability of Alex, Irene Pepperberg's gray parrot, to understand abstract numerical concepts.
- identify the variables and basic experimental strategies needed to test your hypothesis about Alex's numerical conceptual abilities.
- discuss the ways in which the findings of such experiments affect our fundamental understanding of the uniqueness of human thought and language.

Exercise 10.4

MONEY IN THE BANK? *Practical Problem Solving*

Heuristics are strategies we use to organize our world and to help us make decisions. Although this approach allows for rapid processing of information and decision making, it is not always accurate. In fact, a heuristic can make you quite prone to errors. Heuristics are especially tempting when time is of the essence—when you think you don't have the time to extensively or exhaustively review all the available options.

The world of high finance demands the rapid processing of large amounts of information. Imagine that you are a consultant, hired to work with investors to help them make the wisest choices with their money. How could you use an understanding of the risk of using heuristics to help your investors make, rather than lose, money? How does the use of heuristics relate to confidence or overconfidence in decisions? If you need a suggestion to help you get started, focus on the availability heuristic. Identify what the availability heuristic is, how it might lead to errors that could cost the investors money, and what strategies the investors might use instead of relying on this heuristic.

What would you tell the investors about heuristics? _____
_____
_____
_____

What could you tell them about overconfidence and the way it might affect their investing decisions? _____
_____
_____
_____

What is the availability heuristic and how does it specifically affect investment decisions? _____
_____

How have you seen these concepts reflected in your own money-handling experiences?
_____
_____
_____
_____

After completing this exercise, you should be able to
- describe how heuristics and overconfidence play a role in decision making.
- discuss the way in which these concepts affect decision making in the area of financial investing.
- discuss a specific example of the availability heuristic and its influence on investment reasoning.
- recognize how these concepts are reflected in your own money-managing experiences.

Exercise 10.5

SEEING IS BELIEVING *Psychological Reasoning*

You may have already experienced this phenomenon in the course of reading your textbook. Chances are that at some point in your reading, you have read, or will read, some research findings that directly contradict what you know to be true from your own experience. Most people tend to believe the validity of their personal experience over the findings of research, even when the scientific evidence is very compelling.

How would you use what you've learned about making decisions and forming judgments to explain this tendency? (A solid answer will discuss at least two different concepts from this chapter.) _____

_____

_____

_____

_____

When might it be appropriate to rely on personal experience more than other sources of information when making decisions? _____

_____

_____

When would it not? _____

_____

_____

_____

After completing this exercise, you should be able to

- describe how heuristics, overconfidence, belief bias, and belief perseverance can result in an over-reliance on personal experience when making judgments and decisions.
- identify situations when it might be appropriate to weigh personal experience more heavily than other sources of information when making decisions.
- understand the complexity of the process of forming judgments and making decisions.

Exercise 10.6

POOR JOHN AND MARY *Creative Problem Solving*

John and Mary were found dead in a locked room. The following objects were found in the room with them: some water, a table, a dog, a chair, and a broken glass. How did John and Mary die?

This riddle illustrates many principles underlying the creative process. To solve the riddle, we must first *define the problem* by establishing the facts as we know them. John and Mary are dead. They have been found in a locked room with some objects. Our task is to determine how the deaths occurred. That seems straightforward enough.

As you begin to *analyze the problem,* pay careful attention to the components that you can *observe.* Do any solutions jump out? Probably not, which means we must approach the problem from another angle.

One important aspect of creative problem solving is careful scrutiny of inferences and assumptions. Have you drawn any *inferences* that will either help you solve the problem or—perhaps—just get in your way? Consider these assumptions:

- John and Mary died in the room.
- The objects—or some of the objects—are involved in their deaths.
- Because the room was locked, the possible causes of their deaths must be limited.

How can you find *relationships* among the facts of the case so that you will be able to *solve the problem?* You might ask whether all the objects are essential to their deaths. Are some objects more important than others? Did John and Mary die at the same time? Why was the glass broken? As you examine the relationships, you may reach a tentative *conclusion.*

All manner of hypotheses have been proposed to solve this problem, although there is really only one elegant solution. Perhaps John and Mary had a mutual suicide pact . . . but then how was the pact enacted? Perhaps the dog was rabid . . . but death by rabies takes a while, and how probable is it that both would die at the same time? Perhaps John and Mary drowned . . . but that would require a great deal of water.

The process we go through when solving riddles involves problem-solving processes and creativity in characteristic phases. Sometimes we have to think a long time before a solution comes to mind. This process is called *incubation.* When a solution arrives, we have *insight.*

What is *your* conclusion about John and Mary's deaths? If you haven't reached one yet, here is a hint: The water was once in the glass. Try asking yourself these questions: What kind of water? What kind of glass? Was the glass once a bottle? A dome? A pitcher? A vase? An aquarium?

Did the hint help? Are you closer to solving the riddle? (See Answer Key.)

_____
_____
_____

After completing this exercise, you should be able to
- summarize the steps that are apparent in riddle problem solving.
- identify the roles that incubation, insight, and functional fixedness play in creative problem solving.
- describe how assumptions can limit our problem-solving abilities.
- recognize how practical problem-solving processes fit with everyday life.
- generate at least one proposal for John and Mary's murders.
- drive your own friends and family crazy figuring out who killed John and Mary.

11

Intelligence

What, exactly, is intelligence? This question is at the core of a long-standing discussion in psychology. Although there is no one simple answer, most psychologists agree that it is not a specific or concrete entity of which individuals have some easily specified proportion; rather, intelligence is a set of abilities used to adapt to the environment. The potential to reason logically, to solve problems, and to learn from experience are only some of the diverse abilities that are typically included under the general heading of "intelligence." The activities in this chapter will help you understand and appreciate the diversity that is inextricably a part of any discussion about intelligence. We also address the challenge of measuring intelligence and the consequences of making judgments based on those tests.

Exercise 11.1

"CHARACTER"ISTICS OF INTELLIGENCE — *Pattern Recognition*

Historically, intelligence was defined as a specific set of cognitive abilities used primarily in academic settings. Contemporary theories of intelligence, however, tend to stress "multiple intelligences," suggesting that mental abilities are too diverse to fall under one label. Although there is some disagreement over the exact nature of these different intelligences, Robert J. Sternberg, Richard Wagner, and some of their colleagues have described three different intelligences: academic, practical, and creative. Academic problem-solving skills are those measured by more traditional intelligence tests and focus on an individual's ability to answer well-defined problems with objectively correct answers. Practical intelligence is often termed "common sense"—the ability to successfully complete the often ambiguous and complex tasks that are a part of everyday life. Creative intelligence involves seeing unexpected patterns and solutions when presented with novel situations.

Below are some classic literary and cinematic figures. Using the triarchic classification of the Sternberg and Wagner framework of intelligence, analyze each character's intellectual profile. Provide a rationale for each answer. Then, pick some of your own favorite characters and identify their intelligences (and lack thereof).

Character	Academic	Practical	Creative
Scrooge	Strong: his career as an accountant dictates good analytic skills	Strong: his money-making abilities attest to his street smarts	Weak: he conforms to conventions to an extreme degree
Mary Poppins			
Sherlock Holmes			
Winnie the Pooh			
Don Quixote			
Your example			
Your example			

After completing this exercise, you should be able to
- explain the components of Sternberg and Wagner's theory of multiple intelligences.
- identify the intellectual strengths and weaknesses of fictional literary figures.
- apply the theory of multiple intelligences to new examples.

Exercise 11.2

CHALLENGING QUESTIONS *Perspective Taking*

Since the early 1900s, intelligence tests have been used in a variety of educational settings. Beginning with Alfred Binet and Théodore Simon's work in France in 1904, and continuing with Lewis Terman's later adaptation of their work in California, intelligence tests have become a popular way to predict the probable academic performance of children and to identify those children who might benefit from special attention. You have probably undergone significant experiences with testing that can be traced back to these early pioneers.

Today, psychologists use testing predictions to make decisions about the ways specific children should be educated. For example, a child who scores below 85 might be offered special support services while remaining in a traditional classroom. A child scoring below 70 might be placed in a special classroom, program, or school.

How might such an approach be advantageous for a child? _____

_____

_____

_____

_____

How might it be detrimental? _____

_____

_____

_____

_____

What are the underlying values inherent in this approach and what impact does it have on society? _____

_____

_____

_____

_____

_____

Are there any corresponding differences in the way the academically gifted are treated?

_____

_____

_____

_____

_____

After completing this exercise, you should be able to

- discuss the history of the development of intelligence tests.
- recognize that intelligence tests were designed to measure the potential for academic success rather than some inborn trait.
- speculate about the effects that separating children based on academic ability has on the children involved and on society.
- identify some of the underlying values related to intelligence testing and the resulting educational practices.

Exercise 11.3

TO RETEST OR NOT TO RETEST? *Scientific Problem Solving*

Taking achievement and aptitude tests has become a standard practice in American culture. Performance on achievement tests often determines whether you will gain access to the next level of training in a variety of fields. For example, at the end of high school, you probably took a Scholastic Assessment Test (SAT) or the American College Test (ACT) to determine whether colleges would admit you.

Sometimes our performance on achievement and aptitude tests is disappointing. Test-takers who are strongly motivated to move to the next level of training then face the unsettling decision of whether to repeat the test. In principle, retesting should not influence a test-taker's score on an aptitude test. Nevertheless, we occasionally hear anecdotes about individuals who retested and scored startling gains on the second try. Sometimes these anecdotes are accompanied by compelling testimony in praise of some course in a particular aptitude or achievement area. The stories cause the power of additional training and the advantage of additional testing to seem very appealing. However, these stories rely on testimony, not on objective evidence derived through well-designed experimentation.

Your task in this exercise is to design an experiment. You are to imagine yourself as a psychology major nearing the end of your undergraduate education. You have decided that you want to attend graduate school in psychology to become an experimental researcher. Unfortunately, your scores on the Graduate Record Examination (GRE) were disappointing. They weren't dreadful, but they were low enough to disqualify you from some of the best programs, which were your first choices. Should you take the exam again? Or should you spend time enhancing other areas that might make up for low scores?

The experiment you will design will help you and others determine whether test-takers would be wise to retake an achievement exam if they were dissatisfied with their original results. You have been able to round up 100 volunteers who are willing to retest or retrain, regardless of their original scores. To begin setting up your experiment, answer the following questions. (See Answer Key.)

What is your hypothesis? _____

_____

_____

What is the independent variable? _____

What is the dependent variable? _____

How will you assign volunteers to test conditions? _____

_____

What elements of the experience will you need to control? _____

_____

Although listening to a powerful commercial and deciding what to do on the basis of the strength of testimony may be easier than searching for objective evidence, such a decision-making process doesn't represent good science. Controlled comparisons contribute more objective data to assist in making such an important decision.

After completing this exercise, you should be able to

- generate a hypothesis consistent with the goal of evaluating the effects of retesting.
- identify an appropriate, simple dependent variable.
- recognize the complexity of extra variables that need to be controlled if alternative hypotheses are to be ruled out.
- understand that well-designed research processes are complicated and time consuming.

Exercise 11.4

WHEN TO TEST   *Practical Problem Solving*

Testing is an entrenched part of contemporary life. You have been tested at various stages of your educational experience. Chances are good that as you seek employment, you will have other opportunities to be tested. However, as a well-informed consumer of psychological services, you should also be equipped to spot faulty uses of testing. This ability should prepare you to challenge inappropriate uses of tests or to build solid rationales to get the testing services that you need.

Examine the problem situations on the next page and construct your best argument about the course of action that you think would be most satisfying. Keep in mind that the strongest arguments will rely on the principles of test design and fair use. The best practical strategies should address standardization, reliability, or validity of testing. What strategies can you develop for the following situations?

Your prospective employer is interested in asking you to take a polygraph test to ensure that you won't steal office supplies. _____

_____

_____

_____

Your little brother had a serious cold on the day that achievement tests were performed. His results suggest that he needs placement in a classroom for mildly retarded children.

_____

_____

_____

A graduate program offers admission only to students who score in the top 10 percent on the GRE. They do not factor in other academic performance indicators. _____

_____

_____

_____

Although you worked very hard on your English literature essay, you got back a "D" with no explanatory feedback. Your friend, who partied heavily the night before the paper was due, got back an "A" with no explanatory feedback. _____

_____

_____

_____

An employer is deciding between the use of two tests for selecting sales representatives. The content of each test is complex but she's leaning in the direction of selecting the one that is less expensive and has a prettier cover. _____

_____

_____

_____

Exercise 11.5

BRAVE NEW WORLD — *Psychological Reasoning*

In *Brave New World*, Aldous Huxley described a society in which everyone was sorted into groups based on engineered characteristics that were then enhanced through specific experiences and educational practices. Although most people would agree that seeking ways to sort individuals for the purpose of limiting opportunities is not appropriate, we often do so unintentionally when we value certain characteristics more than others. (If you have trouble envisioning this, consider why aptitude, achievement, and intelligence tests are used, and what the result of their use often is.) Our society places great importance on analytic and academic skills but may be less interested in other dimensions of intelligence. Imagine a world in which creativity was valued above all else. Using the five components of creativity—expertise, imaginative thinking skills, a venturesome personality, high intrinsic motivation, and a creative environment—identify the creative components that seem to be more genetically determined than environmentally influenced. In other words, which of the five seem to be more environmentally influenced, so that an individual's creative expression could be enhanced by the right environment? For each component, put an X in the column that you think best explains whether nature or nurture most strongly influences the creative dimension:

Creative Characteristics	Primarily Heritable	Primarily Environmental
Expertise		
Imaginative thinking skills		
Venturesome personality		
High intrinsic motivation		
Creative environment		

Describe how knowing the heritability of certain factors related to creativity might influence how creativity would be produced in the population, as well as how a home or educational environment could be designed based on understanding the role of environmental components in the expression of creativity: _____

_____

_____

_____

_____

_____

How appropriate do you think such actions would be? Why? Is it ever appropriate to sort people based on their expression of specific traits? _____

_____

_____

_____

_____

_____

After completing this exercise, you should be able to
- reflect upon the ways in which we use intelligence and related characteristics to place people in different categories.
- identify the five components of creativity.
- articulate genetic and environmental contributions to the development of creative expression.
- speculate about how information about genes and the environment could be used to sort people and enhance creativity in a culture that valued creative expression above all else.
- make some judgments about if and when it is appropriate to sort people based on the expression of specific characteristics.

Exercise 11.6

JUST TOO COOL — *Creative Problem Solving*

One dimension that often becomes the basis on which we judge others is how "cool" they are. Of course, the problem with that concept is that it is not entirely clear whether what "cool" is for one person would be the same as it is for another. Being cool may be a particular dimension of social intelligence, but it probably varies a great deal by context. For example, a cool young adult probably differs in characteristics and behavior from a cool senior citizen.

Join with a group of students who are your age peers. See if you can construct a strategy for the measurement of "cool." First, you must operationally define what it means to be cool for the target group. Then try to develop a measurement strategy that would allow you to sort people on the basis of their relative cool. Finally, reflect as a group on the ease or difficulty of the assignment.

Operationally define what it means to be cool: _____
_____
_____
_____

What strategies could you use to sort people according to levels of being cool?
_____
_____
_____
_____

Why was this assignment particularly challenging? _____
_____
_____
_____

After completing this exercise, you should be able to
- describe the process of developing an operational definition and explain its importance in testing.
- generate some viable strategies for measuring and comparing a dimension of behavior.
- reflect on the difficulties connected with test construction and use.
- articulate ethical concerns related to the comparing and labeling of people.

12

Motivation

Why do we get up in the morning? Why do we study hard to be successful in a college course? Why do we shrink with horror from the sight of a grisly car accident? Why do we pursue a dream?

All of these questions represent the terrain psychologists describe as motivation. Research in motivation explains how we meet our needs, select our goals, adopt our beliefs, and make our decisions.

Exercise 12.1

THEORIES OF MOTIVATION — *Pattern Recognition*

In the history of psychology's exploration of the motivating factors behind behavior, three theoretical perspectives have proven the most influential: instinct theory, drive reduction theory, and arousal theory. Instinct theory came out of the growing evolutionary understanding of the origins of behaviors. It assumes that some complex behaviors are not learned and can be explained by a genetic predisposition to the behavior. This approach is most often applied to explain species-typical behaviors. Drive reduction theory states that a physiological need creates a psychological state that pushes the organism to behave in ways that reduce the need. Arousal theory suggests that some behaviors are motivating because they increase arousal; that is, that they stimulate the organism or individual in some needed fashion.

See the next page for a list of motivated behaviors. For each behavior, identify which theories could be used to explain why the behavior occurs and describe how that theory would explain the behavior.

Behavior	Theories	Explanations
A human infant rooting to find the mother's nipple		
Getting a glass of water when you are thirsty		
Going for a walk when you are worried or restless		
Working on a difficult jigsaw puzzle		
Studying hard to pass an exam		
Crying when hurt or upset		
Developing a lasting, intimate relationship		

After completing this exercise, you should be able to

- identify the three main theoretical perspectives used to explain motivated behaviors.
- use instinct theory, drive reduction theory, and arousal theory to explain why certain behaviors occur.
- recognize that motivated behaviors can be interpreted through more than one theoretical perspective.

Exercise 12.2

HUMANISTIC HISTORY *Perspective Taking*

During the turbulent 1960s, Abraham Maslow suggested that some human needs take precedence over others. The more immediate the need, the stronger the motivation to meet that need. For example, you might have a need to be successful and so would work very hard to accomplish this goal, but if you did not have enough food to eat, you would probably divert most of your energy to finding food to eliminate your hunger. Hunger, on the other hand, might lose its significance if you were deprived of air. Maslow speculated that physiological needs were the most essential; once these needs are met, needs for safety, belongingness, love, esteem, and the need to live up to one's fullest potential become motivating factors. Maslow's hierarchical framework was intuitively very appealing and became one of the most popular explanations of human motivation.

As the century came to a close, psychologists began to question the validity and usefulness of Maslow's approach. Critics have begun to generate examples of situations in which Maslow's hierarchy does not provide a solid explanation. Can you think of an example from contemporary life that would challenge the validity of Maslow's hierarchy?

After completing this exercise, you should be able to

- describe Maslow's hierarchy of needs.
- recognize that there are differences in the way that individuals prioritize needs and are motivated to achieve them.
- generate a disconfirming example to weaken Maslow's theory.
- speculate about factors that contribute to an individual's prioritization of motivations and needs.

Exercise 12.3

CHICKEN OR EGG? *Scientific Problem Solving*

In 1991, researcher Simon LeVay reported evidence from autopsies that suggested the brains of homosexual men were different than the brains of heterosexual men. Specifically, he identified a region of the hypothalamus in which a cell cluster was larger in heterosexual men than in women or homosexual men. More recently, other researchers have used brain imaging techniques to identify potential differences in the brains of homosexual and heterosexual individuals (Gladue, 1994). For example, the corpus callosum in homosexual men was reported to be up to one-third larger than the comparable structures of heterosexual men (Allen & Gorski, 1992).

It is currently unclear whether the scientific community finds this evidence persuasive, particularly because the topic is fraught with political sensitivity concerns. However, even if these differences turn out to be reliable and significant, many questions still need to be answered. One of the most critical questions is related to the causal link between the behavior (hetero- or homosexuality) and the neuroanatomy. Which came first? Can one be the cause of the other? For example, we already have evidence from a wide variety of developmental studies demonstrating how one's experiences mediate the development of visual neural pathways. Given the difficulty of establishing the direction of causality (which comes first—sexual behavior or neurological structure?), this research sets the stage for serious ethical dilemmas.

Assume that you are serving on an institutional review board which has been given the charge of determining whether additional funding should be devoted to research of this type. Formulate your position about whether such research should continue. If you believe funding is justified, what additional ethical safeguards should be put in place and why?

After completing this exercise, you should be able to

- identify some potential links between brain anatomy and sexual orientation.
- recognize the role of an institutional review board in providing ethical oversight of research.
- formulate and defend an ethical position regarding politically and personally sensitive research.

Exercise 12.4

THE DIET RIOT — *Practical Problem Solving*

Dieting is an American obsession. Although there is growing evidence that changes in American diet and lifestyle have led to an increase in the percentage of people who are significantly overweight, some of the dieting craze is a result of a societal trend toward an ideal body type that projects "thin is in."

Using what you have learned about hunger, design an educational program that would help people make good decisions about weight loss. What would you teach about the physiology of hunger that might help your program members understand the purpose food serves for their bodies? What role might their current weight play in their feelings of hunger?

Given what you have read about the psychological component of hunger, what practical suggestions for maintaining healthy eating habits and a healthy weight might you suggest? _____

_____
_____
_____
_____
_____
_____
_____
_____

What information might you share with them about eating disorders? Why?

_____
_____
_____
_____
_____
_____
_____

After completing this exercise, you should be able to

- describe the physiology of hunger, relying on terms such as metabolism, body chemistry, and set point.
- discuss some of the cultural, environmental, and individual factors that play a role in an individual's experience of hunger.
- identify the variety of cultural and individual factors related to the development of eating disorders.
- provide realistic and practical suggestions about developing and maintaining healthy attitudes and behaviors related to food.

Exercise 12.5

THE WEIGHT-LOSS COUNSELOR — *Psychological Reasoning*

Jim has been attempting to lose weight for many months. No matter what weight-reduction method he attempts, he seems unable to lose and sustain his loss. Although some methods are initially effective, the weight returns, and within weeks the excess ounces become the "ten pounds from hell" that simply won't go away.

This exercise asks you to imagine that you have found employment after college as a weight-loss counselor. Some students who graduate with a psychology major find this a suitable entry into a helping career. In your new role, you will attempt to isolate as many variables as possible in trying to help Jim reach his objective.

Begin by considering all the behavioral, physical, and social influences that could undermine Jim's weight-loss efforts. From these influences, identify six variables that may prevent Jim from reaching his goal. For each of the six variables, formulate a question you could ask Jim to evaluate the impact of the variable. (See Answer Key.)

Variable 1: _____

Question: _____

_____

Variable 2: _____

Question: _____

_____

Variable 3: _____

Question: _____

_____

Variable 4: _____

Question: _____

_____

Variable 5: _____

Question: _____

_____

Variable 6: _____

Question: _____

_____

The number of factors you address in the problem-solving process is likely to influence your success as a weight-loss expert. Interpreting these variables as questions will add significantly to the available raw material you can draw on as you counsel your clients.

After completing this exercise, you should be able to
- recognize that weight management is a complex behavior.
- isolate variables that influence weight control.
- transform variables into questions that shape problem-solving processes.

Exercise 12.6

THE CREATIVE CONSULTANT *Creative Problem Solving*

Advertising professionals are specialists in human motivation. They usually start with a product, create a campaign to stir our impulse to buy, and wait to see if their expertise on human motivation will pay off in larger sales for their clients.

In this exercise, pretend you have been hired as an advertising consultant to develop an ad campaign to promote a new toothpaste. The toothpaste inventor believes his particular toothpaste will effectively reduce cavities. If you have ever studied the toothpaste section of a well-stocked grocery store, you will recognize how hard it might be to interest consumers in a new choice. How would you design your client's campaign to make this toothpaste more attractive than its competitors?

Your task is to identify four motives that you could exploit in developing the campaign. For each motive, select a name and an advertising image that will link the product and the motive. Then describe an approach based on that link. After you have described four approaches, select the one you believe would have the greatest success in generating customers for your client. Justify your choice by explaining why it could be more effective. (See Answer Key.)

Motive 1: _____

Product name: _____

Advertising approach: _____

Motive 2: _____

Product name: _____

Advertising approach: _____

Motive 3: _____

Product name: _____

Advertising approach: _____

Motive 4: _____

Product name: _____

Advertising approach: _____

Which of these four approaches would, in your judgment, be the most successful in generating new business for your client? _____

Why would this approach be more effective than the others? _____
_____

After completing this exercise, you should be able to
- identify four motives relevant to the challenge of selling a product.
- articulate any assumptions that might influence how you begin problem solving.
- generate some preliminary plans for advertising campaigns.
- show greater awareness of the way existing advertising campaigns link motives, product names, and advertising approaches in their attempts to influence consumers' purchasing habits.

13

Emotions

In its common usage, the word *emotion* is synonymous with *feeling*. For psychologists, however, studying emotion involves more than examining feelings—it also includes exploring and explaining the physiological states, cognitive experiences, and measurable behaviors that are components of those feelings. The challenge of research in this area is synthesizing the uniqueness of the individual emotional experience to create a common ground of definitions and classifications that are amenable to study; one of this area's many rewards is the opportunity to explore and understand some of the most intriguing and mysterious areas of human experience. The exercises in this chapter are designed to help you practice the skills of defining and observing emotions and behaviors, and to consider the significant role emotion plays in our interactions with others and with our environment.

Exercise 13.1

TOURIST TRAP — *Pattern Recognition*

Over your lifetime you will develop a remarkable ability to interpret the communications of others. You will be able not only to understand the spoken language addressed to you but also to decode the body language other members of your culture use to add visual emphasis to their communication. With practice, your interpretive processes will become so automatic that you will hardly pay conscious attention to what is communicated verbally versus what is communicated nonverbally.

This exercise offers you several examples of nonverbal behavior. Your task is to describe the behavior and then interpret it by stating the meaning our culture typically assigns to the behavior.

This task isn't as simple as it looks. Because these examples are familiar, your interpretation of them may be so automatic that you will find it hard to restrict yourself to simple behavioral descriptions. There is an interesting way to test whether your description is free from interpretation. Once you have derived your answers to the following set of questions, ask yourself, "If others had not grown up in my culture, would they describe this behavior in the same way?" Think about how a tourist to America might describe the sample behavior. Good *descriptions* of behavior should be similar across cultures; *interpretations* of behaviors may differ across cultures. (See Answer Key.)

Chapter 13 Emotions

(holding a thumb up)

Description of behavior: _____
_____
_____

What meaning do North Americans assign to this nonverbal gesture?
_____
_____

Would tourists from other countries describe the behavior similarly?

Yes _____   No _____

(phone call)

Description of behavior: _____
_____
_____

What meaning do North Americans assign to this nonverbal gesture?
_____
_____

Would tourists from other countries describe the behavior similarly?

Yes _____   No _____

(extending an apple with left hand)

Description of behavior: _____
_____
_____

What meaning do North Americans assign to this nonverbal gesture?
_____
_____

Would tourists from other countries describe the behavior similarly?

Yes _____   No _____

(looking down)

Description of behavior: _____
_____
_____

What meaning do North Americans assign to this nonverbal gesture?
_____
_____

Would tourists from other countries describe the behavior similarly?

Yes _____   No _____

(shaking head "no")

Description of behavior: _____
_____
_____

What meaning do North Americans assign to this nonverbal gesture?
_____
_____

Would tourists from other countries describe the behavior similarly?

Yes _____   No _____

("ok" sign)

Description of behavior: _____
_____
_____

What meaning do North Americans assign to this nonverbal gesture?
_____
_____

Would tourists from other countries describe the behavior similarly?

Yes _____   No _____

You may be surprised to learn that these nonverbal gestures were selected for a specific purpose. Each gesture has a very distinctive meaning in the culture shared by most people who live in North America. You probably interpreted that meaning quite accurately. However, each gesture also has a decidedly different interpretation in other cultures. Turn to the Answer Key to see the kind of trouble that might result if you casually used these gestures in other lands. The idea for this exercise was based on material in Roger Axtell's *Gestures: Do's and Taboos of Body Language Around the World* (New York: John Wiley, 1991).

After completing this exercise, you should be able to

- restrict your descriptions of behavior to a level that would be described similarly by individuals from any culture.
- describe how difficult it is to observe behavior without interpreting it.
- recognize how easily two individuals from different cultures could misinterpret each other.
- prepare more cautiously for foreign travel.

Exercise 13.2

FORGET YOUR TROUBLES *Practical Problem Solving*

Happiness is an elusive feeling, according to psychologists who conduct research in emotion. Yet most of us harbor secret wishes about the things, events, or conditions that we believe would make us happier. In the mythical story of "Aladdin and His Magical Lamp" a genie grants the holder of the lamp three wishes. In this exercise, assume you've captured the genie. First, identify three wishes that you think would increase your happiness. Justify your wishes by explaining why you would be happier if each wish were granted. Finally, speculate about the impact of your good fortune—how long will your happiness endure?

Wish 1: _____

Justification: _____

_____

Speculated impact: _____

_____

_____

Wish 2: _____

Justification: _____

_____

Speculated impact: _____

_____

_____

Wish 3: _____

Justification: _____

_____

Speculated impact: _____

_____

_____

Although fantasies about generous genies are fun, they don't provide much serious help in promoting happiness. The *adaptation-level principle* suggests that happiness is fleeting, no matter what wonderful things happen to us. When we make significant strides in being happy, we tend to adapt, adjusting our expectations by setting new goals that continue to make happiness somewhat elusive.

The *relative deprivation principle* offers more hope about putting our wishes in perspective. This principle suggests that we may feel better about our circumstances if we purposefully review situations that are far worse than the ones we are currently experiencing. This review can help us feel better or happier as we think of how much worse things really could be.

Select just one of your three wishes and review the wish. What kind of scenario or comparison might help you feel better about your circumstances and let you capture elusive happiness for a little while?

_____

_____

After this exercise you should be able to

- recognize the differences between the adaptation-level principle and the relative deprivation principle as regards views of happiness.

Exercise 13.3

PINOCCHIO'S LEGACY *Creative Problem Solving*

One of the great mysteries of childhood is how your parents could always tell when you were not telling the truth about something. If you think back on those moments, you probably can recognize that your parents were not practicing extrasensory perception. They were merely watching you carefully for telltale signs of discomfort (e.g., averted gaze, scuffing the ground with one foot, pausing). Although your nose didn't lengthen like Pinocchio's when you told a lie, your nonverbal behavior broadcast that you were trying to get away with something.

Speculate about what would happen if there were some observable physical or behavioral changes when you told a lie. Let's assume your nose might really swell noticeably every time you told an untruth. Try to generate three creative ideas about what might happen to social behavior if such an outrageous outcome were possible.

Outcome 1: _____

_____

Outcome 2: _____

_____

Outcome 3: _____

_____

Exercise 13.4

WHAT IS THIS THING CALLED LOVE? *Scientific Problem Solving*

Songwriter Cole Porter once asked, "What Is This Thing Called Love?" That question has plagued psychologists interested in emotions and intimate relationships. How can one research a phenomenon that seems to be as unique as love? Psychologists can't exactly conduct experimental research on how people fall in love. (Imagine trying to set up a controlled observation in which you randomly assign individuals to "heartbreak" and "no heartbreak" conditions!) However, psychologists can try to study aspects of the phenomenon, although that, too, is a challenge.

Your task in this exercise is to figure out just what would be measured if you tried to quantify falling in love. Join with a group of students who are about your age. How many different indicators can you generate that might be evidence of falling in love? Why is there so little uniformity across individuals in such an important emotional experience? Of those indicators, do any particularly reveal the measure that is most relevant to your own experience?

Indicators: _____

_____

_____

_____

Why is there so much variability across people? _____
_____
_____

Which indicators are most relevant to your own experience? _____
_____
_____

Exercise 13.5

EXPRESS YOURSELF!   ***Psychological Reasoning***

Self-help books and therapists alike regularly promote the conviction that expressing your emotions is nearly always preferable to keeping your feelings in check. Expressing emotion is a vehicle for solving problems as well as staying connected to others. However, there are situations in which expressing the fundamental emotions of fear, anger, sadness, and happiness might not be in one's best interest. Identify at least one situation for each of the emotions listed below in which the expression of the emotion might not be such a wise course.

Fear: _____

Anger: _____

Sadness: _____

Happiness: _____

After this exercise you should be able to:
- distinguish whether you believe that the expression of emotion can be dictated by situation.

Exercise 13.6

HONESTY IS THE BEST POLICY   ***Perspective Taking***

We don't always need polygraph machines to detect liars. Much to the amazement of guilty children parents can be very reliable judges of whether their children are lying. Parents often recount very specific cues they watch for—such as a change in the child's tone of voice or a failure to return eye contact or some exceptional body position. Both business and government rely on honesty for their success, and both would welcome a magic machine that offered these early parental skills. This quest for a magic box has led to an unfortunate and unjustifiable reliance on polygraph tests.

Although the American Psychological Association has advised the public about the limits of polygraph testing, professional lie detection in America is big business. The polygraph machine, which monitors physiological arousal, cannot distinguish "little white lies" from whoppers, but it can indicate that the person being tested is decidedly uncomfortable. This discomfort is assumed to be caused by lying. The examiner begins the test by establishing a resting level or base rate of arousal. To do this, he or she asks several questions that are assumed to provoke an honest response, such as "What is your name?" "Where do you live?" and "How long have you worked for this organization?" After establishing the baseline, the examiner asks a question designed to catch a liar. A significant increase in arousal is presumed to be caused by the strain of the moment and the fear of getting caught.

The use of lie detection as part of normal business practice is controversial and has been legally challenged. Your task in this exercise is to develop arguments for and against using lie detection in business settings and to identify the values that might underlie each of these positions. (See Answer Key.)

An Owner's Pro-Use Position

Assume that you are the owner of a shoe store and that for the last two weeks your cash register hasn't been balancing at the end of the day. You are certain that someone is shorting the cash drawer, but you have no evidence to suggest which of your employees is guilty. You propose a broad screening using a polygraph machine to try to narrow the field to a few probable culprits. What arguments could you use to persuade your employees to submit to the screening? What values are at the core of your plan of action?

Value(s): _____

_____

Arguments: _____

_____

_____

An Employee's Anti-Use Position

Now assume you are an innocent employee working at the same store. You have not seen anyone shorting the cash drawer, although you recognize that someone could easily do so because business practices are quite loose in the store. You are being asked to submit to a broad screening, but you find the idea offensive. What key points would you propose in your opposition to the plan? What value(s) might reinforce your position?

Value(s): _____

_____

Arguments: _____

_____

_____

After completing this exercise, you should be able to
- develop two opposite positions about polygraph use in business settings.
- identify possible value systems supporting each position.
- recognize the connection between values and arguments.
- understand how two positions could be effectively justified and still be diametrically opposed.
- predict what you might do if asked to submit to a polygraph test.

14

Personality

Personality is a puzzle. We can be alternately crabby or charming, aloof or appealing, abrasive or ingratiating. Although we may experience many variations in the social self that we present to others, psychologists prefer to study our enduring traits or characteristics in order to describe, explain, and predict how we will behave. Psychologists, of course, are not the only ones interested in describing personality. Astrologers, handwriting analysts, and fortune tellers also specialize in developing portraits of personality that, although they may be appealing, fall far short of the scientific standards psychologists observe.

Exercise 14.1

FREUD MEETS MOTHER GOOSE *Pattern Recognition*

Sigmund Freud was a man of singular accomplishments. His speculations about the structure and motives of human behavior have always generated significant controversy. His ideas were initially unpopular because they suggested that sexual motives were much more responsible for human behavior than his own Victorian culture would easily tolerate. Despite Freud's controversial beginnings, many of his contributions to understanding human behavior have endured.

Part of Freud's work was a stage theory of human development that organized significant stages around pleasurable activities. First is the *oral stage*. Freud suggested that infants derive pleasure through oral exploration. Further, he indicated that disturbances in the weaning experience will contribute to distinctive personality structures as the children mature into adults. Oral challenges to personality involve management of eating patterns and overall activity levels, whether impulsive (excessive) or restrictive (deficient).

Next is the *anal stage*, in which the child's attention shifts to the pleasures of elimination. Strain in the anal stage usually results in characteristic styles of handling possessions and orderliness, whether uncontrolled and sloppy or overcontrolled and precise.

In the third or *phallic stage*, children are attentive to the pleasures derived from sexual and gender identification. Fixations in this stage tend to produce exaggerated sexual responses, whether overactive or underactive.

In the *latency stage*, according to Freud, children's sexual motives go underground, waiting only for adult maturity for complete sexual expression.

The final stage is the *genital stage*. People who escape fixations at earlier stages are able to experience mature sexuality. Freud was quite pessimistic about the number of people who could realize this stage of development without scars from early developmental trauma.

Another of Freud's most interesting contributions is the concept of the defense mechanism. Freud suggested that we cope with our anxieties by converting them into more socially responsible activities that symbolize the original conflict. He called this conversion process *sublimation,* and he believed sublimations were responsible for many socially acceptable achievements.

In this exercise, we are going to assume that sublimation has been at work in the creation of the nursery rhymes that you probably learned as a child. For example, what psychoanalytic insights could you propose about the author of the following nursery rhyme?

> *Jack Sprat could eat no fat.*
> *His wife could eat no lean.*
> *And so between them both,*
> *They licked the platter clean.*

One might propose that oral fixation dominates this nursery rhyme about eating. Jack is probably thin. His wife is probably fat. However, they appear to spend all their time fretting about food, a characteristic of those who are orally deprived. The theme of this nursery rhyme may present some frustrations the author experienced in the oral stage. Freud would suggest that the author might be inclined in adulthood to show other problems related to oral fixation. Orally fixated adults show one of two patterns. They may be focused on oral stimulation—taking in food or performing other behaviors—such as sucking on pens, chewing ice cubes, and kissing—that will stimulate the pleasure center of the mouth. Or they may avoid oral stimulation and lose conscious interest in eating or other pleasurable mouth activities.

Assuming that each of the following nursery rhymes represents sublimation, analyze how Freud might interpret the real motives that lie behind the author's creation of the story. Identify the stage in which you think the creator of the nursery rhyme was fixated; then speculate about the kind of personality the creator might have had. (See Answer Key.)

Jack and Jill

> *Jack and Jill went up the hill*
> *To fetch a pail of water.*
> *Jack fell down and broke his crown,*
> *And Jill came tumbling after.*

Likely developmental stage at fixation: _____

Justify your answer: _____

_____

What might characterize the creator's adult personality structure? _____

_____

_____

Three Blind Mice

Three blind mice. Three blind mice.
See how they run. See how they run.
They all ran after the farmer's wife.
She cut off their tails with a carving knife.
Did you ever see such a sight in your life?
As three blind mice?

Likely developmental stage at fixation: _____

Justify your answer: _____
_____

What might characterize the creator's adult personality structure? _____
_____
_____

Mary, Mary, Quite Contrary

Mary, Mary, quite contrary,
How does your garden grow?
With silver bells and cockle shells
and pretty maids in a row.

Likely developmental stage at fixation: _____

Justify your answer: _____
_____

What might characterize the creator's adult personality structure? _____
_____
_____

After completing this exercise, you should be able to

- speculate about a significant Freudian theme around which literary works are written.
- support speculations of Freudian interpretation, using appropriate examples.
- use Freud's ideas to make some predictions about the adult personality of the writer, based on your speculations about the fixations.
- recognize that fixations can produce different patterns of adult behavior.

Exercise 14.2

MATCHMAKER, MATCHMAKER *Practical Problem Solving*

One of the more compelling and popular approaches to explaining personality patterns is the framework referred to as the Big 5. This approach suggests that there are five fairly stable dimensions on which we can make judgments about personality. Not only are the dimensions stable, but they appear to have some cross-cultural applicability, as well. According to this theory, we can evaluate personality along the following five dimensions:

Conscientiousness .... Irresponsibility

Stability .... Neurosis

Extraversion .... Introversion

Open to experience .... Closed to experience

Agreeableness .... Hostility

Suppose that you decide to set up a dating service based on the Big 5 principles. What kind of potential could occur when you match extremes on each of the dimensions? How would you predict the following matches would turn out?

a. Conscientious + Conscientious: _____
   Conscientious + Irresponsible: _____
   Irresponsible + Irresponsible: _____
b. Stable + Stable: _____
   Stable + Neurotic: _____
   Neurotic + Neurotic: _____
c. Extravert + Extravert: _____
   Extravert + Introvert: _____
   Introvert + Introvert: _____
d. Open + Open: _____
   Open + Closed: _____
   Closed + Closed: _____
e. Agreeable + Agreeable: _____
   Agreeable + Hostile: _____
   Hostile + Hostile: _____

After completing this exercise, you should be able to
- describe the Big 5 theory of personality.
- predict how the Big 5 characteristics might differ in other cultures.
- speculate about the interaction potential of mixed styles according to the Big 5.
- recognize what a foolish business enterprise this would be!

Exercise 14.3

PSEUDOSCIENTIFIC PERSONALITY — *Creative Problem Solving*

Many people believe in pseudoscientific methods of describing personality or predicting the future. From fortune cookies to palm reading, many individuals seem especially vulnerable to simplistic approaches conveyed by clear and concrete descriptions of personality. Many believers can offer powerful testimonials about the incredible accuracy of the predictions of their favorite astrologer. Psychics now offer their services by phone, charging by the minute. The popularity of these false sciences truly attests to P. T. Barnum's famous appraisal, "There's a sucker born every minute."

The purpose of this exercise is to use your creative processes to develop your own abilities to "read" people and to predict their behavior. (See Answer Key.)

The Stock Spiel

You will begin by generating a *stock spiel*, a trait description so general that few people could deny that it applies to them. Try to include at least five observations that anyone might find believable about himself or herself. Keep in mind that the more credible spiels are not entirely positive; some mild negative characteristics tend to enhance the realism of the statement.

_____

_____

_____

_____

_____

_____

Inferences From Physical Cues

To maximize the effectiveness of the ruse, you can personalize the stock spiel by adding other elements to the interpretation, based on inferences you make from physical cues offered by your "client." Can you think of five different inferences that could be justified by a person's physical traits, language, clothing, or behavioral cues, and that could enhance the credibility of your personality assessment?

Inference 1: _____

Derived from what kind of cue? _____

Inference 2: _____

Derived from what kind of cue? _____

Inference 3: _____

Derived from what kind of cue? _____

Inference 4: _____

Derived from what kind of cue? _____

Inference 5: _____

Derived from what kind of cue? _____

Can the generic comments (the stock spiel) and the inferred characteristics be combined to make the pseudoscientific interpretation more powerful?

After completing this exercise, you should be able to

- identify five characteristics that would appeal to most people seeking pseudopsychological explanations.
- recognize the role of incorporating some negative characteristics to enhance the realism of the description.
- personalize the descriptions by generating some personal characteristics based on typical physical or behavioral cues.
- challenge pseudoscientific explanations of behavior.

Exercise 14.4

YOU CAN'T CHEAT AN HONEST MAN *Scientific Problem Solving*

One of the most challenging problems that trait personality theorists face is that human beings may not always produce consistent behavior patterns across situations. For example, you probably consider yourself an honest person, but are you *always* honest? What are the factors that affect how honest (or not) you are in your interactions with others? Identify four variables that could influence honest dealings with others, that you might need to address in research designed to examine the trait of honesty. What would be the complications in trying to conduct research in this area?

After completing this exercise, you should be able to

- discuss why personality research is challenging.
- isolate how context factors can make a difference in how individuals behave.
- recognize the potential for ethics conflicts in conducting the research.

Exercise 14.5

RORSCHACH'S FATE *Psychological Reasoning*

Projective testing is one of the activities that distinguishes the clinical psychologist as a mental health professional. Only psychologists undergo the intensive training required to use tests such as the Rorschach inkblot test to make diagnostic judgments about personality. You have probably seen this practice parodied in movies and on television. The psychologist presents a nondescript symmetrical blob of ink on a card and instructs the client, "Tell me what you see." After taking copious notes on the client's responses, the psychologist will make some interpretations of those statements by comparing the responses to normative judgments. The patterns in the Rorschach can determine how the psychologist will judge the relative normality of the client.

The use of the Rorschach in making diagnostic decisions is controversial. Many research scientists believe that the Rorschach practices simply do not live up to the criteria of good science. That is, Rorschach results produce neither reliable nor valid findings. On the other hand, seasoned practitioners express enormous faith in the accumulated successful experiences that they have had in interpreting Rorschach findings. These practitioners point to the popularity of the instrument in making decisions that are sometimes critical to the outcome of court cases.

Would you agree to having a Rorschach conducted as part of a psychological evaluation? Are there some circumstances in which the questionable validity and reliability of the Rorschach would make you less inclined to rely on its findings?

After completing this exercise, you should be able to
- describe which mental health practitioners can and cannot use projective test techniques.
- explain the basic procedure involved in Rorschach protocol and interpretation.
- describe why the Rorschach is controversial.
- speculate about circumstances in which the use of the Rorschach would be personally acceptable.

Exercise 14.6

IS IT HOPELESS—OR NOT? *Psychological Perspective Taking*

As we explore the various perspectives on personality development, you may notice that theorists differ on the degree to which change is possible. Psychologists refer to this as the principle of "determinism." Review the list of theorists below and categorize each theorist's position as "deterministic" (personality is fixed) vs. "nondeterministic" (personality is flexible).

Theorist	Deterministic	Nondeterministic	Why?
Freud			
Skinner			
Rogers			
Maslow			

After completing this exercise, you should be able to
- explain the principle of determinism.
- discuss how four major personality theorists can be categorized based on the principle of determinism.
- develop your own views about the degree to which personality is determined.

15

Psychological Disorders

Scholars in psychiatry and psychology collaborated in an unprecedented manner to produce the fourth version of the *Diagnostic and Statistical Manual (DSM-IV)*, which offers a comprehensive description of every significant variation in behavior that falls outside normal expectations. Although the diagnostic compendium is somewhat controversial, the *DSM-IV* offers an impressive range of disorders that remind us of how fragile normal experience can be. It may be impossible to cruise through life without experiencing some of the disorders captured in the *DSM-IV*. The following exercises address the problems psychologists encounter when they attempt to make diagnostic judgments about normal versus disordered behavior.

Exercise 15.1

AND THE WINNER IS . . . *Pattern Recognition*

It is commonly said during Oscar season that the best way for an actor to win an Academy Award is to play a deeply disturbed person. A recent example of this strategy was Jack Nicholson, who played a remarkably endearing writer with obsessive compulsive disorder in the film, *As Good As It Gets*.

See if you can develop a list of performances in movies by gifted actors and try to identify the disorders that they are skillfully portraying.

If you have time during this part of the semester, you might benefit from renting a film and studying the treatment of the disorder. But, watcher beware! Sometimes artistic portrayals of psychological disorders may not truly capture the complications caused by the problem or the heroic measures their sufferers take in coping with the disease.

The answer key describes some classic performances and offers a roster of good movie watching.

After completing this exercise, you should be able to

- discuss why actors might prefer to take roles of those with psychological disturbances over those with normal behavior.
- recognize how syndromes can be portrayed in a variety of contexts.
- speculate about the nature of research an actor might need to complete to be effective in a role portraying a psychological disorder.
- identify specific performances that capture psychological disorders.

Exercise 15.2

ALL I NEED IS AN AGENT! *Creative Problem Solving*

In the last exercise you explored the ways that actors have portrayed various psychological disorders in film. In this exercise you become the writer. Review the chapter on psychological disorders and pick one of the problems described. Identify the psychological disorder and list its symptoms. Then draft a story line that would demonstrate the full range of difficulty someone with that disorder might experience.

DSM-IV diagnosis: _____

Characteristics: _____

Plot: _____
_____

After completing this exercise, you should be able to

- describe one psychological disorder thoroughly.
- speculate about the kinds of difficulties that disorder would cause the person who suffered from the disorder.
- develop reasonable empathy for persons afflicted with the specific psychological disorder you explored.
- evaluate your potential for screenwriting!

Exercise 15.3

THE END *Practical Problem Solving*

You have been worried about your friend Morgan for some time. He seems easily upset and filled with gloom. Few things make him smile. When he does talk, he makes vague references about his capacity to surprise people, and he often says that someday the people who have disappointed him will be "really sorry." The challenge Morgan is offering is the possibility that he might be one of the 25,000 people in the United States who will end their lives by suicide this year.

The purpose of this problem-solving exercise is twofold. First, you will try to identify aspects of Morgan's history that might help you evaluate how serious the threat of suicide is in his case. You'll generate a list of questions that might allow you to assess whether he will try to kill himself as a way out of his depression. Second, you will apply a decision-making process to determine the risk involved in either of two courses of action: (1) confronting Morgan with your concerns and following through with appropriate support and action or (2) rejecting your original suspicions about the significance of the depressive signs and hoping for the best.

Questions

Begin by formulating five questions whose answers might enable you to make a wiser judgment about the course of action you should take. Designing your questions may be easier if you think about the possible variables or characteristics that could contribute to depression and suicide decisions. Some of these are health status, disappointment, crisis, relationship strain, discouragement, revenge, and employment challenges. Can you think of others?

1. _____

2. _____

3. _____

4. _____

5. _____

Risk Analysis

When you must make a decision, you can sometimes structure the decision in a matrix, as follows. There are four possibilities, or conditions. In two of the four conditions, you have the potential to be right (a "hit," in decision-theory terminology). In the remaining two conditions you will be wrong (a "miss").

	Morgan is suicidal.	Morgan is not suicidal.
You predict Morgan is suicidal.	correct diagnosis	incorrect diagnosis
You predict Morgan is not suicidal.	incorrect diagnosis	correct diagnosis

Real Situation Alternatives

As the matrix shows, Morgan (as the potential suicide) and you (as the diagnostic problem solver) can each make one of two choices. He can either kill himself or stay among the living. You can either decide that he is suicidal or judge that he is depressed and upset but not suicidally so.

The next part of your task is to consider these four conditions and describe the advantages and risks involved in each of them. As you do so, consider the consequences for you and for Morgan. (See Answer Key.)

A "hit": Morgan is suicidal and you correctly identify his intentions.

Advantages: _____

Risks: _____

A "hit": Morgan is not suicidal and you correctly identify his intentions.

Advantages: _____

Risks: _____

A "miss": Morgan is suicidal and you don't correctly identify his intentions.

Advantages: _____

Risks: _____

A "miss": Morgan is not suicidal and you don't correctly identify his intentions.

Advantages: _____

Risks: _____

After completing this exercise, you should be able to
- identify variables that may influence suicidal intentions.
- formulate questions that might lead to more insight into the choices that prompt suicide as a solution.
- examine decisions in terms of "hits" and "misses."
- plan how you might intervene if you were confronted with this problem as a real challenge.

Exercise 15.4

I'M JUST NOT MYSELF TODAY   *Scientific Problem Solving*

The psychological disturbance called multiple personality disorder (MPD) or dissociative disorder is one of the most fascinating patterns that confront scholars of abnormal psychology. How could it be that a seemingly normal-looking individual could shelter multiple entities with separate interests and talents? When MPD first emerged in diagnostic circles, the problem was thought to be quite rare. However, the frequency of MPD dramatically increased through the 1970s and 1980s. MPD even emerged as a defense in murder trials. Most curiously, one young woman brought charges against a sexual partner when she indicated that only one of her personalities was in agreement with the sexual proposition.

In the late 1980s and in the 1990s, the diagnostic validity of MPD was challenged. Some patients were challenged about using MPD symptoms to try to escape legal consequences. Some patients accused their therapists of exploitation after having been convinced in therapy that they had MPD. Even some of the classic cases of MPD might have been fraudulent.

How can we use the benefits of experimental design to address this problem? Some enterprising researchers recruited patients who had been diagnosed as having MPD and conducted Positron Emission Topography (PET) scans on those patients. PET reveals thermal activity in the brain based on degrees of glucose use. The researchers asked the patients to do similar kinds of activities when they were experiencing different personalities and noted significant differences in the blood flow to different parts of the brain depending on their personality status. The researchers' preliminary assumptions indicated that thermal activity on a given task should be reflected in the same areas in an intact brain but might show up in different areas if MPD produced a different physiological infrastructure for each personality. Preliminary results showed different thermal activity in the same brain of an individual reporting to be functioning out of different personalities.

Based on your knowledge of experimental design, is this evidence sufficient to conclude that MPD causes the brain to become differentiated in MPD? Justify your answer.

After completing this exercise, you should be able to
- describe the controversy surrounding the validity of Multiple Personality Disorder.
- formulate your own position of the validity of the disorder.
- discuss the rationale of Positron Emission Topography in capturing brain activity.
- apply experimental design principles in forming a judgment about scientific evidence.

Exercise 15.5

THE LABELING CONTROVERSY — *Psychological Reasoning*

Clinical psychologists confront a challenging task each time they sit across from a new client. Every individual has a unique story to tell—often filled with pain, confusion, and other symptoms that in most cases will be interpreted as a specific diagnosis.

Although the use of diagnostic labels is a widely accepted practice, it is still somewhat controversial. Fueling the controversy, David Rosenhan conducted a field study in which he and his friends became "pseudopatients" in various inpatient settings. By reporting some symptoms that were interpreted by hospital staff as auditory hallucinations, the researchers found that they could easily be admitted as hospital inpatients: however, when they continued to act normally, they couldn't get out.

In this exercise you will do a critical analysis of the Rosenhan study by arguing both sides of the controversy: *The Rosenhan study is or is not a valid (trustworthy) test of the problems associated with labeling.* First establish two arguments to support each side of the argument. Then decide which side of the controversy you find more convincing.

The Rosenhan study is *a valid test of the problems associated with labeling.*

Argument 1: _____

_____

_____

_____

Argument 2: _____

_____

_____

The Rosenhan study is not *a valid test of the problems associated with labeling.*

Argument 1: _____

_____

_____

_____

Argument 2: _____

_____

_____

Which side of the controversy most closely represents your own beliefs about labeling? Why? _____

_____

_____

_____

_____

_____

After completing this exercise, you should be able to

- recognize the relationship between the Rosenhan study and the problem of labeling in mental health today.
- identify some elements of the Rosenhan study that can be challenged.
- develop an adequate defense of Rosenhan's approach to the labeling problem.
- speculate about the role of preconceptions in making sense of psychological disorders.

Exercise 15.6

WHY Y2K? *Psychological Perspective Taking*

As the last century came to a close, we witnessed near frenzy that challenged our views of what constitutes normal behavior. Many individuals believed that predicted massive computer malfunctions would produce an apocalypse. Consequently, they stockpiled supplies, in case there were a significant disruption of services. They put in supplies of canned food and bottled water. Some bought generators. Unfortunately, some stockpiled gasoline and propane, which created new risks through increased threats for fire hazard.

Because the arrival of the new year 2000 brought no sign of the disturbances predicted by the news media, the individuals who stockpiled supplies and predicted doom and gloom seemed in retrospect "abnormal" and perhaps even a bit silly. In fact, the *DSM-IV* probably gives you some ideas about how extreme cases of Y2K fear might be diagnosed.

a. What *DSM-IV* diagnosis comes the closest to capturing the abnormal pattern of stockpiling goods in anticipation of doomsday?

b. How people responded to the Y2K threat gives us an opportunity to explore the notion of a continuum of disorder. Based on the stories that you heard about how people prepared to cope with Y2K, develop a set of descriptions that reflects a continuum of severity of the stockpiling problem, from "no difficulty" to "extreme difficulty." How might the behavior of a person who had no Y2K fears differ from those whose fears were incapacitating?

No difficulty: _____

Minor difficulty: _____

Moderate difficulty: _____

Serious difficulty: _____

Extreme difficulty: _____

c. Finally, what if the stockpilers had been right? It seems rather easy in hindsight to label the problems of Y2K fanatics as disordered. However, if predictions of gloom and doom had been right, those who had not prepared in dramatic ways for the apocalypse would have been at a distinct disadvantage. In fact, they might be perceived as the abnormal ones. Assuming that Y2K fears were justified, what *DSM-IV* labels would be useful in explaining how underprepared individuals ignored all the obvious signs of impending doom and failed to protect themselves and their families?

16

Therapy

The stereotyped image of therapy usually involves a patient lying on a couch unraveling personal stories about life's injustices to a concerned but well-trained listener. In contemporary therapies, reality is likely to be far different. Freud's "talking cure" has evolved into a remarkable array of therapy modes, most involving therapists in active collaboration with the client. Therapy is more than listening. Helping others professionally provides an opportunity for the exercise of refined critical thinking skills, from selecting the right therapeutic strategy through designing outcome studies that demonstrate therapeutic effectiveness. The exercises in this chapter offer a simulation of the processes researchers and practitioners employ in therapy.

Exercise 16.1

HOW DOES THAT MAKE YOU FEEL? *Pattern Recognition*

You may have been surprised to find that therapists practice clinical arts in so many different ways. Estimates of the distinguishable "schools" of therapeutic treatment vary, but there may be as many as 200 different psychotherapeutic approaches to solving human problems in therapy. The exercise below will give you an opportunity to match the school of therapy to the statement most representative of a practitioner from that school. See if you can determine how specific phrases reveal the practitioner's preferred approach.

Statement	Options
__ 1. "Tell me about your earliest memories from childhood."	a. Token economy
__ 2. "What were the consequences that happened after you punched your boss?"	b. Cognitive therapy
__ 3. "Rank order the things that frighten you from 'least' to 'most'."	c. Gestalt therapy
__ 4. "Let's explore how your role as a daughter, mother, and wife might influence the problem."	d. Freudian therapy
__ 5. "Have you been having recurring dreams?"	e. Feminist therapy
__ 6. "In what ways do you think you have fallen short of your ideals?"	f. Behavior therapy
__ 7. "Pretend that your grandmother is sitting in the chair over there and tell her how you feel."	g. Adlerian therapy
__ 8. "You have developed a very powerful mental set that you are a loser."	h. Humanistic therapy
__ 9. "If you can refrain from losing your temper, you'll get two red stars."	i. Jungian therapy
__10. "Let's try to figure out how your feelings of inferiority might be linked to your family."	j. Systematic desensitization

After completing this exercise, you should be able to

- identify key characteristics of schools of therapy.
- use appropriate terminology in connection with a school of therapy.
- describe the main schools of therapy that are currently popular.
- explain why there might be more than one way to address a psychological disorder.

Exercise 16.2

EVEN DOMESTIC ENGINEERS GET THE BLUES — *Practical Problem Solving*

Ellen looked awful. She said she had spent three relatively sleepless nights and had eaten little, and it showed. She couldn't sleep because she felt tormented by feelings of shame, guilt, and loss. She thought that it had nothing to do with her family. She had been "happily married" for nine years. The family members were all healthy. The family was financially stable and seemed to have a strong network of support in the community. Nothing was really wrong with them. Oh, sure, the kids and her husband weren't home much. He worked overtime very often. The kids were always running to soccer or other commitments. But that was the way it was supposed to be. Ellen thought her "blues" had more to do with her brother. She hadn't been able to escape strong feelings of self-recrimination since her brother died. They had had a serious fight the night before his car accident, and she had never had a chance to apologize. The last few months had been a nightmare because of the impact her unrelenting sadness was having on Ellen and her family.

The purpose of this exercise is to experiment with matching a client with an appropriate therapy. You will do this by considering the characteristics Ellen is bringing into her first clinical session and by determining the advantages and disadvantages that each of seven schools of therapy might offer her. After considering the seven frameworks, select the one that might be most helpful for the symptoms Ellen is presenting. (See Answer Key.)

Psychoanalysis

What would you expect the therapist to focus on or to do? _____

What would be the advantages of using this approach? _____

What would be the disadvantages of using this approach? _____

Person-Centered Therapy

What would you expect the therapist to focus on or to do? _____

What would be the advantages of using this approach? _____

What would be the disadvantages of using this approach? _____

Aversive Conditioning

What would you expect the therapist to focus on or to do? _____

What would be the advantages of using this approach? _____

What would be the disadvantages of using this approach? _____

Cognitive Behavior Therapy

What would you expect the therapist to focus on or to do? _____

What would be the advantages of using this approach? _____

_____

What would be the disadvantages of using this approach? _____

_____

Drug Therapy

What would you expect the therapist to focus on or to do? _____

_____

What would be the advantages of using this approach? _____

_____

What would be the disadvantages of using this approach? _____

_____

Family Therapy

What would you expect the therapist to focus on or to do? _____

_____

What would be the advantages of using this approach? _____

_____

What would be the disadvantages of using this approach? _____

_____

Electroconvulsive Therapy

What would you expect the therapist to focus on or to do? _____

_____

What would be the advantages of using this approach? _____

_____

What would be the disadvantages of using this approach? _____

_____

Which framework would you select for Ellen? _____

Justify your answer: _____

_____

_____

_____

After completing this exercise, you should be able to

- identify general differences in the activities that would take place in different therapeutic approaches.
- for each of the seven possible therapeutic frameworks, specify one advantage.
- eliminate some choices of therapy for this client, based on their disadvantages.
- understand how therapists may select elements of various frameworks as they develop treatment strategies.
- clarify the characteristics of therapy schools that you might find personally helpful if you needed to seek treatment in the future.

Exercise 16.3

THERE MUST BE 50 WAYS TO LEAVE YOUR SHRINK — *Creative Problem Solving*

Psychotherapists endure a lot of criticism about keeping their clients or patients longer than they really need to as a way of sustaining their own practices. Although some less-than-ethical therapists might engage in keeping clients over time, the majority of practitioners take on new clients with the express intent of making themselves dispensable.

But how do you know when you are ready to go? What if the therapist doesn't pronounce your work completed? Try to generate five "indicators" that might help you determine that your therapy has been effective. (And it wouldn't hurt if you added some humor to your answers!)

After completing this exercise, you should be able to

- recognize the inevitability of completing psychological treatment.
- describe multiple strategies for ending a significant relationship.
- question the ethics of therapists who may engage in protracted treatments that cannot be justified by the symptoms.
- demonstrate flexibility in planning personal expression.

Exercise 16.4

OUT, DAMNED SPOT — *Scientific Problem Solving*

Suppose you had just developed a revolutionary new treatment for compulsive hand washing. Preliminary results with your own clients suggest that your approach is not only effective (it makes the chronic hand-washing rituals go away) but also efficient (it makes the rituals go away faster than does any other approach currently being tried).

To gain the attention of the mental health community, you will need to demonstrate that your method is effective. Assuming you could get 100 people who suffer from compulsive handwashing to volunteer for an experiment, how would you design an experiment that would demonstrate the superiority of your methods? (See Answer Key.)

What is your hypothesis? _____

What is your independent variable? _____

How will you assign subjects to treatment conditions? _____

How will you measure your dependent variable? _____

What other elements will you need to control in order to rule out alternative hypotheses? _____

If all proceeded as planned and you obtained the results you intended, would your study offer proof of the superiority of your treatment? Justify your answer.

_____

After completing this exercise, you should be able to

- isolate the independent variable and create treatment conditions that reflect your emphasis.
- identify a strategy that will measure the dependent variable while accurately reflecting changes in the anxiety condition.
- specify important influences that need to be controlled to rule out alternative explanations.
- describe whether such a design would offer definitive evidence of the superiority of a new technique.

Exercise 16.5

NOT-SO-CLEVER HANS *Psychological Reasoning*

Hans Eysenck created a huge controversy early in the history of clinical psychology by publishing a study in which he concluded that therapy was no more effective than the passage of time in producing improvements in psychological disorder. He conducted what is now referred to as a meta-analysis. He synthesized the results of many treatment studies by comparing the improvement in symptoms of those who received treatment with those who were placed on a "waiting list," the equivalent of a control group. Eysenck said that psychological therapy was relatively ineffective. He thought it was just as effective to wait for time to heal psychological wounds.

The treatment community was up in arms. Eysenck's finding certainly didn't fit with their own experiences in treatment offices, and they appropriately began to question the procedure that Eysenck used to come to his conclusion. More recent meta-analytic studies have concluded that many therapy forms produce significant symptom reduction and contrast starkly with Eysenck's early observations.

What kinds of questions would you raise about the process Eysenck used to produce his controversial finding? Identify at least three variables that a good outcome design would need to address before it could allow making broad conclusions about the overall effectiveness of therapy.

After completing this exercise, you should be able to

- describe Eysenck's early findings and indicate why they were so controversial.
- identify the function and complexity of a meta-analysis.
- consider why seeking therapy rather than waiting for time to improve conditions may be more adaptive.
- isolate variables that need to be controlled in well-designed outcome studies.

Exercise 16.6

WHO'S GOT THE CHECK? *Perspective Taking*

The right to good mental health care is somewhat controversial. Despite significant evidence that psychological therapy is effective, many insurance policies restrict the number of sessions to which their insured members are entitled. Because health care costs regularly increase, those who don't support the right to mental health treatment emphasize that insurance premiums could be reduced if policies didn't include coverage for mental health.

Access to good quality mental health care is especially problematic for people without insurance resources. Psychologists are regularly criticized for electing to work with the "worried well," rather than people who are in greater need of the kind of assistance psychologists could provide.

Think about your own position in relation to mental health care and its funding. Should this treatment be a regular part of health insurance? Should it be part of a national health care plan? How committed are you to equal access to good mental health care? Come up with three justifications to support your point of view. Whatever your position, try to anticipate the critical elements of the opposite side. Try to think of three justifications to support the opposite side. Finally, does a more thorough evaluation of both sides affect your original position?

After completing this exercise, you should be able to

- describe the current national status of funding for mental health care coverage.
- articulate the arguments "pro" and "con" for increased funding and access to mental health care.
- justify your own position regarding improved access to mental health care.

17

Stress and Health

Our ancestors in more primitive times probably experienced stress as they faced the challenges of survival—securing sufficient nutrition and avoiding danger. Although the goal of survival in contemporary life is the same, the array of sources of stress is much richer. We have a wider selection of possible goals as well as broader ranges of stimulating and threatening experiences. As a result of our knowledge about the relationship of stress to the quality of life, many people conscientiously learn all they can about ways to reduce stress and promote healthy lifestyles.

Exercise 17.1

BETWEEN A ROCK AND A HARD PLACE *Pattern Recognition*

A very commonly used metaphor for being placed in the difficult position of choosing between two unattractive alternatives is "being caught between a rock and a hard place." Although you have two distinct choices, the negative impact will be virtually the same, no matter which one you choose. Psychologists refer to this problem as an *avoidance-avoidance conflict*, since either selection produces frustration, conflict, and withdrawal.

Ironically, choices do not need to have a negative impact to promote stress. *Approach-approach conflicts* challenge the individual to choose between two *attractive* alternatives. However, selecting one means losing the other.

A third variation, the *approach-avoidance conflict*, also generates feelings of stress and strain. In this case, the individual is confronted by only one attractive option, but that option has some distinct negative features attached to it. By pursuing this goal, you guarantee some unpleasantness as well as a positive experience.

In this exercise, you will personalize your own response to stress by predicting the intensity of stress that various conflict situations would generate. For each situation, label the conflict pattern it represents (approach-approach, avoidance-avoidance, or approach-avoidance), and estimate how much stress each situation would generate for you personally. (See Answer Key.)

Going to the Dentist to Have an Aching Tooth Repaired

Type of conflict _____

Your stress-intensity rating

_____
not at all   mildly   extremely
stressful   stressful   stressful

Choosing Between Chocolate-Chocolate Chip and Rocky Road Ice Cream

Type of conflict _____

Your stress-intensity rating

_____
not at all   mildly   extremely
stressful   stressful   stressful

Discovering That Your New and Very Attractive Dating Partner Has Bad Breath

Type of conflict _____

Your stress-intensity rating

_____
not at all   mildly   extremely
stressful   stressful   stressful

Choosing Between a 7 A.M. and an 8 P.M. Class

Type of conflict _____

Your stress-intensity rating

_____
not at all   mildly   extremely
stressful   stressful   stressful

Deciding Between a One-Week Vacation at Disney World and a One-Week Camping Trip in the Mountains

Type of conflict _____

Your stress-intensity rating

_____
not at all   mildly   extremely
stressful   stressful   stressful

Choosing Between Breast Removal and Chemotherapy After a Diagnosis of Breast Cancer

Type of conflict _____

Your stress-intensity rating

_____
not at all   mildly   extremely
stressful   stressful   stressful

Selecting One of Two Highly Rated Colleges That Have Admitted You

Type of conflict _____

Your stress-intensity rating

_____
not at all						mildly						extremely
stressful						stressful					stressful

As a Vegetarian, Being Asked Whether You Want Steak or Ribs

Type of conflict _____

Your stress-intensity rating

_____
not at all						mildly						extremely
stressful						stressful					stressful

Deciding Whether to Buy a Low-Priced, Beautiful Used Car That Needs a Major Repair on Its Engine

Type of conflict _____

Your stress-intensity rating

_____
not at all						mildly						extremely
stressful						stressful					stressful

Having Plastic Surgery to Correct a Bump on the Bridge of Your Nose

Type of conflict _____

Your stress-intensity rating

_____
not at all						mildly						extremely
stressful						stressful					stressful

After completing this exercise, you should be able to

- distinguish the three kinds of conflict that generate stress about making choices.
- recognize that stress can be generated even by positive choices.
- describe variations in stress intensity among individuals.
- speculate how stress ratings may change over time.

Exercise 17.2

HEALTHY LIVING   *Perspective Taking*

Stress is a word that has many uses in everyday conversation. In the technical vocabulary of psychology, however, it refers to the process an organism uses to evaluate and respond to the threats and challenges in the environment. As you learned in your study of perception, the stimuli in the environment are interpreted through the senses and expectations of the perceiver. This means that any two individuals, when experiencing the same event, may interpret and respond to it differently, depending on their personalities, personal habits, level of social support, and personal appraisal of the situation. Individuals who see most of life's events as a challenge, who are optimistic and easygoing, with plenty of social support and who get plenty of exercise, don't smoke, and eat nutritious foods are more likely to be healthy than individuals who see these same events as threats, who are depressed or pessimistic, without a strong social support network and who smoke, are sedentary, and follow a poor diet.

For the scenario given below, assume that your tendency is toward health, and describe how you might react to the situation. Be as specific as you can, identifying your appraisal of the event, your personality, personal habits, and relationships with other people. Once you have done this, assume that your tendency is toward illness, and show how your response would be different. Again, you should be as specific as possible, describing the same factors of appraisal, personality, personal habits, and social supports.

Scenario: You are a 42-year-old working woman with two teenage children and a husband. During your annual review at work, your boss tells you that you are up for promotion. The new job is one that you've always thought you'd like, and the salary is significantly higher than what you are making now. The job involves a tremendous amount of travel, however, and you would be on the road approximately two weeks out of every month. Your teenage children are involved in many different school and social activities, and your husband also works a full-time job. In particular, your daughter is one year away from college and is beginning to plan and visit the schools in which she is interested. You have two weeks to make your decision.

Describe how you spend your two weeks if your general tendency is toward health.

___

How do you spend these two weeks if your tendency is toward illness? ___

Which of the characteristics you have described above is similar to the way that you deal with life events? Can you identify ways in which you can approach decisions and activities in a healthier fashion? _____

_____

_____

_____

_____

_____

_____

After completing this exercise, you should be able to

- define stress, stressor, and stress response.
- recognize that the same event can have different effects on an individual's well-being based on that person's interpretation of the event.
- identify the factors that influence a person's perception of a stressful event.
- describe health-prone and illness-prone responses to a given event.
- consider ways in which you can respond in health-prone ways to your own life events.

Exercise 17.3

ENHANCING IMMUNE FUNCTION   *Scientific Problem Solving*

In a series of experiments with rats, Ader and Cohen (1985) demonstrated that the immune system can be classically conditioned. After many pairings of sweet water with a drug that suppressed the immune system, the sweet water suppressed the immune system when presented by itself. With the immune system suppressed, the rat was much more likely to acquire a variety of illnesses. Many researchers think that if it is possible to condition immune suppression, it should also be possible to condition immune enhancement. This could help people fight off illness and lead healthier lives.

Because our understanding of the factors that enhance immune function is less well defined than our understanding of those that suppress immune function, operationalizing and selecting the variables for experiments testing immune enhancement is difficult. Assume that you are part of a team working on research in this area. Your team has decided that the placebo effect—improvement in a person's condition with treatments that have no physiologically significant effect—may be the result of conditioned immune enhancement. In other words, because medication administered in the past has resulted in improved immune function, similar administration of something an individual believed was medication also improved immune function. Working from this hypothesis, your team decides to modify the way in which the placebo is given in one set of medication trials to make it less like other experiences individuals have with medication. One of the placebo groups will be given the placebo in pill form (traditional group), while the other will receive it dissolved in a cup of coffee (novel group).

Given this basic design, what are some of the extraneous variables your team needs to consider? _____

_____

If the results show a significant difference between the two groups, what conclusions might you reasonably draw? _____

_____

What are some ethical considerations in using placebos in experiments dealing with people's health? Do you think the benefits justify the methods? Explain your answer.

_____

After completing this exercise, you should be able to
- describe experiments demonstrating classical conditioning of the immune system.
- identify extraneous variables that might influence classical conditioning of immune function.
- interpret the results of a hypothetical experiment of classically conditioned immune response.
- discuss the ethical considerations of placebo studies.

Exercise 17.4

HEALTHY EXECUTIVES *Practical Problem Solving*

You are a consultant being hired by a large investment firm to set up an on-site wellness program. The company has noticed that its health insurance rates are increasing because of the high utilization of the health insurance by their employees. Many of the health concerns of the employees are related to high blood pressure, coronary artery disease, obesity, and other illnesses that might be stress-related. They have asked you to help them create fitness and wellness programs designed to decrease the negative stress responses of their employees and to help them become more fit. This is a particularly challenging project because of the fast-paced work atmosphere. Most of the employees work 10-hour days and only take 30 minutes or so out for lunch or a break.

Based on your understanding of psychology and the specific needs of this type of organization, design a stress-management program that takes into consideration the special needs of this group. You should have at least two different components to your program; very strong programs will have three or more. _____

_____
_____
_____
_____
_____
_____
_____
_____
_____
_____
_____
_____

How might your program design have been different if you had been working with a group of teachers instead of investment executives? _____

_____
_____
_____
_____
_____
_____
_____
_____
_____
_____
_____
_____

After completing this exercise, you should be able to

- identify the risks of a high-stress lifestyle.
- create a stress management program that includes exercise, relaxation, and social support components.
- recognize the ways in which a program must fit the needs of the individuals for whom it is designed.

Exercise 17.5

STEP ON THE GAS   *Psychological Reasoning*

Despite the fact that there are many different types of stressors to which an organism can respond, the stress response itself follows a predictable pattern. Hans Selye (1976) called this pattern the General Adaptation Syndrome (GAS). Selye said that there are three phases of stress response. The first is the alarm reaction, in which the sympathetic nervous system is suddenly activated by the detection of the stressor. During the resistance phase you cope with the stressor, and the sympathetic nervous system remains aroused to provide energy and protection against illness. The final stage, exhaustion, occurs when the body's energy is depleted. During this stage the organism's resistance to illness is diminished, and energy levels are low.

Using this framework, explain your own reaction to a significant stressor in your life. Make sure that you clearly identify each stage with your accompanying physical, emotional, and cognitive experiences. _____

_____

_____

_____

_____

_____

_____

_____

_____

_____

_____

_____

Given your knowledge of this process, what might you do to minimize the negative effects of stress the next time you are in a stressful situation? _____

_____

_____

_____

_____

_____

After completing this exercise, you should be able to
- describe Selye's General Adaptation Syndrome.
- use the GAS to explain a significantly stressful event in your own life.
- speculate about how you might use your understanding of this process to minimize the negative effects of stress in future stressful situations.

Exercise 17.6

THE GAME OF LIFE *Creative Problem Solving*

At some point during your educational career, you have probably been presented with one of a variety of fictional dilemmas asking you to make choices based on your value system. They generally follow the format of "If you can only save 10 of the following 50 people from some disaster, who would you save and why?" This activity is similar to those others you may have seen. You must select a given number of items from the following lists of stressors, with the intention of maximizing your health and resiliency. Once you have made your selections, explain why you chose the items you did, and what impact you would expect them to have on your health and happiness. Compare your answers with those of your classmates and discuss the differences in personality, event appraisal, and personal habits that led to your decisions.

Category I (choose 1)	Category II (choose 3)	Category III (choose 5)
Living in a country experiencing war	Death of a close relative	Getting stuck in construction traffic and being three hours late getting home
Living through a major earthquake	Getting married	
	Losing a job	Waiting in line at the post office for one hour to mail in your taxes
Losing your home and possessions because of a fire	Having triplets	
	Living 2,000 miles from family	Having two exams the day before your sister's wedding
	Moving to a new city	
Living near a nuclear disaster site	Developing a serious illness	Locking your keys in the car
	Buying an expensive house	
Having a close relative die in a plane crash	Getting a promotion at work	Forgetting your notes for a presentation
	Having a 2-hour heavy-traffic commute every day	Getting a speeding ticket
	Getting divorced	Losing your keys on the morning of a big job interview
		Having a fight with your roommate
		Bouncing a check
		Having to find a new apartment

Take a look at the items you selected. What effect would you expect them to have on your health and well-being? _____

_____

_____

_____

_____

_____

Would your health be affected differently if these things happened at different points in your life? How might you respond differently if the event you chose from Category I happened when you were 8 instead of as an adult? _____

_____
_____
_____
_____
_____
_____
_____

After completing this exercise, you should be able to
- discuss the effects that various stressors might have on your health.
- identify the ways in which your own personality, event attributions, and personal habits affect the ways in which you respond to various stressors.
- speculate about how catastrophic stressors affect individuals differentially based on their stage of development.

18

Social Psychology

Human beings are uniquely social organisms. Social psychologists study the systematic patterns that emerge as human beings interact with one another. Examples include the factors that increase obedience to authority figures, the influence of social roles and contexts on behavior, and even the variables that make people love each other. The exercises in this chapter, highlighting different specialized areas in social psychology, address critical thinking attitudes as well as critical thinking skills.

Exercise 18.1

PRIDE AND PREJUDICES — *Pattern Recognition*

Prejudice represents an enduring attitude that predisposes a favorable or unfavorable response toward a group. It is remarkably easy to acquire prejudice. Because our brains detect patterns in what we experience, we may be able to generate prejudicial conclusions based on very little evidence. Negative experiences with even one representative of a group can engender lifelong beliefs, emotions, and behaviors toward members of that group.

Many college students (and professors, too) deny that they have prejudices. Chances are that such broad claims are simply not true. For example, how would you rate your degree of prejudice toward the following?

Police Officers

very negative	neutral	very positive

Cheerleaders

very negative	neutral	very positive

Convicted Child Molesters

very negative	neutral	very positive

Preachers

very negative	neutral	very positive

Psychologists

very negative	neutral	very positive

High School Vice Principals

very negative	neutral	very positive

Redheads

very negative	neutral	very positive

Bald Men Who Wear Wigs

very negative	neutral	very positive

Hunters

very negative	neutral	very positive

AIDS Patients

very negative	neutral	very positive

You can see the trend here. It is hard, if not impossible, to live a bias-free life.

How does prejudice develop? We can acquire prejudice (either positive or negative) by generalizing from direct experience with one person to a group and through observation and imitation of the attitudes of others. Both social and cognitive factors encourage and sustain prejudice.

Social Factors

Social factors that promote prejudice include the following:

- *Social inequalities* encourage perceptions that justify discriminatory beliefs and treatment.
- The *in-group bias* causes us to favor arbitrarily those we perceive to be like us.
- *Scapegoating* suggests that our frustrations are reduced when we can blame someone else for our problems.

Cognitive Factors

Cognitive processes can also sustain patterns of prejudice.

- *Categorization* encourages us to simplify the world by making people and events as predictable as possible. Categorizing sometimes produces stereotypes that offer the illusion of predictability.
- *Vivid cases* determine those instances in which we are likely to overgeneralize from a few exceptional cases to a group expectation.
- The *just-world phenomenon,* also known as *hindsight bias,* allows us to blame the victim, thereby offering reassurance that good people will triumph and bad people will meet appropriately wretched ends.

Now revisit your prejudice ratings and determine which explanations may have influenced your ratings on the target groups for which you registered either a positive or negative bias. See if you can identify the likely sources of prejudice by checking those that may have contributed to your ratings. The manner in which the prejudice develops probably has some bearing on whether the prejudice can be modified.

	Social Inequality	In-Group Bias	Scape-goating	Categori-zation	Vivid Cases	Just-World Phenomenon
Police Officers						
Cheerleaders						
Convicted Child Molesters						
Preachers						
Psychologists						
High School Vice Principals						
Redheads						
Bald Men Who Wear Wigs						
Hunters						
AIDS Patients						

An honest assessment of the possible sources of your own prejudices can determine how open you might be to changing your point of view. William James, the father of American psychology, argued that the function of a good education is the "rearrangement of prejudice."

After completing this exercise, you should be able to

- identify at least some target groups for which you had either a positive or negative predisposition.
- designate your individual profile of preferences and the sources from which these may have developed.
- speculate about the way in which a type of source may give rise to the prejudice as well as how modifiable the prejudice might be.
- discriminate between prejudices that might have negative, positive, or neutral impacts.

Exercise 18.2

DEAR ABBY — *Practical Problem Solving*

Dear Abby,
I have been dating a young woman for about eight months. I fear she is losing interest in me. We attend different universities, so I can't spend as much time with her as I would like. I'm afraid she may have fallen for some other guy. Can you give me some advice about how to win her back?
Signed,
Worried and Weary

Abby has gone on vacation. The column editor, who knows you've been studying principles of physical attraction and love at school, has asked you to pinch-hit. He thinks you'd be just the right person to advise Worried and Weary. How could you use the following concepts from social psychology to make some recommendations that will help Worried and Weary with his romantic dilemma? (See Answer Key.)

How would *proximity* principles influence your advice? _____

What could you recommend regarding *physical attractiveness*? _____

How would *similarity* principles influence your advice? _____

How would you incorporate *arousal* in your recommendations? _____

How would you address the importance of establishing *equity* in enduring relationships? _____

What role should *self-disclosure* play in securing the relationship? _____

From these principles, draft your response to Worried and Weary:

Dear Worried,

_____
_____
_____
_____
_____
_____

Signed,
Glad When Abby Gets Back!

People vary in the ease with which they offer advice about managing the behavior of others. Evaluate your comfort level in serving as Abby's substitute:

_____
_____
_____
_____
_____
_____

After completing this exercise, you should be able to

- apply principles of liking and attraction to create some meaningful advice.
- distinguish the relative effectiveness of these principles for developing a romantic strategy.
- question the use of psychology in influencing or manipulating the lives of others.
- determine whether knowledge of liking and attraction principles will influence how you proceed in your own relationships.

Exercise 18.3

BUT MY TEACHER *MADE* ME DO IT! *Creative Problem Solving*

A standard assignment in social psychology is to ask you to violate a norm that governs social behavior and report the responses of people who observe you doing the violation. This exercise asks you to perform a norm violation but adds four simple requirements:

1. Do the exercise in pairs. One individual should be the norm violator and the other the helper who can watch the reaction of observers. Then switch roles to see if the responses of the observers are the same.
2. The norm violation should not put you at risk for arrest.
3. Explain how this exercise demonstrates *attribution theory*. Contrast how you and your partner would explain the violation of the norm with how the observers would interpret it.
4. Your norm violation should be more creative than facing the rear wall in the elevator. Challenge yourself to come up with something that might be worthy of *Candid Camera*.

Your report:

Norm violation attempted: _____
_____

Observations: _____
_____
_____

Using attribution theory, how would you explain your motives for norm violation?
_____
_____

How would an onlooker explain your norm violation? _____
_____
_____

After completing this exercise, you should be able to
- define norms and the roles they play in social interaction.
- describe behavior without adding interpretation.
- apply attribution theory terminology to distinguish how actors and observers explain their own motivations.
- explain why extremes in norm violation often involve the police.

Exercise 18.4

HOW CAN I HELP? *Scientific Problem Solving*

Social psychologists have long been intrigued by the conditions that give rise to helping behavior. For example, the horrifying case study of Kitty Genovese, in which a New York apartment dweller was killed while more than thirty people looked on, suggests that people will deny help if they can assume that someone else will come to the rescue. On the other hand, people are more likely to spring into action if they have the impression that no one else is around to take action. There are gender differences in forms of helping, too. For example, men may be more likely to take personal risks than women when a situation feels physically unsafe to help another.

Suppose we want to find out helping factors in loaning notes from a missed class in college settings. Design an experiment that will help you test a hypothesis about a factor that is most likely to elicit a helpful response from a college student. Describe your experimental design by following these steps:

First, brainstorm some variables that might influence the decision to loan class notes:
_____
_____

Select one variable and work with the following questions to develop an experimental design on altruistic behavior:

What is your hypothesis regarding "class note-loaning behavior?" _____
_____

Who should be the participants in the study? _____
_____

What would be the dependent variable and how would you measure it? _____
_____
_____

Describe your procedure, including any elements that you would attempt to control: _____
_____
_____

What independent variable would you be testing and why does that variable appeal to you?
_____

Do you think the experiment would confirm your hypothesis?_____
_____
_____

After completing this exercise, you should be able to
- speculate about variables that influence altruistic behavior.
- design a simple experiment that can explore a hypothesis about loaning class notes as a form of altruism.
- correctly distinguish between independent and dependent variables in social psychology experiments.
- reflect on your own sensitivity about being helpful to peers who make this request of you in the future.

Exercise 18.5

FOR THE SAKE OF THE CHILDREN   *Psychological Reasoning*

Many social critics are arguing about the best way to deal with violence in our children's schools. Many people, including psychologists, have offered suggestions to school systems to prevent future violence. Below we list several suggestions that have been proposed to help with the problem. Use psychological concepts from the social chapter of your book to explain each suggestion's potential for effectiveness. Then offer some criticisms (both positive and negative) about the likelihood that the suggestion would be effective.

1. Metal detectors at the school entrances:
    a. Related psychological concepts: _____
    b. Positive criticism: _____
    c. Negative criticism: _____
    d. Predicted success: _____

2. The requirement to wear school uniforms:
    a. Related psychological concepts: _____
    b. Positive criticism: _____
    c. Negative criticism: _____
    d. Predicted success: _____

3. Sensitivity training built into the curriculum:
   a. Related psychological concepts: _____
   b. Positive criticism: _____
   c. Negative criticism: _____
   d. Predicted success: _____
4. Holding parents accountable for the violent actions of their children:
   a. Related psychological concepts: _____
   b. Positive criticism: _____
   c. Negative criticism: _____
   d. Predicted success: _____

After completing this exercise, you should be able to

- discuss the relationship between basic principles of social psychology and the phenomenon of violence in the schools.
- evaluate the feasibility of a proposed solution to a social problem by weighing both its positive and negative features.
- predict likely success of a social intervention through reasoning.
- feel some empathy for the challenge that children may be facing today due to the threat of violence as a part of expected school experience.

Exercise 18.6

PEOPLE WERE STUPID BACK THEN — *Perspective Taking*

In the early 1960s, Stanley Milgram conducted a unique demonstration of the perils of obedience to authority. His ingenuity in design captured the attention of the scientific and lay communities alike. By thrusting unwitting volunteers into the position of "teacher" in a seemingly random selection process, Milgram was able to demonstrate that a majority of normal individuals would go to extraordinary lengths to harm another person when they were encouraged to do so by an authority figure.

Despite the power of the demonstration, the impact of the original work can be hard to grasp. Students often exempt themselves from the obedience patterns that Milgram described. Some even claim that "people were stupid back then."

The purpose of this exercise is to put yourself in the shoes of the "teacher." Read the following description and try to imagine the thoughts and emotions of the teacher (the real subject in the Milgram research) so that you can develop an appreciation for the impact of conforming to the social expectations and demands of authority figures. (See Answer Key.)

> *You are ushered into a room with another volunteer who is a middle-aged man. Another man is already in the room; he is wearing a white coat, and he introduces himself as "the doctor" in charge of the experiment. He seems kindly enough. He begins to explain the procedure to you and the other volunteer. He suggests that the procedure that will follow may involve some pain from electric shock.*

What do you think and feel? _____
_____
_____

The explanation continues. By a toss of a coin, you become the teacher. Your job will be to help the other volunteer to learn pairs of words. You will do this by punishing each of his mistakes, using an electric shock.

What do you think and feel? _____

_____

The researcher takes both of you to a small area away from the main room, and he begins to attach some electrodes to the other volunteer. The volunteer explains that he has a heart problem and wonders if that will be a problem in the procedure. The researcher says, "Not really."

What do you think and feel? _____

_____

The researcher demonstrates the shock by administering it to you at mild levels, telling you that this will give you an idea of the potential discomfort you will be administering. The level of shock you feel is fairly low, as demonstrated on the control box, but it is uncomfortable.

What do you think and feel? _____

_____

You return with the researcher to the main room where he explains your job as the teacher. You will punish incorrect word associations, which you will recognize by consulting a list you hold in your hand. You will be required to increase the voltage every time the learner makes an error.

What do you think and feel? _____

_____

You begin your role as the teacher. The learner's first few answers are accurate, but then he begins making mistakes. You hit the appropriate shock levers, and the learner protests mildly.

What do you think and feel? _____

_____

You turn to the authority figure with a questioning look. He calmly reassures you that it is important for you to continue for the sake of the experiment.

What do you think and feel? _____

_____

As you increase the shock levels, the learner's protests become louder. Eventually, the learner's protests stop altogether. When you turn to the researcher, he nods to affirm that this is the proper procedure and encourages you to continue. He states that he will assume full responsibility.

What do you think and feel? _____

_____

Just how far might you have taken the process? _____

_____

Psychological testing on the Milgram participants indicated that they were neither unusually mean-spirited nor abnormal in their relationships with others. Yet a large number (66 percent) increased the shock levels all the way to the end of the available range—despite clear warnings on the shock control mechanism that such an action could be dangerous. Can you generate some explanations of why this result—which no psychiatrists anticipated prior to the experiment—would occur? (See Answer Key.)

How did the setting contribute? _____
_____
_____

How did the behavior of the learner contribute? _____
_____
_____

How did the emotional state of the true subject (the "teacher") contribute? _____
_____
_____

How did the teacher's experience of being shocked contribute? _____
_____
_____

How did "luck" contribute? _____
_____
_____

How did the demeanor of the researcher contribute? _____
_____
_____

Were people more stupid back then? _____
_____
_____

Most of the teachers were so engrossed in the situation that they didn't think critically about the situation. If they had, they might have been less vulnerable to the pressures of authority. For example, why would the researcher even need the teacher? If the goal was to find out the impact of punishment on learning, the researcher could have administered the shock himself. The critical thinking that did occur, as you may have demonstrated in your explanation, may have been much more focused on worry and fear about the impact of the actions than on the right of the researcher to require another person to perform harmful actions on others.

After completing this exercise, you should be able to

- describe the process used in the Milgram "obedience to authority" study.
- infer the kinds of thoughts, feelings, and actions the teacher probably experienced in the Milgram demonstration.
- state how many features in the demonstration converged to form a powerful incentive to obey the authority figure.
- speculate about the impact that your knowledge of this demonstration may have on your own obedience to authority figures.

Answer Key

1

ANSWER KEY

Thinking Critically with Psychological Science

Exercise 1.1

THE CASE FOR INTERFERENCE — *Pattern Recognition*

The Problem of Child Abuse: *Correlational*

When social scientists study existing records of foster care children, they are not interfering in the normal process. They are making careful observations of the reports that describe the children's lives. In effect, they are combining many individual case studies and trying to define their common characteristics. Therefore, this approach is correlational. Although it will not produce strong cause-effect conclusions, a correlational study may provide some direction about the most important factors in the development of foster care children. Also, child abuse is an area in which it is extremely difficult to do experimental research. Scientists would be ethically opposed to constructing controlled conditions in an experiment that might place any child at risk for physical abuse or merely not exercise sufficient protection of children.

Charlie's Weight Loss: *Experimental*

Charlie's ambitious weight loss plan represents a good experimental approach to understanding weight management, if he carefully imposes the limitations he describes from the outset of his plan. In effect, his approach simulates something called a single-subject design. In this case, Charlie's eating behavior is "interfered with" in a systematic fashion. He carefully records his progress and then is able to make a reasonably sound conclusion about the relative effectiveness of one method over another. This advantage assumes that Charlie is successful in abiding by the conditions he has established.

The Curious Teacher: *Experimental*

Ms. Tucker's strategy for evaluating teaching methods represents a good classroom experiment. There are some interesting problems with her design that threaten the validity of her conclusion. For example, she may be an advocate of active learning and may inadvertently construct her final exam to be easier than the midterm. Experimenter effects of this kind threaten the validity of conclusions. However, she does propose a controlled comparison, which would qualify as an experimental approach.

The Lucky Pen: *Neither Experimental nor Correlational*

Peter's observation that his pen is lucky is a good example of superstitious behavior. Human beings are inclined to reach unfounded conclusions of this nature because our brains are geared to find patterns even where patterns do not exist. Although this description sounds like it might be correlational because it does not show interference by a scientist, it does not qualify as correlational because it does not take a systematic approach to the problem. The observations are haphazard and there is no attempt to quantify the relationships.

The Best Neighborhood: *Correlational*

Because the researcher is working with existing records, a careful comparison of SAT performance with geographic location represents a good correlational approach. The researchers are not interfering with the process but merely reporting existing relationships. However, as often happens when nonscientists try to make sense of the data, the researchers go too far by pronouncing the superiority of one school district over another. There are simply too many variables (e.g., parental income, access to computers) that might explain the superiority of one sector over another. This is the risk with correlational approaches: We cannot be confident in the cause-effect relationships that they suggest.

Copycat Crime: *Correlational*

It may be tempting to conclude that watching a violent film can induce violent behavior, but we do not have sufficient controlled evidence in this case to make that pronouncement. The reporter is not manipulating conditions in this situation (no interference), so the interpretation would be based on correlational methods. The relationship established would be that teens who see the violent example in the film would be more likely to commit a similar violent act than teens who had not seen the film. Obviously, we would be loathe to construct an experiment to narrow down the cause-effect relationship suggested by this finding.

Doctor's Choice: *Experimental*

This interesting physician appears to be embarking on an experimental approach to evaluate the effectiveness of a new expensive medication. He does many things right, including random assignment to conditions by using a coin toss. However, no matter how good his intentions are, the physician does violate ethical protocol for the protection of research participants. His patients have the right to know that they are being "experimented" upon and that there are other treatment options.

Exercise 1.2

YOU NEED AN OPERATION *Practical Problem-Solving*

The Sloppy Roommate: "I can't stand living this way!"

Jack could operationally define the problem as follows:

Jack is unhappy because Ed

- leaves his clothes in inappropriate places.
- does not do the dishes on an equitable basis.

1. "It seems to me that you are not picking up your things. You have a lot of clothes in the living room that could be moved to your bedroom."

2. "I have done the dishes for the last five days straight. You need to take your turn doing the dishes if we are going to be able to share the apartment."

The Surly Boss: "Why don't you like me?"

Joe could operationally define his problems with his boss as
- receiving no feedback.
- getting looks from his supervisor that he cannot interpret.
- observing his supervisor laugh and wondering if the laughter is about him.

1. "Although I think I've been doing a good job, I haven't received any formal feedback from you in the last six weeks. May we please set up a time where we could review my work?"
2. "I don't think you and I are making a good connection. I noticed this week on three occasions that you seemed to be staring at me, and it made me think that something was wrong."

Bonnie's Worry: "Emily seems slow."

Bonnie will be more helpful to Emily's parents if she can articulate her concerns about Emily more precisely:
- playing alone 80% of the time.
- taking toys from other children.
- talking to herself more than to other children.
- focusing on single objects and tasks longer than other children.

1. "Emily spends a greater proportion of her time talking to herself than she does talking to other children. Does that ever seem to be a problem at home?"
2. "Sometimes Emily spends long periods of time at a single task. This makes it difficult for her to participate in all of the activities the other children enjoy."

Exercise 1.3

THE LIMITS OF NURSERY RHYME REASONING *Creative Problem Solving*

The limits here are only those of your creativity. Were the concepts of hindsight bias and overconfidence apparent in your nursery rhymes? Were you playful with your treatment of these concepts?

Exercise 1.4

DESIGNING CAREFULLY CONTROLLED RESEARCH *Scientific Problem Solving*

The Colorful Boss

Focal behavior: Work production among clerical staff, operationally defined as projects completed.

Hypothesis: Environments painted blue cause workers to produce a greater volume of completed work than will environments painted yellow.

Independent variable: Color of paint used in the environment (blue versus yellow)

Measurement of dependent variable: Number of projects completed by clerical staff

Controlled variables:
- New paint applied to cubicle walls of two departments
- Productivity measured over the same time period

Uncontrolled variables:
- Absence of random assignment creates the possibility of alternative explanations for different volumes of work produced by the two groups.
- Knowledge of boss's hypothesis may have influenced worker performance so that workers in the preferred-color environment outperformed those in the nonpreferred environment.
- Number of tasks may differ from department to department. Without better control procedures, the boss is comparing blueberries and bananas.

Valid results?: No. Perhaps this boss should find something more important to do than experimenting with the effect of color on work production.

The Bad Driver

Focal behavior: Frustration-induced aggression in drivers, operationally defined as speed in horn honking.

Hypothesis: People will show their frustration more quickly with low-status drivers than with high-status drivers and will do so by blowing their horn after a shorter delay if the driver blocking their path is a low-status driver.

Independent variable: Presumed status of driver (high versus low)

Dependent variable: Duration in seconds from onset of green light until driver honks the horn operationalizes the level of aggression demonstrated by the participant drivers.

Controlled variables:
- The driver
- The neighborhood
- The afternoon
- The length of time in car

Uncontrolled variables:
- Time of day (the 3 to 5 time slot may include rush hour traffic)
- Subject drivers (not randomly selected)
- Condition of experimenter's cars (undented versus very used).

Improvement:
1. Use two drivers following a similar course during the same time on the same day.
2. Have the same driver follow the same course during the same time on two days similar with regard to weather and time of year.
3. Use brand new cars that differ only in the socioeconomic status represented by the car, not the condition of the car.

Did you spot any other improvements?

Going for the Gold

Focal behavior: Preparation of Olympic athletes

Hypothesis: In developing award-winning athletes, self-esteem training during sleep is superior to diet and steroid use and to no preparation.

Independent variable: Type of training (self-esteem sleep training, versus diet and steroid preparation, versus control).

Dependent variable: Number of gold medals three groups of athletes win in the Olympics

Controlled variables:
- Amount of time at camp
- The setting
- Random assignment to conditions, which minimizes the systematic influence of other variables.

Uncontrolled variables: Condition 2 is poorly defined. Manipulating both diet and steroids reduces the comparative statements the researcher can draw. In addition, the use of steroids creates serious ethical problems.

Would you fund this experiment? No. The ethical and economic concerns present significant obstacles to adopting Rita's proposal. Design flaws limit the usefulness of the results. The study could be improved as follows:

1. Eliminate steroids from the experimental design.
2. Reconsider other dependent variables to measure training effectiveness.
3. Control for the order in which the experimental groups are treated.
4. Ensure that the group assigned to the self-esteem tape condition actually does play the tape while sleeping.
5. Ensure that the group assigned to the self-esteem tape condition gets the same amount of sleep the other groups get.

Can you think of other ways to improve the design?

Exercise 1.5

CONSUMER SAFETY *Psychological Reasoning*

The Tanned Rock Queen

Principle 2: Don't settle for cause-effect statements without sufficient evidence.
Personal testimony is not effective evidence even when it is given by someone famous. How do you know the rock star isn't fresh from a cruise to the Caribbean?

The Moralizer

Principle 1: Don't expect simple cause-effect relationships.
Violence is a complicated behavior that has multiple causes.

Principle 4: Don't mistake correlation for causation.
Two alternative explanations are (1) that heavy metal music reflects a violent culture rather than causing violence within the culture, and (2) that both heavy metal music and violence are caused by other variables.

The Laundry

Principle 5: Do look for experimental comparisons that involve control conditions.
Although television Moms do demonstrate questionable reality testing, this test included good controls in design; if all conditions were equal, the experiment should provide valid evidence that the new detergent is more effective.

The New Car

Principle 6: Do examine how behaviors are defined or operationalized.
Just what does "pizazz" mean? How does the company operationally define the goal? Will you have more dates? More intense contacts with loan officers? More challenges to drag race? More speeding tickets?

Halloween Wisdom

> *Principle 2: Don't settle for cause-effect statements without sufficient evidence.*
> What is the psychologist's evidence? Did a well-designed study lead to these conclusions? Even though a person's credentials seem impressive, we should not suspend appropriate criteria in evaluating a cause-effect claim.

One Bad Apple

> *Principle 2: Don't settle for cause-effect statements without sufficient evidence.*
> Subjective experience with one representative of a group is likely to be insufficient in making judgments about all the representatives of a group. Beware of making generalized conclusions about groups based on experience with one representative. This is sometimes referred to as the "*n* of 1" error, where *n* represents sample size.

The Blind Date

> *Principle 3: Don't confuse interpretations of behavior with behavior itself.*
> Recycling discarded cans on a date could represent a serious commitment to the environment, but it could also mean that your date is just broke (or cheap). Remember to distinguish actual behavior from the inferences or conclusions you draw about the behavior.

Burglars

> *Principle 4: Don't mistake correlation for causation.*
> Even though a "full moon effect" may be an appealing explanation for unlawful or extraordinary behavior, there is a simpler and more plausible explanation than unexplained lunar forces. A full moon may provide more light, enabling burglars to see better and to break in more easily.

Exercise 1.6

PSYCHOLOGY'S PERSPECTIVES — *Perspective Taking*

Drug Abuse

> *Neuroscience:* Psychologists in this area are interested in the physiological processes underlying emotions, memories, and sensory experiences. Questions from this framework would include:
> - How do particular drugs affect the way that the brain sends and receives messages?
> - How does long-term cocaine use damage the brain?
> - How does LSD cause hallucinations?
>
> *Evolutionary:* When using this framework, psychologists focus on how traits have enabled organisms to survive and pass along their genes to future generations. When studying drug abuse, this perspective might lead one to ask:
> - How might addictive behavior patterns have enabled our distant ancestors to survive?
> - Does the tendency to seek stimulation through drug use confer any survival advantage?
> - What influence does widespread drug abuse have on the quality of the gene pool?
>
> *Behavior Genetics:* This perspective asks to what degree do our genes and our environment contribute to our individual differences. Psychologists in this area might ask questions such as:

- To what extent is the propensity toward addiction inherited?
- What are the environmental and genetic risk factors for drug abuse?
- Does gene therapy show promise for treating drug addiction?

Behavioral: Psychologists in this area are interested in how we learn our observable behaviors. In the area of drug abuse, the following questions could be posed:

- What reinforcing contingencies encourage teenagers to use heroin?
- How important are role models in developing addictive behavior?
- How can we design effective drug treatment programs to help people overcome addiction?

Cognitive: Because they are interested in how individuals process, store, and retrieve information, cognitive psychologists might ask the following:

- How do individuals assess the risk of drug use?
- What kind of problem-solving strategies do drug addicts use to obtain their drugs or hide their addictions from friends?
- What is the best way to educate people about the dangers of drug abuse?

Social-Cultural: Psychologists interested in how behaviors and thinking differ across cultures and situations might ask:

- Why is the rate of alcoholism higher in the United States than in Sweden?
- Why do groups from different cultures and ethnic backgrounds have differing rates of abuse for various drugs?
- How do different peer groups affect a teen's choice to use drugs?

Love

Neuroscience: Questions with a physiological focus could include:

- What neurotransmitters are involved in our experience of love?
- What roles do different brain areas play in falling in love?
- Are there drugs that could serve as a "love potion?"

Evolutionary: When exploring how organisms pass along their genes, evolutionary psychologists might ask:

- How does falling in love help perpetuate the species?
- Are people who experience love strongly more likely to successfully reproduce?
- What physical characteristics seem most important in mate selection?

Behavior Genetics: Psychologists working from this perspective explore behaviors that could be influenced by genes. Their questions could include the following:

- Can the tendency to easily fall in love be inherited?
- What genetic and environmental factors promote falling in love?
- Is there a genetic basis for how quickly an individual can rebound from a broken heart?

Behavioral: A behavioral psychologist, interested in how consequences shape behavior, could ask any of the following questions:

- How do we learn socially appropriate ways to express love?
- How are the actions of love different from the actions of kindness or friendship?
- How do behaviors differ with different love objects (family, friends, significant others)?

Cognitive: Some of the questions of interest to researchers who study thinking and problem-solving include:

- How is thinking different when a person is in love?
- How might loving someone change the way we interpret that person's actions?
- Does being in love influence the capacity to empathize with others?

Social-Cultural: When investigating situational and cultural differences in love, psychologists might ask questions such as these:
- How are dating/courtship rituals different in different cultures?
- Do differences in family structure explain how young adults develop intimate relationships?
- What is the relationship between sex and love in different cultures?

Intelligence

Neuroscience: A neuroscientist would be interested in exploring questions such as the following:
- Do differences in brain structures account for differences in intellectual abilities?
- How do neurotransmitters assist in the accurate storage and rapid retrieval of information?
- What role does the frontal cortex play in making connections among novel concepts?

Evolutionary: Some examples of questions of interest to individuals working from this perspective include:
- What types of intelligence make survival more likely?
- How does intelligence affect survival rates?
- Under what circumstances might low intelligence be considered adaptive?

Behavior Genetics: The contribution of genes and the environment to intelligence would be of interest to psychologists in this area as illustrated by the following questions:
- Is intelligence inherited?
- How successful is providing a stimulating environment in raising IQ scores?
- What are the relative contributions of genetics and environment to various measures of IQ?

Behavioral: The behaviorist's questions would focus on observable behaviors and their consequences. Questions might include:
- How can we measure intelligence?
- How might an educational system be designed to encourage effective learning strategies?
- What rewards are most effective in promoting learning?

Cognitive: Cognitive psychologists would seek to answer questions such as:
- What is the relationship between intelligence and memory?
- Is there any difference in the way that highly intelligent individuals store and retrieve information?
- What are the cognitive processes involved in different types of intelligence?

Social-Cultural: Social-cultural psychologists would be interested in how different cultures define and measure intelligence. Their questions might include:
- Are there meaningful differences between the overall intelligence of men and women?
- How do some individuals from impoverished backgrounds overcome these conditions to have successful, productive lives?
- What factors account for stable performance differences across ethnic groups on IQ tests?

2

ANSWER KEY

Neuroscience and Behavior

Exercise 2.1

HOW DID YOU DO THAT? — *Pattern Recognition*

Here are some examples of how brain components could contribute to the leisure activity of playing bridge.

Brain Site	Function?	Involvement?
Hypothalamus	Maintaining autonomic nervous system	Yes. Regulates body temperature and appetite (popcorn and soda intake)
Occipital lobe	Processing visual information	Yes. Registers cards dealt and body language of opposing players
Reticular formation	Controls arousal and attention	Yes. Maintains vigilance even during boring plays
Cerebellum	Coordinates voluntary movement and balance	Yes. Holds you upright in the chair and supports appropriate card selection
Parietal lobe	Processes sensory input through sensory cortex	Yes. Prompts subtle shifts in movement when body parts "go to sleep"
Corpus callosum	Connects two hemispheres	Yes. Keeps unified eyes on players on both sides of the table
Medulla	Controls heartbeat and breathing	Yes. Increases heart rate during exciting play and promotes breathing even through challenging play
Temporal lobe	Processes auditory information	Yes. Monitors the bidding voices of other players

Brain Site	Function?	Involvement?
Frontal lobe	Manages speaking and muscle movement. Makes plans and judgments	Yes. Determines proper bidding, announces bid, and judges when to be pleased or irritated with partner's performance
Thalamus	Directs messages to the sensory areas in cortex and transmits replies to motor areas	Yes. Coordinates images of cards played with motor movements involved in own selection
Amygdala	Involved in governing emotion	Yes. Many bridge players work hard to manage their emotions for more controlled play
Hippocampus	Processes explicit memories for storage	Yes. Monitors thoughts of "what beats what"

Exercise 2.2

THE SPLIT-BRAIN PROBLEM *Practical Problem Solving*

Studying concepts from psychology is primarily a left-hemisphere activity *(L)* because most concepts presented in your book are presented verbally. However, textbook illustrations and graphics also involve the right hemisphere *(R)*, though to a lesser extent.

Drawing a map of your campus engages both hemispheres *(L and R)*. The left hemisphere interprets the labels and the right hemisphere interprets the images.

Daydreaming about a holiday trip is primarily a right-hemisphere *(R)* function. Our fantasies generally take the form of images, which are processed on the right side of the brain.

Listening to a piano concerto is essentially a right-hemisphere activity *(R)*. The absence of lyrics leaves the left hemisphere less involved.

Listening to rap music engages both hemispheres *(L and R)*; the right hemisphere attends to the powerful tempo and musical elements of the music while the left interprets the lyrics.

Thinking about your next "night out" draws on the right hemisphere *(R)* because the activity involves fantasy, which is processed primarily on the right.

Reading junk mail usually engages the left *(L)* hemisphere, unless the junk mail contains fancy attention-getting graphics to capture your attention.

$6 \times 4 - 2 + 5 =$ This sequence, like other mathematical expressions, is processed and evaluated by the left hemisphere *(L)*.

Redecorating your room engages the right hemisphere *(R)*, this is a highly spatial activity.

Doodling engages the right hemisphere *(R)* in processing spatial stimuli; however, a right-hander's motor control in executing fine motor movements of the right hand will be governed by the left hemisphere *(L)*.

Completing this form probably starts out as a left hemisphere *(L)* event, activated by processing the words on the page. However, you may have to picture in your mind the image created in the words, this shifts some thinking to the right hemisphere *(R)*. Writing down your answer again involves both hemispheres, through language processing and fine motor movement.

Exercise 2.3

| **THE NEW SUPERHEROES** | *Creative Problem Solving* |

Here are some possible examples of creative new superheroes:

Thermostatman: This superhero is capable of voluntarily shifting his temperature to adapt to his surroundings. The augmented brain structure is the hypothalamus. Thermostatman would be especially helpful in tolerating extreme temperatures, rescuing volcano or arctic research teams whose missions have gone awry.

Scribewoman: This superhero is able to retain every detail spoken to her. The augmented brain structure is the hippocampus. She is the perfect team member to have on complicated projects, particularly a spy mission when obvious note-taking might endanger the group.

Vigilboy: This superhero could stay awake for extended periods of time. The augmented brain structure is the reticular formation. Vigilboy would excel at surveillance sessions.

These three examples demonstrate how you can use your imagination to come up with new arrangements. Once your superhero emerges from your creative process, you apply appropriate criteria to determine whether your creation is satisfying. How original and playful are the examples provided in this text? How original and playful are your examples?

Exercise 2.4

| **THE ADDICTED BRAIN** | *Scientific Problem Solving* |

There are many brain areas that could be responsible for contributing to the addict's behavior and experiences. Some of these include:
- The medulla—responsible for heartbeat and breathing
- The reticular formation—responsible for arousal
- The amygdala—responsible for aggression and fear
- The frontal lobe of the cerebral cortex—responsible for forming judgements and making plans (especially the prefrontal area or association areas)

Your hypothesis statement will depend on the brain area and behavior you chose. It should have a specific prediction and be written so that the independent and dependent variables are clear. In the same way, your experimental design should describe your variables operationally and briefly outline how you might conduct your test.

Animal studies are an important part of psychology. Although many psychologists study animals simply out of an interest in animal behavior, many more use them to explore questions in which it is difficult or impossible to study humans directly. This is a good example of such a question. Although a rat's brain and bodily processes are not identical to those of a human, they are similar enough in structure and function that scientists are able to use rats to learn about basic metabolic, physiologic, and behavioral responses to drugs. Nevertheless, such studies give only a limited understanding of the role that higher cognitive functions play in mediating basic responses. For example, although studies with rats can tell us that a drug has an excitatory effect on a particular brain structure, they cannot tell us how a human being's perception of, and cognition about, the experience could minimize or magnify that effect. In this exercise, it probably would be unethical to conduct an experiment on human beings. Psychology's code of ethics would prohibit a psychologist from administering a drug that would cause permanent harm or from damaging brain areas as part of an experimental control. What we must also remember is that many of these guidelines apply to animal research. In all cases in which animals are used, it is important that the experimenter not use them recklessly and that care be taken to provide them with humane conditions and procedures that are as pain-free as possible. Experimenters must always balance the knowledge that they can gain with the potential harm to the animal.

Exercise 2.5

PHANTOM PAIN — *Psychological Reasoning*

This young man's pain is probably phantom pain and is the result of the neural reorganization underway in his somatosensory cortex. As the neurons in the motor cortex that would have received the signals from the arm die from lack of stimulation, other motor neurons take advantage of this new space to extend their neural branches. However, because there are still neural connections between the motor cortex and sensory cortex, the area of the sensory cortex responsible for the missing arm receives information from these new connections. Other areas of the brain interpret these signals as pain.

The most likely sources of the new neural signals are the areas adjacent to those that were connected to his arm: the neck, forehead, or eyebrow.

Exercise 2.6

CARING FOR PHINEAS — *Perspective Taking*

Describe how Phineas and his family and friends might have perceived these changes.

Whatever your answer, you should recognize that the sudden change would have been difficult for everyone. His family would have been faced with the shock of his injury, his likely frightening physical appearance (at least initially), and his bizarre behavior. They would have had to get to know the "new" Phineas; a task made more difficult by the fact that this new person was not all that likeable. They may have even disliked him and then felt guilty because the change was not his fault. If they thought Phineas *did* have some control over his behavior, and that he was simply acting inappropriately, then they might have been angry and ostracized him.

Phineas may or may not have been aware of the changes in his personality and behavior. Given that there was nothing wrong with his memory, however, he probably was aware of them. Because he had been a well-liked and respected young man, the change in how people felt about him probably was disturbing. He might well have felt frightened and angry over his lack of control. He might even have been angry at himself, wondering *why* he couldn't control his behavior. It would have been very easy for him to want to be by himself, especially when others were probably not anxious to be with him.

If you were a social worker assigned to this family now, what types of services might you offer them?

The services could include counseling for both Phineas and the family to help them develop new strategies for relating to each other and dealing with feelings of anger and guilt. You might refer him to a physician who might be able to offer medical options to help him manage his behavior through the use of drugs or surgery. Phineas would probably function best in a structured environment, so you could help the family explore educational and supervised living arrangements that would allow him to be as independent as possible. Phineas would always need care, so assisting the family in arranging for Medicare and SSI and coordinating resources with Workman's Compensation would be an important part of your job.

What would be your expectations for the rest of Phineas' life? Why?

Your opinion of Phineas's future should recognize that Phineas would always need some form of care and assistance. Because the areas of his brain that are responsible for judgement and planning were permanently damaged, he would need supervision to function safely at work and home. Because his behavior would now be impulsive and often socially inappropriate, he would need continual guidance and reinforcement in order to maintain and develop healthy relationships. His life would be very different from the one he formerly led, but it might be possible for him to eventually establish a new life with dignity and some degree of independence.

Speculate about what other kinds of changes might have occurred in Phineas' recovery if the tamping rod had pierced the brain at a different location.

If the rod had gone through the back of his skull and damaged the occipital lobe, Phineas would have probably lost his vision, and his recovery would have been focused on learning how to function without this sense. If the rod had injured the hindbrain, particularly in the area of the medulla, he would not have survived because the areas responsible for controlling vital functions such as breathing and heart rate would have been damaged. Injury to the side of his head, in the area of the temporal lobe (Broca's area), could have interfered with Phineas's hearing or speech. Injury to the top of his head in the area of the motor cortex or somatosensory cortex would have interfered with motor function or sensation. Memory impairment would have been the result if the hippocampus and other structures in the limbic system had been damaged. Damage to the limbic system could also result in excessive aggression, fear, or significant changes in sexual behavior.

What other areas and impairments did you identify?

ANSWER KEY

The Nature and Nurture of Behavior

Exercise 3.1

NATURE OR NURTURE? *Pattern Recognition*

The key to successfully completing this exercise is recognizing the assumptions about how we become who we are that underlie each statement. For example, the assumption upon which "Handsome is as handsome does" is based is that behavior, not a particular configuration of features, is attractive. In other words, genetics is not what determines beauty, learned patterns are. This, then, is a nurture argument. Can you identify the assumptions for each of the following?

"Sugar and spice and everything nice, that's what little girls are made of . . ."	NATURE
"Handsome is as handsome does."	NURTURE
"Like father, like son."	NATURE
"You can't teach an old dog new tricks."	NURTURE
"Early to bed and early to rise, makes a man healthy, wealthy and wise."	NURTURE
"Boys will be boys."	NATURE
"You are what you eat."	NURTURE
"Blood will tell."	NATURE
"All men are created equal."	NURTURE

What examples did you come up with?

Exercise 3.2

KEEP ON TRUCKIN' *Practical Problem Solving*

Social learning theory: This theory states that children learn gender-linked behaviors based on the consequences of their imitation of the behaviors they have observed in adults. A young girl giving a doll a pretend bottle may be told, "You are such a good mommy," whereas a boy doing the same thing might be told, "Why don't you go play with your trucks?" Similarly, a boy crying might be told that "boys don't cry," whereas a girl might be comforted or consoled. Such patterns lead children to adopt the behaviors that are "appropriate" in the eyes of the authority figures in their lives.

Example: Boys are given trucks and cars as gifts and are encouraged to learn how engines work. Men who are good with cars or trucks are seen as desirable and "manly." Girls are often discouraged from getting dirty or being loud, activities that are a natural part of playing with cars and trucks or learning about engines. All of these things combine to make it less likely that a girl or woman would adopt the activities and skills around cars and trucks that boys and men might.

Gender schema theory: Gender schema theory suggests that individuals develop a gender "lens" through which they view the world. There are concepts of maleness and femaleness in every culture, and children learn the appropriate gender-typed way to act by comparing their own behavior with these concepts. Individuals also compare the behaviors of others with these concepts and can judge the "appropriateness" of these others' behaviors with the standard set by the culture. Cultural ideals are presented through the media, use of language, and the actions of adults.

Example: Truckers are portrayed as big, tough, and often a little grubby. In our culture, this is more compatible with the image of masculinity. The image of femininity is a little softer, more sensitive, cleaner, and neater. Women truckers might then be seen as not very feminine, or thought to have something wrong with them. They might also be seen as less competent at their work, even if that is not the case.

What plan would you suggest to the owners? How does it use either social learning theory or gender schema theory? An example that promotes social learning theory might involve getting authority figures for male truckers to endorse the benefits of having women in the occupation. Similarly, male truckers might get some incentives for agreeing to train or mentor new female truckers. Social learning theory requires that reinforcers for desirable behavior must change. Gender schema themes requires changing the lens through which one filters experience. You might place posters that show men and women who otherwise fit the cultural gender schema performing tasks that are not gender typical. Perhaps they could show a big, burly man holding a baby or taking care of an elderly woman; other posters might depict an attractive woman firefighter or trucker. These images could help expand the employees' perception of gender-appropriate roles, both for themselves and the people they work with. Did you come up with a different strategy?

Exercise 3.3

CHARACTER BUILDING *Creative Problem Solving*

This person needs to be sensitive enough to deal with witnesses and victims; tough enough to stay alive in the face of bombs, hired killers, and guard dogs; intelligent enough to break secret codes and outwit the criminal mastermind; and witty enough to be interesting and to find the humor in devastating situations.

Sample biography: Private eye Jo Hardison was a skilled detective whose distinguished police record *(nurture)* made her a natural at solving mysteries in the private sector. The eighth of nine children, she had developed some wiley strategies to help her get her way in her crowded family *(nurture)*. Somehow Hardison still managed to get into trouble on a regular basis. Her father's harsh punishment tactics helped her develop the resilience and persistence *(nurture)* she used to cope with her most challenging cases. Her father's love of physics *(nature)* and her mother's quick Irish wit *(nature/nurture)* seemed to find a perfect outlet in Hardison's deft handling of evidence and clients. All of her siblings were successful in high-pressure, professional occupations *(nature/nurture)*, so Hardison always felt some extra pressure to do the job right *(nurture)*.

Exercise 3.4

SEEING DOUBLE — *Scientific Problem Solving*

There are quite a few possible hypotheses that you could have created. Whatever your hypothesis is, it should be stated as a question for which you could find an answer. Both the dependent and independent variables should be obvious from the question. Examples of possible hypotheses include:

- Is an individual's level of extraversion greater when raised in a family with more than four children?
- Is an individual less likely to be extraverted when raised in an urban community?
- Is an individual's level of extraversion higher when parents are also extraverted?
- Is an individual more extraverted when exposed to diverse educational settings in the primary school years?

The design that you outlined should take into account the fact that identical twins have the same genetic information and that environments include factors like socio-economic status, family structure, educational opportunities, as well as the more obvious ones like geographic location and race.

Numerous ethical issues make such experiments impossible. It is not ethical to take children away from biological parents able to provide for their needs and assign them to new parents. It is not ethical to separate children who share strong biological and emotional ties that would prove supportive to their development. It is not ethical to place children into potentially less than ideal circumstances simply for the purpose of seeing what happens. It is not ethical to give couples or individuals children who are not their own and for which they may not be prepared and force them to raise these children. The list goes on and on. So, given these necessary ethical restrictions, what alternative experiments are there?

One alternative is to use animal studies. It is possible to take animals like voles, rats, mice, or fish that have multiple offspring at the same time and to give those offspring to different foster parents to raise. Those foster parents can live in different environments and have different resources at their disposal. Although there are limits on the conclusions that one can draw from such experiments, their results can be combined with other correlational and naturalistic observations of human experience to provide a more complete picture of the issue. Did you propose other alternatives?

Exercise 3.5

WHO'S TO BLAME? — *Psychological Reasoning*

When this shocking episode occurred, the public was quick to find culprits who contributed to the actions of the six-year-old killer. Many critics suggested that lax controls in the school were somehow to blame *(nurture argument)*. Many more individuals pointed to the more compelling explanation of the absence of a significant careprovider *(nurture argument)*. At age six, this child had already learned to fend for himself and to make judgments without adult supervision. Even if he had received attention, he was raised in the home of a drug dealer so he might have had questionable moral instruction *(nurture argument)*. Given that his mother's life had gone badly awry, there is also the possibility that the child could have some genetic predisposition for poor judgment *(nature argument)*.

Exercise 3.6

IT'S ALL IN THE GENES   *Perspective Taking*

Assuming that the premise of the program would still be to facilitate the success of low-income children in school, children would probably be given an IQ test to determine who had the innate (genetic) ability to succeed academically. Administrators of the program might also examine the school records of the parents of the children; in this framework, children with academically successful parents would be more likely to be successful themselves. Little or no consideration would be given to the way that the children's environment, health, or general well-being might affect their performance. The children's success would be seen as a product of their innate ability and not much affected by outside influences. It also would be unlikely that the program would solicit the involvement of the community or the parents.

If this philosophy were continued in the public school system, funds would not be available for those special services designed to facilitate the performance of children who do not easily succeed in traditional academic settings. For example, there might not be any special education programs or programs for students with learning disabilities. Taken to its extreme, there would not be any meal programs; after all, environment doesn't affect academic performance.

You may hold any one of a number of different views about the role genetics plays in intelligence. Maybe you think that intelligence is primarily inherited. If so, many of the ideas in the preceding two paragraphs will make sense to you. You might think that intelligence is strictly a product of the environment and that, if the environment were equal for everyone, everyone would perform equally well. Most likely, your views fall somewhere in between. Regardless, you will have the opportunity to explore this issue more when you work with Chapter 11, later in the term.

The Developing Person

ANSWER KEY

Exercise 4.1

WHEN BAD CHILDREN AREN'T BAD — *Pattern Recognition*

Holiday Toys: Children under the age of two are most interested in exploring their world through their actions. Manipulating everyday objects is a great delight. What makes this example even more exciting is that this girl has recently discovered that objects exist even if she can't see them (object permanence). This makes the game of peeka-boo a potential marathon event.

The Scary Boyfriend: This young infant also has realized that things exist outside of his presence. In this case, he knows that this person is new and would much prefer to be with his aunt or other familiar caretaker. Piaget called this stage "stranger anxiety." This fear may be exaggerated by the presence of unfamiliar features, such as a mustache, but children in this stage can shriek at any person who is perceived as "not Mom" or some other familiar caregiver.

The Flying Bottle: This child has learned a simple cause-and-effect relationship and is delighting in experimenting with it. Not only does the bottle hit the floor every time he throws it, but Mom picks it up so he can do it again. This is lots of fun! This ability is a result of the infant developing object permanence. He can recognize that the bottle in his hand and the bottle on the floor are one and the same, but it can take a long time for him to get it.

The Card Game: The younger sister has not yet developed the concept of conservation: the ability to recognize that the same number of cards exist regardless of arrangement. As far as the girl is concerned, if her cards take up more space, then there are more of them and she wins.

Juice, Please: This is also an example of a child who does not understand the concept of conservation. Even though the same amount of juice went into the bigger glass, she was happy because the glass looked bigger.

Twins' Toys: This is a classic example of egocentrism. Young children cannot perceive things from another person's point of view, so everything is as they see it. They are not able to understand how another person feels, only how *they* feel. Although giving the lecture may make the father feel better, it is unlikely that the children have sufficient cognitive sophistication to profit from his wisdom.

Exercise 4.2

| **THE SITTER'S DILEMMA** | *Practical Problem Solving* |

The 9 month old will be interested in games that focus on looking, touching, and putting things into his mouth. This might include watching a mobile, playing with stackable blocks, or eating Zwieback Toast. Because of a newly acquired awareness of object permanence, peekaboo is also favorite game.

The 2 year old will probably enjoy activities that allow her to explore her growing ability to use words and "make-believe." Many children of this age like puzzles; they have the motor skills necessary to put large pieces together and can anticipate what the picture will be. Games of pretend—house, store, princesses—will be a big hit. Telling stories and making up words with funny sounds should also keep her out of trouble.

The 5 year old will enjoy many of the same activities as the 2 year old. In addition to this, he will enjoy telling simple jokes and playing those games that don't require a long attention span; Candy Land, Chutes and Ladders, and Hi Ho! Cherry-O are all examples of board games that appeal to children of this age.

At 9 years, the oldest child will have more abstract reasoning skills and will enjoy games with complex rules. Monopoly will probably be a favorite, and her sense of humor will be quite sophisticated. Word and number puzzles might be appealing, as will some basic science experiments.

Activities that can be approached at many different levels are your best bet. Reading stories is a possibility; have the 9 year old read to the younger children. Have the children make up their own stories. Each child can contribute an idea as you verbally tell the story, or the older children can make up stories to tell to the younger ones. You could even turn this into a play, with the older children acting and the infant and you serving as audience. If all of this fails, hit the kitchen. While the infant bangs pots and pans, and the 2 and 5 year olds pretend to make a cake, you and the 9 year old can find a simple cookie recipe over which you can supervise while she follows the recipe. Everyone will have fun, and you will end up with a bedtime snack!

As the younger children go to bed, the activities can become more complex and abstract. Instead of Candy Land, for instance, you could play Yahtzee or Monopoly. Instead of *Goodnight Moon* you might read *Charlotte's Web*.

Exercise 4.3

| **DEVELOPMENTAL DELIGHTS** | *Creative Problem Solving* |

These are only examples. Your toys and activities may be very different, depending on what potential relationships you saw among the different objects.

Objects: drinking straws, cardboard, large plastic cups, string

Children: 6 months: Make a caterpillar by alternately stringing straws and cups for the body and using the cardboard to make feet.

4 years: Fill the cups with water and blow bubbles through the straws; make it even more fun by blowing patterns of water onto the cardboard to make pictures.

7 years: Make a telephone, using the cups and string, and a telephone booth out of the cardboard.

Objects: 4-quart pot, spoon, measuring cups, sink full of water

Children: 9 months: Turn the pot and cups over in the sink, and let the child beat on them with the spoon to make "music."

3 years: Play restaurant and wash the pot, cups, and spoon in the water; then make pretend soup.

10 years: Make spaghetti sauce from scratch and then clean up the mess (okay, the cleanup part is less fun).

Objects: 2 chairs, pillows, several books, large blanket

Children: 12 months: Put the chairs close together, with the pillows underneath. Practice climbing on the chairs. You could also play peekaboo with the books and the blanket.

2 years: Play preschool. Sit on the chair and read the books; then pretend it's nap time and sleep on the pillows with the blanket.

9 years: Make a fort out of the chairs and the blanket. Curl up inside with the pillows and read.

Exercise 4.4

ON DEATH AND DYING — *Scientific Problem Solving*

Note: These answers are samples only. They may overlap with the hypotheses you generate, or you may be able to derive other approaches not listed here.

Characteristics of the illness

Variable 1: Type of illness

Hypothesis It is easier to sustain denial of impending death if symptoms develop gradually. Illness with sudden, dramatic symptoms may be easier to adjust to and accept than gradual-onset illness.

Variable 2: Amount of pain

Hypothesis: More painful terminal conditions produce reports of more intense anger than those found in less painful conditions. Conditions that involve greater pain may be more difficult to bear for the dying person and for the individuals in the support system.

Characteristics of the person

Variable 1: Personality structure

Hypothesis: People with stronger control issues in their lives might have a more difficult time moving beyond denial. Optimistic people may be more inclined to bargain, or they may more readily accept their own death, believing that it is a blessing.

Variable 2: Gender

Hypothesis: Men may demonstrate more visible anger responses to terminal illness; women may demonstrate more depressive responses.

Variable 3: Age

Hypothesis: Children may spend less than bargaining than adults spend.

Variable 4: Religious belief

Hypothesis: Some religions do not regard death as an enemy. Where death is regarded as a more natural part of life, perhaps we wouldn't observe the grief reactions described by Kübler-Ross at all.

Variable 5: Experience with death.

Hypothesis: Being present at the death of a loved one might influence a person to be more accepting of his or her own death.

Characteristics of the environment

Variable 1: Social support

Hypothesis: Those with a strong social support system are likely to demonstrate acceptance more quickly.

Variable 2: Culture

Hypothesis: Cultures differ in their responses to death. In cultures where death is seen as natural, people may show less anger about a terminal illness and the predicted death.

Exercise 4.5

UNDERSTANDING TEEN PREGNANCY — *Psychological Reasoning*

1. However you approach this problem, you should take into consideration the biological, social, and cognitive issues of adolescence. Physically, people of this age become sexually mature. Girls develop breasts and have their first menstrual cycle, and boys experience their first nocturnal emission; both grow additional body hair. This process happens rapidly, generally over about two years. If it happens earlier or later than for others in the peer group, young people may feel uncomfortable about the changes. Reasoning powers continue to develop and it is at this point that teenagers begin to be able to reason abstractly and to question the reason of others. As they develop their own sense of right and wrong, adolescents begin to try to separate themselves from their parents. Trying out different roles, changing one's appearance, and forming strong peer relationships are part of the job of the adolescent.

    Many of these changes could explain higher-than-expected teen pregnancy rates. Because their bodies are changing so rapidly, teenagers may not understand how their new bodies work and how they can avoid pregnancy. Also, because their bodies look adult, adolescents often experiment with adult behavior as they try out different roles in an attempt to find a personal identity. Although their reasoning powers are improving, they may still not be able to interpret accurately abstract statistics or relate those statistics in a concrete way to their own actions. Finally, all of the above, when combined with the teenager's desire to separate from parents, means that teenagers are notoriously poor at seeking out answers to questions about sex and pregnancy prevention from reliable sources.

    Adolescence is an unique developmental stage. The adolescent is not a big kid or a small adult. Any program that takes this into consideration and finds ways to create developmentally appropriate educational opportunities will have a higher rate of success than those that deal with adolescents as either big children or small adults.

2. You can make a case for many useful statistics. Make sure that you clearly state the rationale for your choice. For example, if you believe that using contraceptives is necessary to reduce the teen pregnancy rate, then looking at the numbers of teens having unprotected sex may be your statistic of choice.

Exercise 4.6

PIAGET MEETS SANTA CLAUS   *Perspective Taking*

What are the general characteristics of the sensorimotor stage child?

In the sensorimotor stage, children have not acquired many meaningful concepts. Their primary activities involve experiencing and exploring the physical world and discovering the abilities and limits of their growing bodies. Sensorimotor stage children would not have learned the concept that Santa Claus represents.

On encountering Santa, what would the sensorimotor stage child

- *observe?*

On first encounter, Santa's image is likely to be discrepant with anything that is familiar. His image is a mass of bright red and white. He makes deep booming sounds. Santa's lap is soft and his beard tickles. If the child is receptive to the experience, the nature of the interaction will stimulate the child's senses, the basis of the sensorimotor period.

- *think and feel?*

Sensorimotor stage children think and respond to Santa Clause in different ways. Many identify this new acquaintance as distinctly strange (think about it—a huge, oddly dressed, hairy guy who belly-laughs all the time) so that the first visit with Santa often ends in fright and tears. Other sensorimotor stage children may be drawn to the novel person. Their curiosity fuels interest and excitement as they experience their first ritual visit.

- *believe?*

Children in the sensorimotor stage have no relevant organizing schema to interpret Santa, so belief in his existence is not an issue.

What are the general characteristics of the preoperational stage child?

In the preoperational stage, children have acquired some stability in their ideas about how the physical world works; however, their ideas may not correspond to physical realities.

On encountering Santa, what would the preoperational stage child

- *observe?*

In this stage, children have comfortably acquired the concept of Santa Claus if that tradition is part of their culture. They observe consistency in his attire and his demeanor. They observe his generosity and jolliness.

- *think and feel?*

Santa encourages children to behave well since he knows who's "naughty and nice." Children think Santa has the capacity to watch over them and evaluate their behavior. Parents rely on this phenomenon, sometimes invoking Santa's presence during the holiday season to encourage the preoperational stage child to behave. The preoperational stage child feels excited about encounters with Santa and may create obnoxiously long lists of wishes that she expects Santa to fulfill via his reindeer-drawn sleigh.

- *believe?*

The preoperational stage child truly believes in the physical reality of Santa. Santa lives at the North Pole? No problem. After all, that's where the toy workshop is. Besides, Santa can stay warm in his fur-trimmed red outfit and black boots. All elements of the culture tradition make sense to the preoperational child, making it easy to believe.

What are the general characteristics of the concrete operational child?

Children who begin to demonstrate concrete operations develop a much more accurate picture of operations in the physical world. Their cognitive skills improve, not just in conservation skills (for example, recognizing that mass doesn't change merely by changing an object's shape) but also in understanding causality and in developing reliable categorizing strategies.

On encountering Santa, what would the concrete operational child

- *observe?*

The concrete operational child begins to recognize inconsistencies in Santa's appearance. A concrete operational child might ask, *"How can there be so many Santas all over town?"* or *"Why are some Santas thins?"* More refined observational skills set the stage of Santa's downfall.

- *think?*

As concrete operational children come to understand some physical realities about the world, other kinds of questions further undermine Santa:

—*How can Santa get to kids' homes all over the world in one night?*
—*How can reindeer really fly and pull a sleigh?*
—*Wouldn't there be a better place for Santa to live, especially since he's so old?*
—*Just how does Santa keep track of good behavior? . . . Hmm.*

- *feel?*

Discovering principles of physical reality often represents a period of serious disappointment for concrete operational children. Hoewver, they may receive some compensation from making the transition to thinking as adults do around the holidays. They may experience new kinds of fun in actively assisting younger brothers and sisters in continuing their own beliefs.

- *believe?*

Before you know it, the concrete operational thinker is no longer willing to tack up the sock. Concrete operational children abandon their belief in Santa but may still believe that it is important to continue the holiday celebrations. After all, a concrete operational child, capable of conservation skills regarding number, would recognize that the number of presents might be reduced if traditional practices were abandoned.

How do these transitional experiences differ from the characteristics of the formal operational child and adult?

As children move into the *formal operations* stage, they begin to appreciate the cultural custom of Santa. They enjoy Santa as a symbol of seasonal celebration in keeping with their ability to understand abstract ideas. They recognize the importance of shared customs as a means of promoting cohesion in their families and in their culture.

Sensation

Exercise 5.1

CROSSING THE THRESHOLD *Pattern Recognition*

- *"Learn While You Sleep:"* subthreshold
- *Sentry:* detection threshold
- *Father and child:* difference threshold
- *Potatoes:* difference threshold
- *Contact lens:* detection threshold
- *Music group:* subthreshold
- *Pajamas:* difference threshold
- *Hottest chili:* difference threshold
- *Cinnamon chili:* detection threshold

Exercise 5.2

OCCUPATIONAL DESIGN *Practical Problem Solving*

Sensory Profile of a Garbage Collector

	Diminished abilities	Average abilities	Heightened abilities
Vision			X
Hearing		X	
Smell	X		
Touch		X	
Taste		X	
Pain	X		
Balance			X

Justification: An effective and efficient garbage collector would have refined abilities in balance and vision. It would be helpful in the short term if both pain and smell were diminished, though, again, these reduced abilities might cause trouble in the long term. Average performance in other sensory modes would be adequate for this job.

Sensory Profile of a Dessert Chef

	Diminished abilities	Average abilities	Heightened abilities
Vision			X
Hearing		X	
Smell			X
Touch			X
Taste			X
Pain	X		
Balance			X

Justification: Here is an occupation that requires finely tuned abilities in many areas. Dessert chefs need more than effective taste buds; they must also carefully attend to the visual impact of the desserts they create. A well-developed sense of touch will assist in guiding their actions in various cooking modes (such as beating a batter rather than just stirring it). The sense of smell can sometimes rescue creations before they are overcooked. A chef employed in a high-volume restaurant may need an especially keen sense of balance. On the flip side, pain resistance would be an advantage, so a diminished capacity to transmit feelings of pain would be helpful.

Sensory Profile of a College Professor

	Diminished abilities	Average abilities	Heightened abilities
Vision			X
Hearing			X
Smell		X	
Touch	X		
Taste		X	
Pain	X		
Balance			X

Justification: This profile may vary with the college professor's specific field; generally, however, only a few sensory modes need to be heightened in order to promote the most effective performance as a teacher. An acute sense of hearing and vision enable teachers to monitor student response to classroom activities. Balance is probably also an important mode as teachers move rapidly between activities and among students. Taste and touch are probably of little consequence. And pain? Teachers will tell you that grading a stack of essays can stimulate a variety of painful stimuli, so a diminished capacity to experience pain would be helpful in this job also.

Exercise 5.3

REACH OUT AND TOUCH SOMEONE — *Creative Problem Solving*

The only limits here are the limits of your imagination. However you design this new form of communication, it should recognize that the skin senses pressure and temperature. Perhaps you could communicate content using pressure, much like Helen Keller and her teacher would use the manual alphabet, fingerspelling words into each other's palm. Maybe touches on different parts of the body could mean different things. Emotion could be communicated using temperature changes; giving someone an ice cube could mean you are angry, whereas giving a warm cup of tea could mean you are happy.

Long-distance communication would need to rely on the same principles. Using something like a telegraph, one could send Morse code in a way that physically tapped out a message on someone else's hand or arm. Maybe computers could be used to control temperature and pressure changes in a way that allowed one to send a totally different type of email.

What did you come up with?

Exercise 5.4

IT'S A MATTER OF TASTE — *Scientific Problem Solving*

Here is an example of a possible experiment. Although yours may be different, it should have all of the same components and demonstrate your understanding of how to design an experiment, as well as the basic principles of taste.

Example:

- *Hypothesis:* Sweet tastes can be detected on all areas of the tongue.
- *Independent variables:* Areas of the tongue; sweet taste
- *Operational definitions:* Areas of the tongue—the tongue will be divided into four quadrants; sweet taste—a solution of 1 cup sugar in 1 pint water
- *Dependent variable:* Detecting sweet taste
- *Operational definition:* Being able to successfully label a taste as sweet, when given options of sweet, sour, salty, bitter
- *Brief description:* A subject (or subjects) is asked to identify tastes as sweet, salty, sour, and bitter. Plain water, the sweet solution described above, and diluted lemon juice are placed in unlabelled cups. The experimenter then uses a cotton swab to dip in the solutions and apply to different areas of the tongue. Each solution should be applied in different or random orders to each quadrant of the tongue. If sweet can be detected on all tongue surfaces, then the subject should be able to identify the sugar solution correctly in each quadrant.
- *Extraneous variables:* Subjects should not be able to use scent as a cue. Tastes should be applied to different areas within a quadrant. Different cotton swabs should be used each time. Subjects should not have a cold, and should have normal breathing/smelling abilities. Anything that would interfere with your results could be listed here.

Exercise 5.5

PARTS IS PARTS   *Psychological Reasoning*

How do the following entries compare with your lists? If forced to choose, which sense would you give up? Why?

Sense	Energy consequences	Positive consequences	Negative consequences
Vision	Light	• Won't see painful/sad/cruel sights • Won't see when others are making faces at you • Won't need to pay for sunglasses	• Won't see the flowers in the spring, or the changing color of leaves in the fall • Won't see your friends and family smile at you • Won't enjoy seeing the words on the page of a good book
Hearing	Air pressure waves	• Will get more sleep, because you won't hear the loud music the neighbor upstairs plays at 2 A.M. • Won't hear your 8-year-old nephew practicing the violin • Won't hear the chalk squeak on the blackboard	• Will never hear the beautiful precision of a Bach quartet • Won't hear friends or family say "I love you" • Won't hear birds singing
Touch	Pressure/pain Temperature	• Will save money because you won't need a coat in the winter • Won't feel the bruise after you've run into the coffee table • Won't feel the burn from the hot stove	• Will drop objects because you can't tell how hard you are holding them • Won't feel a friend hold your hand • Won't experience the exhilaration of jumping into a cold pool on a hot summer day
Taste	Chemicals	• Won't mind eating cafeteria food • Won't notice the nasty taste of medicine • Will never know that you have morning breath	• More likely to get sick, because won't know if food has spoiled • Will never taste a fresh strawberry • Won't be able to distinguish between vinegar and wine

Sense	Energy consequences	Positive consequences	Negative consequences
Smell	Chemicals	• Won't notice the smell of garbage • Won't mind cleaning out the fridge, because you won't be able to smell last month's leftovers • Will never know if your partner has morning breath	• Will never think of Grandma when you smell baking cookies and bread • Won't appreciate the smells of a Thanksgiving dinner • Will never smell a Double Delight rose

Exercise 5.6

THE EYES HAVE IT *Perspective Taking*

How did it go? How did your experience compare to the experiences of your classmates? What factors seemed to be involved in successfully adapting to the altered visual experience?

Perception

Exercise 6.1

THE BIG PICTURE — *Pattern Recognition*

Selected performance: ballet

Figure-ground. The relationship of the prima ballerina to the other dancers is often one of figure-ground. Her movements are choreographed to be distinctive and different from the movements of others on the stage. The principle is also illustrated when the prima ballerina dances alone: She is the figure, and the scenery becomes the backdrop.

Proximity. Some choreography provides for smaller groupings of ballerinas placed strategically on the stage. We perceive them to be grouped due to their nearness to each other and the distance separating them from other groups.

Similarity. Grouping may rely on similarly constructed costumes or movements that appear to be the same.

Closure. Some elements of ballet introduce actions that demand a sense of completion. For example, a leap into the air must resolve in a return to earth. Some paired dancing steps exploit our expectation that the couple will come back together at some point if the dance is to be satisfying.

Continuity/connectedness. Our inclination to see smooth, continuous patterns is exploited in particular by choreography that creates fluid motion among dancers. For example, we may see a movement ripple through a dance line, as in the classic Rockettes leg movements, and we perceive a strong impression of good form. We are likely to perceive dancers who are touching in some capacity as forming a meaningful subgroup.

Figure-ground. The players in the immediate vicinity of the ball will create the *figure* against the *ground* of the rest of the team. The ball becomes the focal point for your attention unless you happen to be following a preferred player on the team. In that case, your attention may shift to that player as the figure; the rest of the action will be the ground.

Proximity. Teams begin each play in proximity with one other—one team per side. Once the ball is in play, the good form of proximity is sacrificed. The quarterback is challenged to maintain a good "gestalt" in order to maintain the play as team members pursue their assignments in a chaotic field.

Similarity. Uniforms are a distinctive symbol of similarity. Regardless of team members' physical location on the field, their colors identify them as part of the group.

Closure. Each play represents the principle of closure. Once the ball is snapped, we anticipate how the play will end, whether the ball is galloped into the end zone or buried beneath of mountain of shoulder pads and cleats. The end of the play represents the good form of closure, regardless of whether we like the actual outcome of the play.

Continuity/connectedness. A well-executed play represents the principle of continuity. When the team is functioning well, each member contributes to the overall pattern that makes the play successful. More sophisticated fans recognize the role of all players in a successful strategy, demonstrating the continuity of each successful play. When plays are unsuccessful, the group members appear to be disconnected from one another. Signals are missed; errors are made. Despite other elements of grouping (proximity, similarity), the team may not appear to function as a connected whole.

Exercise 6.2

ASSESSING THE ASSEMBLY LINE — *Practical Problem Solving*

Anything that you do to facilitate shape identification and comparison would make the inspectors' job easier. For example, maybe you would color the conveyer belt so that it contrasts with the gidgit; this would make detecting the gidgit and identifying its shape easier. Perhaps you would have all objects facing the same direction as they move down the assembly line to facilitate shape comparison. Perhaps halting the conveyer belt at regular intervals would help people concentrate. Or you might send some obviously different gidgits down the line to reorient people to the task. Taking regular breaks would also help concentration during inspection. The fundamental processes involved in this design correspond to *signal detection theory*.

Exercise 6.3

CHAOS CONTROL — *Creative Problem Solving*

If we weren't able to habituate, the world would indeed be a chaotic environment. Input from all sensory modes would be overwhelming. For example, our figure-ground relationships in the visual field would be problematic. Objects in the environment would all demand our attention as the figure, with few objects staying in the background. We would probably be dizzy from the competing demands of new stimuli constantly breaking through our awareness as new figures. Smells habituate with good and bad effects. Without habituation, every sweet swig of soda would taste equally pleasant. However, the unsavory smells of a "hygiene-impaired" classmate also wouldn't fade. Habituation is especially important to the senses of touch and kinesthesis. Imagine trying to study with complete and constant awareness of how high our socks are or just how many pounds we need to lose.

Without chaos management by our perceptual sets, we would have a challenging time formulating a course of action. As any experienced traveler can tell you, the challenge of a new environment requires vigilance because you do not have routines to fall back on. For example, you don't know how to locate things or you may not know the local customers, so it's easy to make mistakes. Many people enjoy this assault on the routine; others find the challenge overwhelming. Without reasonable perceptual sets, life would be a constant surprise.

Exercise 6.4

CLIFF HANGERS — *Scientific Problem Solving*

There are a variety of monocular and binocular depth cues that infants, kids, chicks, kittens, and other babies could be using to perceive depth. They include: retinal disparity, convergence, relative size, relative height, linear perspective, relative brightness, and texture gradient. Other cues that can be used to perceive depth—such as interposition, relative motion, and relative clarity—are less likely to be potential cues in these experiments because the experimental conditions are not designed to give this information.

Whichever cues you choose to discuss, your hypotheses should be stated as predictions, and the experiments you design should allow you to control when a baby (of whatever species) receives the information about those cues. Be as specific as you can when you discuss how you will control your independent variables. Also, make sure that you are explicit in stating your dependent variables. For most of your experiments, the dependent variable will be whether the baby crawls or walks over the visual cliff. What extraneous variables will be important to consider?

Of the factors that could improve a baby's performance on this task, you should be able to discuss two: biological maturation and experience. The more physiologically mature a baby, the more developed the neural systems that process visual stimuli. A one-day-old kid (baby goat) has more mature visual systems than a one-day-old kitten. In addition, more visual experience stimulates better development of the neural networks within the visual system. Remember the discussion in your text about sensory restriction and restored vision? Kittens and monkeys with limited visual experiences after birth did not develop the same sensitivity to visual stimuli as did those raised in a normal visual environment, even after the restrictions were removed.

Exercise 6.5

THE CASE AGAINST ESP — *Psychological Reasoning*

Music prediction. You may inadvertently narrow the field of available music selections through your listening habits. A song that runs through your mind may be played particularly often during the period in which you experience your uncanny ability. The amount of time you spend humming heavily played popular music probably far exceeds the time spent humming other kinds of music. For this reason you may occasionally "hit" the song about to be played, giving you the impression of extrasensory talent. You probably do not react with the same intensity when a song you are humming does *not* match the next one on the radio, so you become a victim of your own selective perception. To confirm the existence of this telepathic skill, a psychologist would ask if you could perform this event reliably from a wide selection of music or of music stations. That would constitute objective evidence of your extrasensory ability.

Gender prediction. Brenda's chances of being right are 50 percent—not bad odds even in gambling casinos. But does Brenda let people know when she does not predict accurately? Perhaps her reputation does not reflect those failures. She may truly enjoy her position as an adviser to parents-to-be, and she probably won't be reported to the Better Business Bureau if she errs. Oddly enough, even the fancier technologies supporting scientific predictions of gender are not 100 percent accurate.

Lottery-selection skills. As aggravating as lucky lottery players are for those who spend a lot of money in this manner, it does appear that some people are more frequent winners. How could this be? First, we need to look at the frequency with which people like

Eugene play the lottery in order to report one instance of winning? If he plays every chance he gets, then cumulatively his chances of winning will be higher. He has virtually the same chance each time he plays, but the sheer volume of his lottery tickets will increase his opportunity to win. In addition, runs of luck are common in gambling situations. We can explain this occurrence statistically because even unusual events—like chronic winners—can happen. The trick is knowing when to quit, a feat as hard to accomplish as winning is in the first place.

Disaster prediction. Does a disaster happen every time Pat has an "ooky feeling"? To understand this phenomenon, we need to examine how this problem is framed. Disaster happens somewhere on a regular basis. As broadly defined as Pat's skill is, she could probably report a disaster "hit" after watching the evening news. When the clairvoyant feelings prompt Pat to worry about specific loved ones, does she routinely report these concerns to verify her feelings? Or does she confirm that the feelings were present only after an unpleasant outcome is reported to her?

Exam ESP. This explanation has several points of entry. First, Bruce may be quite good at guessing—but not because he has ESP. He may have refined his abilities to observe the professor and to infer the concepts and skills that will appeal most to the professor for exam purposes. (Students sometimes refer to this skill as "psyching out" the professor, despite mild protests from psychologists!) If you wanted to develop this ability, what kinds of indicators might help you pick out the most important ideas in the professor's lecture?

Another explanation might be that one successful examination score does not constitute a reliable ability. *Samples of 1* represent suspicious evidence to most psychologists. Finally, has anyone seen Bruce's report card? He could be lying about his examination success, his grade-point history, and his ability to predict exam construction.

Magician clairvoyance. Were you able to guess how this *illusion* might be accomplished? Magicians refer to this illusion as "one-ahead." A skilled magician merely places an accomplice in the audience. He palms (secretly removes) her index card to make sure that he will not randomly select this card from the pile and read it. When he selects an actual card from a real audience member, he holds it in front of his forehead but he actually reports the agreed-upon worry that his accomplice will claim as her own. He is then free to read silently the card he has held to his head and to report that worry after holding the next card to his head. While our attention is riveted by the accomplice's powerful acting job, we fail to observe that the magician is preparing himself to accurately identify all following cards.

Exercise 6.6

CONTEXT CUES *Perspective Taking*

There is a wide variety of scenarios you could create that would influence what a person perceived in this situation. The best ideas will be those that include both internal and external factors. Here are some examples that can serve as models.

Vase only: If this slide were inserted in a series of slides given to art history students or archaeology students, both internal and external cues would encourage the viewer to see only the vase. In addition to the expectations one of these students has of viewing objects of art and/or pieces of pottery, seeing many other slides with these themes sets the external context as well.

Faces only: This one might be a little trickier. Imagine that the picture were hung in a gallery devoted to portraits of British royalty. Again, such a setting would provide both the external and internal contexts. It would also be helpful if the viewer were an expert on either Prince Phillip or Queen Elizabeth. Perhaps you would present it to the British Historical Society to be part of its annual slide show.

Both vase and faces: Obviously, the primary consideration here is that the viewer know that the picture is reversible. If this is the case, then you could put the picture into almost any setting. You could also set the context so that viewer might be open to looking closely at the picture—perhaps you could hang it in a room with various optical illusions, "Where's Waldo?" posters, or even the new computer-generated pictures-made-of-pictures posters.

States of Consciousness

ANSWER KEY

Exercise 7.1

CONSCIOUS CONTROL? *Pattern Recognition*

There are no hard and fast answers in this rank-ordering experience, but we offer below a general pattern that might help. You may have noticed as you talked over your rank order with others that individuals may differ in the way they experience the degrees of conscious control associated with the states below.

In the *least conscious control* category would be

- f. Quacking like a chicken while hypnotized
- g. Counting backward while being anesthetized
- i. Having one more drink than you should

Demonstrating *a little more conscious control* would be

- a. Nodding off in a boring class
- d. Feeling the effects of having taken a painkiller
- e. Meditating
- j. Driving down the road but realizing that you are two exits past your stop
- k. Praying
- m. Daydreaming

Demonstrating *the most intense conscious control* would be

- b. Preparing to give your first speech in a class
- c. Studying for an exam
- h. Having one social drink
- l. Meeting an attractive person for the first time

Exercise 7.2

PROFESSIONAL PROJECT DARE	***Practical Problem Solving***

Preferred Activity or Profession	Most Dangerous Drug Substance and Predicted Risk
Bicycle messenger	LSD would make navigating busy city streets almost certainly lethal as fantastic pictures, kaleidoscopic displays, and a sense of panic interfere with weaving between buses and darting across busy intersections.
Marathon runner	Any depressant (e.g., barbiturates or opiates); depressants slow down neural activity and can depress physiological functions such as respiration and heart rate through their impact on the brainstem. At the least, such drug use would make it hard to keep up with competitors; at worst, it would be fatal. Depressants are tempting for athletes to use because they can decrease the pain and anxiety that are often a part of this profession.
Artist	Cocaine or crack are risky for the artist for a variety of reasons. Not only do such drugs speed up neural activity so that fine motor control may be difficult to maintain, but the crash that inevitably follows results in headaches, depression, and exhaustion—a difficult state in which to work. Also, these drugs are expensive and could quickly push someone into the "starving artist" category.
Stay-at-home mom	Alcohol is dangerous for the stay-at-home mom because it impairs judgment and slows reaction time, both potentially disastrous effects when small children are present.
Sword swallower	Marijuana has the potential to end a sword swallower's career fairly quickly. Not only does it impair motor coordination, perceptual skills, and reaction time—all of which are critical when putting long pointy objects down your throat—it increases sensitivity to taste and touch stimuli, making gagging a real possibility.
Teacher	Barbiturates are one of the many classes of drugs that would be lethal to a teacher's career (and potentially his or her life, as well). They slow reaction time, impair memory and judgment, and can induce sleep. In large doses, the depressive effects are more likely to cause death than are irate students!
Tightrope walker	The hallucinations caused by LSD would not be an enjoyable experience for someone walking on a narrow rope far above the ground. The sense of being separated from one's body, combined with altered visual perception, would make it impossible for a tightrope walker to make it safely to the other side.
Accountant	Cocaine would be particularly dangerous for the accountant, especially during tax time. Although the rush of energy might seem beneficial, increased aggression would make fistfights with tense customers a real possibility, and the crash following the high would make it impossible to concentrate on the level of detail necessary in this type of work.

Exercise 7.3

ROCK-A-BYE BABY	***Creative Problem Solving***

Was the theory of sleep or dreaming apparent in your adaptation? Do you think your new version or original composition would catch on?

Exercise 7.4

REMEDIES FOR JET LAG — *Scientific Problem Solving*

Your hypothesis. You would attempt to demonstrate the superiority of one jet-lag intervention strategy. For example, the use of meditation may be superior to preventive vitamin B and aerobic exercise. You would design the experiment to demonstrate this difference.

The independent variable. Your experimental design would need at least three, preferably four, groups. Three groups would have an intervention: vitamin use, aerobic exercise, or meditation. The fourth group could serve as the no-treatment control group; this group will illustrate the normal course of jet lag without intervention.

Measuring the dependent variable. Measuring jet lag is a problem. One approach may be to ask individuals how many hours of sleep they would need to feel caught up. Or you could measure how many days elapse until each participant reports feeling "back to normal." Assuming your experimental design includes some treatments that are effective for jet lag, participants in these conditions will need fewer hours of sleep to feel caught up or will report that fewer days are needed to get back to normal. If no treatment is effective and the study has been well designed, the dependent-variable measurements will not differ among the groups.

Controlling other variables. Ideally, the subjects should be matched for age, gender, and travel experience. This process helps to rule out alternative interpretations of any changes reported within the experiment. In addition, all subjects should travel the same distance at the same time of day in a direction that will exaggerate the reaction. All subjects should be randomly assigned to treatment conditions, again to control for alternative explanations.

Once the plane has landed, you should take precautions to ensure that all subjects performed their assigned treatment. You should measure their jet lag at the same time. You should also prevent other activities that would artificially add to the lag (for example, no dancing!).

Exercise 7.5

A MIDSUMMER NIGHT'S DREAM — *Psychological Reasoning*

Peter will begin to feel sleepy and generally lethargic. Over the course of the four days, he will experience a decreased ability to concentrate and will notice impaired creativity, irritability, slowed performance, slight hand tremors, and altered perceptions when performing monotonous tasks. Eventually, he will experience hallucinations and speech and movement problems. He probably will *not* notice a difference in his performance on short, highly motivating tasks (e.g., outrunning rabid seals), however. His immune system will not fight off viral infections with the same efficiency and his body will have increased levels of a variety of pathogens.

When he returns to the land of sleep, Peter probably will experience one or two nights of lengthened sleep and increased REM activity during sleep, but he will then return to his normal sleeping patterns.

Exercise 7.6

THE LIGHT AT THE END OF THE TUNNEL — *Perspective Taking*

Summary: *the spiritual hypothesis.* This position assumes that humans are endowed with a soul that exists apart from the corporeal body. This position is supported by religious traditions in which the promise of an afterlife is prominent. Given this support, the spiritual hypothesis is characterized by a sense of optimism and a belief in the continuity and perhaps even indestructibility of the human spirit.

Summary: *the physiological hypothesis.* This point of view stresses that brain function is governed by physiological principles, regardless of the specific experience reported. Cognitive science proposes oxygen-deprivation hallucination as an alternative hypothesis to explain the reported qualities of the near-death experience. Those who hold this position do not need to posit a special spiritual existence to explain the near-death phenomenon. They are more inclined to see the event as the brain functioning under stress rather than the triumph of the human spirit. They are skeptical that human beings can transcend the physiological limitations of the brain.

Which has greater personal appeal? This answer, of course, depends on your own values and beliefs. Do they more closely match the spiritual hypothesis or the physiological hypothesis?

ANSWER KEY

Learning

Exercise 8.1

THE CLASSICAL CONNECTION *Pattern Recognition*

The Troublesome Shower

Unconditioned response (UCR): pain avoidance
Unconditioned stimulus (UCS): boiling-hot water
Conditioned response (CR): fear and jumping
Conditioned stimulus (CS): sound of toilet flushing

The Water Show

Unconditioned response (UCR): fainting
Unconditioned stimulus (UCS): heat
Conditioned response (CR): dizziness
Conditioned stimulus (CS): organ music

The Trouble With Tuna

UCR: stomach cramps
UCS: tainted mayonnaise
CR: stomach turbulence
CS: sight of tuna fish and possibly the smell, taste, suggestion, menu listing, and commercials of tuna fish (Note the expansion of reactions, due to *stimulus generalization*, the tendency of similar stimuli to elicit aversive reactions.)

Captain Hook's Time Problem

CR: anxiety attack
UCS: croc bite
CS: clock ticking
UCR: pain from loss of hand

(*Note:* Did the changed order of the classical conditioning components make your answers wrong? If you conditioned to the prior order, you may have linked the right components with the wrong labels. If your habit was disrupted by the warning, you may have not conditioned to the order in which the concepts were presented.

Exercise 8.2

POWERFUL CONSEQUENCES — *Practical Problem Solving*

a. +; ↑; positive reinforcement. Although teachers may not often comment on the quality of a classroom contribution, such behavior can be a strong motivator for increasing participation in the classroom.

b. +; ↑; positive reinforcement. The wife is rewarding the husband with a special gesture of thanks. This will be effective—if he likes the flowers.

c. −; ↓; punishment. In this example, the child's academic behavior was met with a negative consequence intended to discourage him from continuing at the same level of performance. Unfortunately, the consequence may influence only the behavior of presenting the report card, not necessarily the level of academic effort itself. Some children avoid punishing consequences by figuring out how to prevent parents from seeing their grades.

d. +; ↑; positive reinforcement. The child's screaming is less likely to be a sign of serious distress than to be a well-learned pattern of manipulation. The child's behavior, which creates pressure on the parent, is positively reinforced with a sucker; consequently, the child learns to repeat this fairly obnoxious behavior.

e. −; ↓; punishment. The spill was followed with physical punishment and the behavior may decline in the future. Or the child may just become afraid of making natural mistakes in front of Mom. Some spills are unintentional, and the commotion and embarrassment that follow them are naturally punishing. Parents may undermine their attempts to teach proper table manners if they don't distinguish between unintentional and intentional messes.

f. +; ↑; negative reinforcement. When we feel pain from a headache, taking aspirin is negatively reinforced when the headache disappears a short time later.

g. 0; ↓; extinction. This dad really missed his opportunity to strengthen appropriate playing behavior. By not offering praise, or a consequence of any kind, he missed an opportunity to reinforce peaceful behavior. The chronically warring children are not likely to be sustained and rewarded by the fun they have together, and so the mutual cooperative play is likely to extinguish rapidly.

h. +; ↑; negative reinforcement. This is a tricky one. Remember, the target behavior here is the surrendering of the parents. When they surrender and hush the spoiled child, they escape the distress generated by having to listen to a screamer. The outcome of this action is therefore positive for them, and these bribery patterns are likely to strengthen and perhaps be enacted even more quickly in the future. In this case, they have exchanged short-term relief for long-term headaches through negative reinforcement.

i. 0; ↓; extinction. Even if Dad's stroll down memory lane isn't particularly exciting, it probably won't have much of an impact. However, if Dad often takes such measures in response to his children's complaints, a different principle (−; ↓; punishment) may be involved.

j. +; ↑; negative reinforcement. Through confession, the spy escapes the torture of the electrical current. Here again, she may have traded in some short-term relief for some bigger woes later on.

Exercise 8.3

| **REINFORCING RHYMES** | *Creative Problem Solving* |

It is hard to predict what kind of rhymes and revisions you came up with to illustrate learning principles. Was the learning mechanism (e.g., negative reinforcement, punishment) obvious in your creative execution?

Exercise 8.4

| **A WORKING HYPOTHESIS** | *Scientific Problem Solving* |

Hypothesis: Using a fixed-ratio schedule (paying for piecework) will result in more royas produced than will a fixed interval schedule (paying a weekly salary).

Independent variable(s): the type of schedule; either FR or FI.

Dependent variable(s): the number of royas produced.

Extraneous variables for which you would control: There are a variety of reasonable answers, including: experience of workers, length of shift, time of shift, working conditions, etc.

Basic experimental protocol: Randomly assign half of each shift during a one-month period to be paid based on either an FR or FI schedule. At the end of that month, the number of royas produced by each group will be counted.

Potential ethical considerations: There are a lot of things that we can do because this is only a pretend experiment. In real life, it would be unethical to pay people differently for doing the same job. Pay for piecework in manufacturing plants was discontinued in the United States many years ago.

Exercise 8.5

| **LITTLE ALBERT REVISITED** | *Psychological Reasoning* |

Someone who believes that the fear is a result of classical conditioning will attempt to extinguish the response by weakening or eliminating the pairing between the CS and the UCS. In this case, treatment would consist of making sure that there were many opportunities for Albert to experience rats without loud noises. This approach stresses extinction as the main mechanism for dealing with Little Albert's fear.

Someone who believed in the operant conditioning model would provide rewarding experiences when Albert experienced rats. Treatment would include giving Albert things he liked or taking away things he did not like. This approach is sometimes referred to as counterconditioning.

With no intervention at all (and no further unhappy accidents with furry creatures), Little Albert's fear might naturally extinguish. However, when people develop fear of some dreaded objects, they naturally avoid circumstances that will bring them into close contact with the object. If Little Albert successfully avoided contact with furry creatures, then chances are good his fears would have been maintained throughout his life.

Exercise 8.6

| **THE DISCRIMINATING DACHSHUND** | ***Perspective Taking*** |

Pavlov's explanation: The tennis ball originally was a stimulus for play. Paired with the painful ant bites (UCS) the tennis ball became a conditioned stimulus (CS), which produced a response of avoidance. Avoiding balls that are similar in shape and size to a tennis ball demonstrates generalization of the response.

Skinner's explanation: The pain of the ant bites serves as an immediate and strong punishment, and decreases the preceding behavior of picking up the tennis ball. Skinner would state that other small balls became discriminative stimuli for pain. Large balls were safe; small balls were dangerous.

ANSWER KEY

Memory

Exercise 9.1

THE MAGNIFICENT SEVEN — *Pattern Recognition*

An encoding problem. A person would be unable to recall the name of a single dwarf if he or she had never properly encoded the fairy tale. People with this problem may simply never have heard the story, as might be the case if they had been raised in a culture other than the American culture. You can't recall details of a story you have never heard.

A storage problem. If a storage problem has occurred, people are likely to encode the target memories insufficiently. The seven names may have been misperceived and the wrong names may have been entered into storage. Upon retrieval, they would get out of memory just what they put in—the wrong names.

An interference problem. The part of the brain that is dedicated to the housing of fairy tales and fictional characters is a pretty crowded place. If people can't dredge up the right names, it might have been easy to substitute some new domestic partners for Snow White.

An insufficient-cueing problem. One minute was not very much time to recall all seven names. Some people might have been able to produce several accurate names if they had been given more time to tap into the context to make the associative network yield the right answers. Or perhaps there weren't enough story details to activate the proper associative network in the first place.

A repression problem. A horrifying experience with mean and evil apple-toting relatives or some hard days in the mines might make this recall task especially difficult. Anything that reminds you of such challenging times might block recall, according to this distinctly Freudian view of forgetting.

Exercise 9.2

THANKS FOR THE MEMORY — *Practical Problem Solving*

Answers will vary.

Exercise 9.3

STORY TIME — *Creative Problem Solving*

Anything goes! Here is one example: *Sally and Mike* went searching for *rental units* (parents) and met *Sam the ant* in the kitchen of one apartment. Not wanting to disturb the local fauna, they continued to look in an exclusive area known as Alphabet City. Driving down *E Lane* in their new *Van*, they saw a log cabin that reminded them of the one that *Laura* and her *sisters* lived in on "Little House on the Prairie." Another house was shaped like a ship that *Christopher* Columbus could have sailed on. "*Uncle!*" they cried. "This is enough!" They finally asked for help from *Melissa and John,* who told them to go down *Grand* Ave. and look for a sign proclaiming "*Uncle Larry*'s Famous Farm," at which they should turn left. After going past two baby goats *(kids)* named Tisha and Devon, they finally arrived at the perfect place to live and decided never to apartment-hunt again.

Exercise 9.4

CREATING CONTEXT — *Scientific Problem Solving*

Independent variable: The context in which the learning and recall occur. In this exemplar it would be the classroom and school cafeteria.

Dependent variable: Student performance. This could be measured in a variety of ways, but test score or number of correct answers are used here.

Extraneous variables for which she should control: Any variable other than the context that might affect student performance should be considered. A short list might include the type of material the instructor is teaching, the mode in which the material is presented (lecture, reading, lab), the time of day, and the type of test. A more complete list could also include things like the gender of the students, their majors, how they take notes, how many days they were present, and how many other classes they are taking this semester.

Outline of a basic experimental protocol: One idea would be to take a class and have half the students take the test in the classroom where the course is normally taught, and have the other half take the test at the same time in the cafeteria. The instructor could then compare the scores of the students who took the test in the classroom (same context) with those who took the test in the cafeteria (different context). Although this would give her the comparison she wants, it also leaves her with several questions. The most serious of these questions is: What if students don't do well in the cafeteria, simply because it is the cafeteria and it is noisy, big, has tables instead of desks, and lots of interruptions?

A more sophisticated design would use two classes of students, one that she teaches in the classroom and one that she teaches in the cafeteria. The instructor would be careful to teach the same material over the same time period to both classes and to control the extraneous variables listed above to the best of her ability. She could then divide each class in half and have half of each class take the test in the cafeteria, and half take the test in the classroom. With this design, she has more information. Half of the students taking the test in the classroom learned in the classroom, and the other half learned in the cafeteria. At the same time, half of the students who took the test in the cafeteria learned in the cafeteria and half learned in the classroom. In this way she can determine if something unique about the setting causes any differences she finds. If all students who take the test in the cafeteria score lower than those who take the test in the classroom, for example, then she knows it is not taking a test in a different context that is the issue (because half of the students taking the test in the cafeteria are testing in the same context), but rather that something about the cafeteria impairs test performance. On the other hand, if the half of the students in the cafeteria who learned in the classroom *and* the half of the students in the classroom who learned in the cafeteria both score lower on the exam, then she can be fairly certain that it is the changing of the context that is responsible for the difference in performance.

By the way, it is very important to note that, although this scenario makes for great discussion, it is *not* ethical unless the students' grades are not affected. Knowingly placing some students at a disadvantage is not appropriate behavior in anything other than a research setting where students are not given grades. Instructors work very hard to encourage the success of all their students, not to hinder it!

Exercise 9.5

ROSEANNE'S DILEMMA *Psychological Reasoning*

Formulate one hypothesis that might explain how a real, traumatic, and previously forgotten event could suddenly be remembered: Most of the possibilities revolve around retrieval cues. Perhaps the person is in a unique context that is similar enough to the earlier event to provide a reminder about that event. An experience with an extreme mood (terror, exhilaration, overwhelming grief) could also serve as a prime for retrieving a forgotten memory. In such cases, however, the cue (emotion, context, or similar event) would be extreme or there would have been multiple opportunities for such remembering to have occurred earlier.

Formulate one hypothesis to explain how people could remember something that never really happened: False memories can arise for a variety of reasons. As demonstrated in the research by Elizabeth Loftus and her colleagues, the associations a person has with words used during questioning about specific events can influence a person's memory for that event. For example, a person questioned about how fast the cars were going when they smashed into each other will remember the speed of the cars as faster than a person asked how fast the cars were going when they bumped into each other. False memories can also arise when a person is given misinformation about an event, or if a person is asked to repeatedly imagine an event that never happened. In addition, it is possible to forget the source of the memory; to forget the context but to remember an event. It is very important to note that, because false memories "feel" like real memories, it may not be possible for the person who is remembering to tell, based on the strength of his or her emotional response or confidence, whether the event occurred.

Describe one strategy that might help distinguish between real and false memories: There is no solid evidence that any particular test or procedure can distinguish between real and false memories. As you may remember from your reading, early work with brain imaging techniques indicates that the left temporal lobe is active when remembering words that were actually spoken and not when inaccurately "remembering" words that were not spoken. This technique is not viable when working with events in the distant past, however. The best way to distinguish between real and false memories in eyewitness accounts is to use questioning techniques that do not provide misinformation or prime for certain types of recollections.

Exercise 9.6

MAKING MEMORIES — *Perspective Taking*

There are many issues that you could discuss here. A strong answer would recognize that basic tasks like answering the phone, doing dishes, going shopping would be difficult or impossible for Patsy because of the many barriers that require explicit memory—knowing what objects are used for, where to put things away, how to get and prepare food, etc. She would need someone to teach her to perform all of these activities of daily living. Patsy also had some rather unusual limitations in her ability to rely on implicit memory, so physical, occupational, and speech therapy might be required for support as she relearned how to walk, tie her shoes, and speak clearly. In addition, there are the emotional challenges of making and maintaining friendships, participating in social and community organizations, and raising a family, if an individual does not know the individuals involved, their roles, the social structures, and culturally appropriate behaviors. Patsy would need support to help re-establish the emotional ties she had with family and friends and to deal with the extreme stress of living in a very frightening situation. Other family members would probably also need professional support as they assumed many of the roles that Patsy previously performed and as they discovered how Patsy's personality has changed. The key criterion for successful treatment is recognizing that true amnesia has the potential to rob the individual of basic functions, and that this will impact the larger family and social structures of which this individual is a part.

10

ANSWER KEY

Thinking and Language

Exercise 10.1

THERE'S GOOD NEWS AND THERE'S BAD NEWS *Pattern Recognition*

Have I Got a Deal For You!

You sell used cars. The best car on your lot has 100,000 miles on it. How could you describe this car to a prospective buyer to make the purchase more attractive?

Many used-car salespeople have opted to describe their products as *pre-owned* to reduce some of the tiredness associated with the term *used*. Another option you may want to examine is framing your description of the mileage in terms of the car's expected mileage over its lifetime. If this model can be run to a lifetime of 300,000 miles, then 100,000 won't sound so bad.

Making the Grade

You're carrying six full classes. You've had a hard semester, and you are about to talk with loved ones about how things have been going. You've excelled in five courses, but you know you won't pass the other course. How do you talk about your experience in this difficult semester?

If your intention is to maximize a sympathetic response from your loved ones, then your wisest choice may be discussing the course that is giving you pain. If your intention is to gain their admiration for your hard work, your best bet is to focus on your success in the five courses and to minimize or omit the news about your most challenging course.

IRS Blues

You've just started working for the Internal Revenue Service. Tax specialists have developed tax brackets to assist in equitable taxation. Will you work with taxpayers by describing how much tax they will pay or by explaining how much income they will keep?

Most taxpayers aren't keen to surrender their money. Even so, they will probably find it easier to hear a description of the percentage of federal tax they will pay (e.g., 28 percent) than to hear that they will be able to keep only 72 percent of their income.

Rain, Rain, Go Away

As a weather forecaster in an area that depends on the tourist industry, will you state your forecast as the likelihood of sunshine or as the likelihood of rain?

Your decision will probably depend on how routine sunshine is in the area. If rain is rare, you may want to forecast rain to prepare tourists to spend their vacation time better. If rain is a common occurrence, tourists may find it more encouraging to hear about the likelihood of sunshine, even if the chances are fairly slim.

Exercise 10.2

IF WE COULD TALK TO THE ANIMALS   *Perspective Taking*

Examples of evidence supporting the viewpoint that animals have the capacity for language:

- Washoe's use of sign language to communicate, including the creation of new words
- The teaching of other chimps to use language without the intervention of trainers
- Lana's use of a computer equipped with word symbols

Examples of evidence challenging the viewpoint that animals have the capacity for language:

- Nim Chimpsky's trainers believe he is merely imitating his trainers.
- The apes' use of language is extremely limited.
- Their behaviors may represent the effect of operant conditioning.
- Interpreting language use may represent more of a human wish than an animal reality.

Your personal choice:
Answers will vary.

Exercise 10.3

ALEX THE ACCOUNTANT   *Scientific Problem Solving*

There are a variety of potential answers. One example is given below. A strong answer will express a testable hypothesis, provide operationalized variables, and clearly describe the experimental design.

Hypothesis: Alex can make comparative numerical decisions, using the concepts of greater than, less than, and equal to.

Experimental design: Alex will be shown a tray on which there are different classes of objects. He will be asked to compare the quantities about any two classes of objects on the tray. For example, if there are blue blocks, red blocks, red rings, and blue rings on the tray, Alex could be asked to compare the number of red to blue things, or the numbers of rings to blocks. Questions should be framed so that some of them ask which has the most, some ask which has the least, and some ask which groups have the same number of objects. The independent variable is the comparative relationships (more, less, and equal to) and the dependent variable is Alex's response. If the hypothesis is supported, then Alex should be able to reply correctly to questions about these relationships at a level significantly greater than chance. It is important to remember that there are other things that can influence Alex's performance on this task. To be a good test of this ability, Alex must be able to distinguish among the objects presented on the tray and be able to group them into the flexible categories needed to answer the questions (for example, a red ring could be either a ring or a red thing). Alex also needs to be able to indicate his answer either through clearly spoken words or some other method that can be understood by any trained, objective observer.

If your hypothesis is supported, how might this change our understanding of human language and thinking? If Alex can do this, then presumably other animals can as well. How might this affect our understanding of what it means to be human? How much of our sense of identity and value arises from our assumptions of intellectual superiority? There are no easy answers to questions like these. Consider discussing these issues with your classmates to see the range of perspectives and to expand your own understanding of what it means to think and use language, and how these are related to our definition of intelligence and humanity.

Exercise 10.4

MONEY IN THE BANK? *Practical Problem Solving*

You could use the availability heuristic to educate investors about the many ways that relying on remembered information is dangerous and how they can avoid making predictable mistakes. For example, just because you see some people making money in computer chip technology, or you saw an article on a successful and profitable computer chip company, doesn't mean that all computer chip technology investments are sound. You can explain that focusing on a particular company's past success rates and separating a specific stock from the general category of stocks (e.g., a particular medical technologies firm rather than medical technology firms in general), would help your investors make more successful choices.

By understanding how overconfidence works, investors can be aware of the human tendency to explain away failures to confirm strongly held beliefs. Instead of ignoring the poor quarterly profit report of a particular company because "that company always does well," perhaps they will be able to see it as the first sign of a turnaround and then sell while its stock is still desirable.

Did you see these tendencies in your own money management experiences?

Exercise 10.5

SEEING IS BELIEVING *Psychological Reasoning*

Many of the concepts in your text could help you explain how people still maintain beliefs in the face of contradictory evidence. Some of the more obvious include:

- *Confirmation bias:* We tend to look only for information that confirms what we already "know." This makes us less likely to question our judgment or look for alternative explanation.
- *Availability heuristic:* We rely on information that is accessible and quickly remembered. This makes us more likely to rely on personal experience than on something that we've read or heard.
- *Overconfidence:* Because we seek to confirm the beliefs that we already hold and we explain away failures, we overestimate how accurate our judgments and beliefs are.

This can contribute to the tendency to rely on our experience, rather than on the collective experience of others.

- *Belief bias:* This concept states that it is easier to see illogic when the conclusions run counter to our beliefs than when they confirm them. Because it is hard to doubt the validity of our experience, we often cannot see where the logic of our conclusions is faulty.

Exercise 10.6

POOR JOHN AND MARY — *Creative Problem Solving*

The solution to this riddle rests in a complete examination of your assumptions and inferences. We can solve the riddle if we first recognize that John and Mary are fish! The dog jumped on top of the table and knocked the fish tank onto the floor and broke it. The fish "drowned" by being unable to extract oxygen from the air. The chair added nothing; it was a decoy.

If you got stuck, you probably experienced a problem called *functional fixedness,* a condition in which we automatically make some assumptions about the elements of a problem, based on our own experience. For example, it was hard to avoid the image of John and Mary as humans in this problem because we don't often assign common human names to goldfish. If the problem specified that Goldie and Fin were found dead in a room, you probably would have had no difficulty solving the problem. Those names are commonly used in our language to communicate the *concept* "goldfish," just as John and Mary invoke the *concept* "human."

11 Intelligence

ANSWER KEY

Exercise 11.1

"CHARACTER"ISTICS OF INTELLIGENCE — *Pattern Recognition*

Character	Academic	Practical	Creative
Scrooge	Strong: his career as an accountant dictates good analytic skills	Strong: his money-making abilities attest to his street smarts	Weak: he conforms to conventions to an extreme degree
Mary Poppins	Strong: her tutoring skills are unparalleled	Strong: she is interpersonally shrewd ("practically perfect") and skilled at solving problems	Strong: her strategies for child care reflected unconventional but successful solutions
Sherlock Holmes	Strong: his detective career offered the opportunity to show off an impressive range of knowledge	Strong: his problem-solving skills were legendary	Strong: he adopted unusual costumes and creative approaches to catch criminals
Winnie the Pooh	Weak: No sign of book-learning for poor Pooh!	Weak: poor Pooh works hard to "think, think, think" but such efforts are rarely successful; he often has difficulty figuring out how to do the tasks of everyday living	Strong: Pooh usually takes an unconventional point of view in coping with the world
Don Quixote	Strong: Prior to his quest, Don Quixote was respected as a learned man	Weak: Don Quixote's problem-solving skills were exquisitely unsuccessful	Strong: Don Quixote's romantic and nonconformist view of the world was impressive

Character	Academic	Practical	Creative
Your example			
Your example			

What were your examples? Did you notice any patterns in either intellectual strengths or weaknesses of the characters you selected?

Exercise 11.2

CHALLENGING QUESTIONS *Perspective Taking*

As with any complex set of questions, there are a variety of possible answers. The advantages and disadvantages you describe will be based on your perspective on the educational practice under consideration, as well as your understanding of, and experience with, educational systems in general.

Some of the advantages that you might think of include the following: the ability to provide individualized attention to students whose needs might be different from the majority of students; providing students with a "safe" learning environment where their academic abilities are not obviously different from the rest of their peers; and increasing the likelihood that teachers will be able to use teaching methods appropriate to the more closely grouped abilities of the students in their classes.

On the other hand, you might also recognize some of the following disadvantages: students less likely to be academically successful will not be stimulated by their more talented peers, nor exposed to them as peer role models; all students will have limited experience with the true diversity of abilities and may find it difficult later to cope with diverse workplace and social settings; and resources may be unequally and unfairly distributed to the detriment of other groups of students.

As for the values that underlie such practices, you might identify success, education, individual growth, and efficiency. These do not always lead to the same set of actions but can compete and pull people in different directions. For example, strongly supporting the value of education would lead one to strive to provide education for all individuals, whereas valuing efficiency might lead one to want to focus educational resources only where they will "do the most good." Valuing success exclusively might support a practice of educating only academically talented individuals, but valuing the growth of the individual makes providing specialized education designed to build on each individual's unique strengths a priority.

Exercise 11.3

TO RETEST OR NOT TO RETEST? *Scientific Problem Solving*

What is your hypothesis?

In experiments, we try to establish differences between groups. Therefore, an effective hypothesis would be that the use of test-preparation courses leads to a significant gain on a second taking of the GRE.

What is the independent variable?

The independent variable is presence versus absence of test-preparation training.

What is the dependent variable?

The dependent variable is GRE score, or the difference in the GRE score from first testing to second testing.

How will you assign volunteers to test conditions?

Volunteers would have to be assigned randomly to the two conditions: test preparation and no test preparation.

What elements of the experiment will you need to control?
- The amount of time between the original testing and the second testing
- The use of the same form of test for all participants
- The test conditions, which must be similar

Exercise 11.4

WHEN TO TEST *Practical Problem Solving*

There are many possible alternatives. Strong answers will provide a clear rationale for each choice, recognizing that appropriate choices consider the relationships of the individuals involved and the tasks that each person will probably need to be able to accomplish in order to succeed within the context of those relationships.

Exercise 11.5

BRAVE NEW WORLD *Psychological Reasoning*

The five components of creativity listed in your text are: expertise, imaginative thinking skills, a venturesome personality, high intrinsic motivation, and a creative environment.

Given current evidence about personality, it would be reasonable to assume that there is a genetic component to a "venturesome" personality. It is probably also reasonable to think about imaginative thinking skills and intrinsic motivation having some very weak genetic component, as well as environmental components. The other aspects of creativity—expertise and creative environment—are probably almost entirely external or acquired through experience and are therefore best thought of as environmental influences.

If you are serious about wanting to perpetuate a desirable trait that has a genetic component, you will want to control breeding. In this case, one could increase the likelihood of producing children with venturesome personalities and imaginative thinking skills by encouraging (or requiring) those individuals possessing these traits to mate with each other. Another alternative would be to collect the eggs and sperm of the "best individuals" and then to implant the resulting embryo in a suitable host.

Arranging the environment in a suitable fashion can also help encourage the expression of creativity. In order to possess expertise, children will need extensive education in a broad range of subjects. Learning the techniques of imaginative thinking skills will also be important. Parents and teachers may be encouraged to teach children how to recognize patterns, see things from different perspectives and solve problems in a variety of ways (sound familiar?). Making sure that external rewards do not become the focus of work and providing students with supportive relationships should also help develop creative expression to its fullest potential. How would you feel about implementing such a program? Chances are, even if you value creativity and think that it is a desirable trait, you would not want to do everything listed above. Where do you draw the line and why? Discuss your answers with some of your classmates and try to establish a set of guiding principles for encouraging the development of desirable characteristics.

Exercise 11.6

JUST TOO COOL *Creative Problem Solving*

Operational definition: This will vary depending on the target group you wish to define. Chances are good that your definition will include elements of practical intelligence or street smartness: knowing how to solve problems, knowing how to create a positive impression, using language that is current or cutting edge, striving to dress in the most widely endorsed fashion.

Measurement strategy: The measurement strategy for each dimension that defines "cool" would differ. Regardless of the dimension selected, you would need to identify some "cool" judges and require them to adhere to the same criteria that define the dimension. Or perhaps you could develop scenarios in which various alternatives could be rated for the degree of "cool" demonstrated in the choice.

What's difficult? The prior two steps should make it clear that it is hard to come to a consensus about the operationalizing of a concept, let alone developing a strategy for its measurement. Because ideas regarding the definition are likely to be diverse, coming up with a reliable and valid way to measure this dimension may not be very feasible. Many people find the process of making comparative judgments among human beings distasteful, further complicating a very difficult task.

12

ANSWER KEY

Motivation

Exercise 12.1

THEORIES OF MOTIVATION — *Pattern Recognition*

Behavior	Theories	Explanations
A human infant rooting to find the mother's nipple	Instinct theory	This is a reflexive behavior that increases the likelihood of survival.
	Drive reduction theory	Hunger creates an aversive state that the infant attempts to relieve through behaviors that increase the likelihood that the mouth will come in closer contact with a food source.
Getting a glass of water when you are thirsty	Drive reduction theory	Thirst creates an aversive state which the person works to diminish by behaving in ways that reduce the need.
Going for a walk when you are worried or restless	Drive reduction theory	The feeling of restlessness or anxiety creates an aversive state that is relieved with activity or a change of scenery.
	Arousal theory	The walk actually increases arousal, which gives the individual the energy to focus or deal with the cause of the anxiety.
Working on a difficult jigsaw puzzle	Arousal theory	Tackling the difficult task increases the intellectual stimulation of the individual in a way that is rewarding.

Behavior	Theories	Explanations
Studying hard to pass an exam	Drive reduction theory	The exam creates an aversive state of anxiety, which studying relieves.
	Arousal theory	Working hard to learn new material or to do well increases arousal because it is intellectually stimulating.
Crying when hurt or upset	Instinct theory	This is a reflexive behavior that increases the likelihood of survival by drawing the attention of others who could provide aid.
	Drive reduction theory	Physical or psychological distress aversively arouses an individual, who releases the excess energy by crying.
Developing a lasting, intimate relationship	Drive reduction theory	Sexual and reproductive needs build and an individual works to find a way to ensure that those needs can be met easily or conveniently in the future.
	Arousal theory	Long-term, intimate relationships with others are stimulating and therefore provide energy for the individuals involved.

Exercise 12.2

HUMANISTIC HISTORY — *Perspective Taking*

Obviously, we cannot anticipate the specific example you will use to demonstrate that the validity of Maslow's hierarchy of needs is questionable. A good example will describe an individual, or group of individuals, who behave in ways that suggest that their priorities of needs are different from those proposed by Maslow. Some of the examples often used to question his theory include examples of altruism—sacrificing one's safety or life for another—and cultural differences in need priorities. What example did you use? If possible, compare your example with those of your classmates. Can you identify any patterns or similarities in the examples used?

Exercise 12.3

CHICKEN OR EGG? — *Scientific Problem Solving*

The job of an institutional review board is to ensure that all experiments are conducted according to the ethical guidelines of the discipline and institution, and that the participants are protected from undue harm or risk. In this case, there are several critical questions you would need to ask yourself:

- What is the benefit of this research?
- Is the research design appropriate? Is the experiment designed so that the data collected will ethically provide an answer to the research question?
- What are the risks to the participants? If these risks are significant, are they explained clearly to the participants? Are the potential benefits important and likely to justify the risks?

It is important to recognize that risks include more than simply the potential for physical harm. Because of the stigma often associated with homosexuality, there are potential social and emotional risks associated with participating in experiments of this type. In addition, the findings from the research could be used to push a political agenda that ultimately would be unacceptable or harmful to those who had participated.

If you, as an institutional review board member, decide that this research should be funded, you must explain how the research is of benefit and how participants can be protected from harm based on their participation in this research. If you decide not to fund the research in this area, your explanation should demonstrate how and why the risks outweigh the potential benefits. You may also decide that some research in this area seems feasible, while some does not. If this is your position, be as specific as you can about the criteria for funding. What is the dividing line between those experiments that will be funded and those that will not?

Exercise 12.4

THE DIET RIOT — *Practical Problem Solving*

There are several components of the physiology of hunger that you might wish to share with people who are interested in changing their eating behavior and/or weight. Hunger pangs are related to the contractions of an empty stomach (although there are also other factors involved). Using water and fiber to fill the stomach decreases the sensation of hunger pangs. Insulin and glucose are also related to feelings of hunger. Insulin decreases the availability of glucose, and decreases in blood glucose levels increase feelings of hunger. Maintaining a consistent blood glucose level will help decrease hunger sensations. It is interesting to note that body chemistry also affects one's choice of food. Some people crave sweet or starchy food when depressed or anxious. The carbohydrates found in these foods help raise serotonin levels and improve mood. Finally, it will be important to discuss the concept of a set point; the natural weight of an individual that the body works to maintain. When the weight drops below this point, feelings of hunger are triggered and the metabolism is slowed to help recover the lost weight. This set point can be changed by a slow and steady weight loss and by maintaining a realistically lower weight until the body becomes accustomed to its new "normal" weight.

There are also other, practical suggestions you can offer about healthy eating. Because some people are sensitive to external cues for eating, keep food out of sight. If it is not visible, people who are externally cued to eat are less likely to consume food when they are not hungry. Consider raising metabolism by increasing activity. Not only does this help build muscle and increase strength, it helps overcome the tendency for the body to decrease its metabolic rate when losing weight.

Because many individuals trying to lose weight have a negative image of their own bodies, and because such negative perceptions are one factor in developing eating disorders, it would probably be a good idea to share a little information about eating disorders with your clients. Eating disorders are becoming increasingly common as the cultural ideal portrayed in the media becomes more unlike the majority of women. Women who have low self-esteem; a high need to achieve; who come from a competitive and protective family; or have a family history of eating disorders, alcoholism, obesity, and/or depression are at higher risk for developing certain eating disorders. These women should be especially careful with their weight loss goals and plans and should be aware of where to seek help if necessary.

Exercise 12.5

THE WEIGHT-LOSS COUNSELOR — *Psychological Reasoning*

Some possible answers:

Variable 1: Food intake

Question: Approximately how many calories do you consume each day?

Variable 2: Genetic influence

Question: Are other members of your family overweight?

Variable 3: Activity level

Question: How much exercise do you get on a regular basis?

Variable 4: Social influences

Question: Are you likely to eat more when you are alone or when you are in the company of others.

Variable 5: Diet history

Question: Have you ever lost weight and maintained your weight loss successfully in the past?

Variable 6: Physiology

Question: Do you seem to have a set point at which your weight can be more easily maintained?

Exercise 12.6

THE CREATIVE CONSULTANT — *Creative Problem Solving*

Some examples of possible answers:

Motive 1: Hunger

Product name: Dee-Lish

Advertising approach: The new toothpaste could be connected with images of people happily eating food and just as happily brushing their teeth with a toothpaste that claims to taste as good as a banana split.

Motive 2: Pain avoidance

Product name: Heavenly

Advertising approach: The toothpaste itself could have some anesthetic quality to address the challenges of those with sensitive teeth. The scenes would emphasize the relief that could be gained from using the product.

Motive 3: Safety

Product name: Refuge

Advertising approach: This campaign could use dental visits in a mildly arousing depiction of the consequences of bad dental care. The campaign could stress prevention as a security measure. This might be especially effective for parents trying to increase their children's tooth-brushing behavior.

Motive 4: Love

Product name: Glow

Advertising approach: This campaign would target the dating crowd. Choosing not to use "Glow" should be linked to increased risk of not having an active love life.

Motive 5: Esteem

Product name: Peak

Advertising approach: Is there a way to link tooth-brushing behavior with the practices of high-status individuals? Could brushing regularly with this product confer some state of grace not available to other toothpaste users? Perhaps reduced cavities represent a type of hygiene achievement that most people can't manage; if so, a good dental record might confer a sense of being special.

All these approaches have been used to promote oral hygiene products. You may have difficulty choosing one approach over the others. The connection between hunger and toothpaste might be difficult to establish. Pain avoidance connections are tricky; potential buyers perceive them as too threatening, and they may form an uncomfortable connection with the new product. Nevertheless, advertising campaigns derive their success from imaginative approaches to the problem of selling an unexciting product. Do you think any of your approaches would work?

13

ANSWER KEY

Emotions

Exercise 13.1

TOURIST TRAP *Pattern Recognition*

Description of behavior: One thumb is held up while the four fingers of the same hand are tucked into the palm.

Meaning: In North America, this is a sign that things are OK or that a person is hitchhiking. In German bars, this gesture will get you one beer. In Japanese bars, it may get you five. In Nigeria, if you use this gesture while hitchhiking you may be beaten by motorists, who will find your gesture extremely insulting.

Description of behavior: The index finger on the right hand is circling the right ear.

Meaning: In North America, this gesture signifies that you believe the receiver of the message may not be mentally stable. In Argentina, however, this gesture alerts you to the fact that you have a phone call waiting.

Description of behavior: An extended left hand appears to be offering an apple.

Meaning: The sender could be offering the apple as a gesture of friendship. Although this example looks harmless enough, woe to the tourist who uses it in Middle Eastern cultures. To use the left hand to offer anything in this manner, whether food or money, is considered a great offense. Why? Because the left hand is reserved for hygiene and is regarded as "soiled," and it should not be used in social transactions of any kind. Offering presents should be done with the "clean" right hand.

Description of behavior: Eyes are cast downward.

Meaning: In North America, a downcast glance represents a loss of self-esteem or shyness. In Japan and Korea, downcast eyes demonstrate respect.

Description of behavior: Head is moving from side to side in one plane.

Meaning: Head shaking substitutes for a negative response in North America. However, in Bulgaria, Turkey, and Iran, you've said "Yes." In India, you've said "Yes, I am listening."

Description of behavior: Forefinger and thumb are joined to form a circle.

Meaning: In North America, this behavior signals that "everything is OK." However, the gesture is interpreted very differently in other cultures. In France, you have implied that something or someone is worthless. In Japan, you've gestured for "coins." In Malta,

Sardinia, Turkey, Greece, and Italy, you've implied an unfavorable comparison to some female body parts.

Exercise 13.2

FORGET YOUR TROUBLES   *Practical Problem Solving*

It would be impossible to predict all the wishes that might have been listed in this exercise; given this culture, however, it is easy to guess that many wishes were for improving material wealth. Research with lottery winners indicates that the adaptation-level principle holds true: The glow of newly acquired wealth is transient. However, the relative deprivation principle could be invoked to ward off this reaction. To invoke it, all you need do to feel happier about your current circumstances is to remember an earlier time when your resources were more limited. If no such time exists, perhaps you could envision some less fortunate circumstances that could occur. Dwelling on worse-case scenarios will make you feel better, perhaps even happier, for a short period of time.

Exercise 13.3

PINOCCHIO'S LEGACY   *Creative Problem Solving*

Here is just a sampling of some possible outcomes of social behavior if lying prompted a swollen proboscis:

- People would develop a stronger value for honesty under all circumstances.
- People who tend to lie would increase their use of phone and E-mail so that their swelling would not be noticeable.
- People with lying tendencies might learn to speak back-to-back instead of face-to-face.
- We would start using metaphors that are nose-related, such as "honest as your nose is long!"
- A nose wardrobe? Perhaps a series of stylish covers coordinated with your clothing would catch on to hide the problem.
- People might pursue plastic surgery, not to enhance beauty but to alter the natural course of swelling.

Were you able to think of any other possible outcomes?

Exercise 13.4

WHAT IS THIS THING CALLED LOVE?   *Scientific Problem Solving*

Some indicators of falling in love:

    loss of appetite → loss of body weight

    increased eye contract → increased time gazing at target

    increased appetite → gain in body weight

    inability to concentrate → minutes off-task

increased conversation → greater time on the phone or on-line

greater excitement → increased heart flutters

Why isn't the experience uniform?

No one really knows the answer to this one . . . yet.

Exercise 13.5

EXPRESS YOURSELF! *Psychological Reasoning*

Here are some suggestions about when it might be a bad idea to express an emotion:

Fear
- when you are giving a speech in which you are trying to be persuasive
- when expressing fear might communicate to a rival or opponent that you are weak
- when you are trying to model bravery for a younger person

Anger
- when the control of your anger might get away from you
- when there are unwarranted risks attached to expressing anger (e.g., being angry at your boss, who is known for having little patience with complaining employees)
- when your anger might contribute to fomenting irrational or dangerous responses in a group

Sadness
- when there are proactive things you can do to relieve the sadness but choose not to
- when the larger context is a joyous one in which the expression of sadness might ruin or diminish the occasion

Happiness
- when the larger context is a sad occasion in which the expression of joy would be deemed inappropriate

Exercise 13.6

HONESTY IS THE BEST POLICY *Perspective Taking*

Possible answers:

An Owner's Pro-Use Position

Values: Protection of investment and profit

Arguments:
- Screening everyone would lift suspicion from those who don't deserve it.
- Employee morale would improve when the thief was exposed and fired.
- Polygraph testing is widely used in all kinds of American businesses.
- The privacy of all those who were questioned would be protected because no one else would know the results.
- The owner is volunteering to submit to the procedure and to be the first person tested.

An Employee's Anti-Use Position

Value(s): Right to privacy

Arguments:

- Federal laws limit the use of polygraph tests.
- The owner's widespread suspicion of the employees has already been a drain on morale.
- Those who can control the symptoms of arousal could fake the results and could therefore divert suspicion to other employees.
- Employee anxiety about the procedure itself might lead to *false positives*—innocent people who appear to be guilty simply because the procedure makes them highly anxious.

14

ANSWER KEY

Personality

Exercise 14.1

FREUD MEETS MOTHER GOOSE — *Pattern Recognition*

Jack and Jill

Likely developmental stage at fixation: Latency

Justification: The assumption of labor performed with a person of the opposite gender. Initial forays into pairing off are met with danger and physical harm.

Adult personality structure: Freud had little to say about the latent influence on human personality; however, the rhyme might portend difficulties in getting along with the opposite gender.

Three Blind Mice

Likely developmental stage at fixation: Possibly the phallic stage

Justification: The innocent mice encounter a symbolically castrating force. In this case, they lose their tails rather than their genitalia.

Adult personality structure: Freud might suspect that the anxieties sublimated in this rhyme would be manifested in adulthood as struggles about sexuality and gender identification. In this case the strivings of a sexually overactive adult might represent some traumatic experience in the author's phallic development.

Mary, Mary, Quite Contrary

Likely developmental stage at fixation: Anal

Justification: Mary's overconcern with tidiness in her garden.

Adult personality structure: Perhaps the creator of "Mary, Mary" would be characterized by the classic anal-retentive personality: These individuals are preoccupied with order and neatness. Freud could also have made a case for an anal-expulsive personality: These slovenly adults disregard order and thrive on chaos.

Exercise 14.2

MATCHMAKER, MATCHMAKER — *Practical Problem Solving*

a. *Conscientious + Conscientious:* A good match. A tidy house, promises kept.

   Conscientious + Irresponsible: Not a good match. The irresponsible partner will forever be disappointing the conscientious partner. The irresponsible one may feel frustration at constantly having to apologize and make amends and fail at that, too.

   Irresponsible + Irresponsible: A good match. Two irresponsible people may function well together, because neither will have high expectations for themselves or the other person involved.

b. *Stable + Stable:* A good match (but maybe a little boring . . .).

   Stable + Neurotic: Perhaps a good match because the unstable partner can bring some variety and challenge to the relationship, if both the stability and the neuroses aren't extreme.

   Neurotic + Neurotic: Probably not a good idea. Two basically unstable people may not be able to offer each other much support and may feed on each other's worries and fears.

c. *Extravert + Extravert:* An excellent match! The only risk is that two extraverts might compete with each other a bit for the attention spotlight.

   Extravert + Introvert: Only a fair match. The strong social needs of the extravert might feel a bit threatening to the introvert, whose needs are to be more solitary.

   Introvert + Introvert: A good match. Perhaps a little quiet, but a good match!

d. *Open + Open:* A good match. These two individuals will spend all their discretionary income on new adventures and travels.

   Open + Closed: Not a good match. The stimulus-seeking adventurer may have to pursue activities without the recliner-bound partner.

   Closed + Closed: A good match. In extreme cases, they can simply sit and look at each other; however, neither might make a good client, because registering for the service would be an adventure.

e. *Agreeable + Agreeable:* A good match. This couple should be flexible enough in times of difficulty to find some common ground and celebrate many anniversaries.

   Agreeable + Hostile: Some possibility for partnership, if the agreeable partner can compensate for the angrier, hostile stance of the other.

   Hostile + Hostile: Not a good idea. This is a combustible combination that is not likely to be very satisfying for either partner.

Exercise 14.3

PSEUDOSCIENTIFIC PERSONALITY — *Creative Problem Solving*

The Stock Spiel

The stock spiel needs to appeal to generalities about personality. The spiel should not be so specific that it enhances your chance of being wrong, nor should it be so negative that it will alienate the person whose character you are trying to describe. The following examples, adapted from astrological predictions, can serve this purpose well:

- You are hardworking, although you sometimes labor without getting attention from others who should notice your work.
- You are generous, sometimes giving when you can ill afford the gift.
- You really enjoy a lively party, but you may find more pleasure in a quiet evening at home.
- You appreciate nature and are surprised at how others take nature for granted.
- You've had some big disappointments in life, but you are able to bounce back without much delay.
- You sometimes feel frustrated by the foolish choices of others, but you are usually patient in the face of this frustration.

Would anyone reject these descriptions as characteristic of their own behavior? If such descriptions are universal, how effective can they be?

Inferences From Physical Cues

The following examples indicate the kinds of cues that would help you determine other "facts" to add to the personality description.

A wedding or engagement ring can serve as the basis for describing challenges in a relationship with a "significant other."

Type of clothes may suggest whether the individual has a formal or casual style; of course, uniforms provide even stronger hints about the kinds of frustration the individual may encounter professionally.

Nail and hand grooming may offer some tips about the person's profession or hobby.

Physical traits, such as gray hair, wrinkles, or acne, can offer hints about particular kinds of stresses that correlate with developmental stages of life.

The format of a check used to pay for your service can hint about values or style. For example, is the check computer-generated, or does it have frolicking kittens displayed prominently?

The type of transportation, especially the type of car, can suggest general aspects of socioeconomic class.

Exercise 14.4

YOU CAN'T CHEAT AN HONEST MAN *Scientific Problem Solving*

There are many complications in research of this type. Most come from the number and types of factors for which the researcher must control, but some come from the topic itself. Most people have a great desire to appear honest, and so they do not act the same way during an experiment (when they know someone is watching) as they might in "real life." An individual's need to demonstrate socially desirable traits can make it difficult to examine traits that *aren't* socially desirable—like *not* telling the truth. Other difficulties include differentiating between when someone is telling a lie and when someone is mistaken or just plain wrong (naturalistic observation) and manipulating internal factors and factors about the other person (laboratory studies). What other complications did you think of?

Factors that might influence honesty can be loosely grouped into three categories: things about you, things about the other person(s) involved, and the situation.

Internal factors: Emotional state—fear, anger

Factors about the other person(s): Relationship to you—stranger, friend, family

Situational factors:

> number of people present
> risk involved in telling a lie
> risk involved in telling the truth
> impact of lie
> duration of harm

Exercise 14.5

RORSCHACH'S FATE — *Psychological Reasoning*

Your answer should reflect some sensitivity to what you have at risk by agreeing to a Rorschach exam. If you have little to risk, it may be more reasonable to allow conclusions from a projective test to contribute to a personality evaluation. However, as the risk increases, for example when custody of children is at stake in a court battle, it may be unwise to submit to a projective test. It is also a bad idea to have projective tests be the sole source of a personality evaluation. If you have little choice in how an evaluation will proceed, at the very least, you (and your attorney) should be aware of the scientifically questionable research support available on Rorschach testing.

Exercise 14.6

IS IT HOPELESS—OR NOT? — *Psychological Perspective Taking*

Freud's belief was that personality is determined. In fact, Freud believed that personality patterns may be fixed as early as age 6.

Skinner also believed that the behaviors that constitute personality are determined. However, he stressed that the causes are strictly environmental.

Rogers believed in a nondeterministic view. He believed human development potential is strong at any age if the conditions are suitably nourishing.

Maslow also was nondeterministic. His humanistic background supported the optimistic view that people can change if conditions are favorable.

15

ANSWER KEY

Psychological Disorders

Exercise 15.1

AND THE WINNER IS . . . *Pattern Recognition*

Some performances and their corresponding disorders

Disorder	Performance	Film
Schizophrenia	Jessica Lange	*Frances*
	Winona Ryder	*Girl, Interrupted*
Antisocial personality	Jack Nicholson	*One Flew Over the Cuckoo's Nest*
	Michael Douglas	*Greed*
	Patty McCormick	*The Bad Seed*
Borderline personality	Glenn Close	*Fatal Attraction*
Mental retardation	Cliff Robertson	*Charly*
	Juliette Lewis	*The Other Sister*
Multiple personality	Joanne Woodward	*The Three Faces of Eve*
	Sally Field	*Sybil*
Autism	Dustin Hoffman	*Rain Man*

Exercise 15.2

ALL I NEED IS AN AGENT! *Creative Problem Solving*

The *DSM-IV* is ripe with possibilities from which you might select material for your creative writing exercise. It is probably easy to see how challenging life might become for a person having to make accommodations around the symptoms described for any of the disorders you might have selected. Keep in mind as you develop your plot lines that the challenges are not isolated with the individual who gets the diagnosis. Families and friends often feel victimized by the existence of serious psychological difficulties. This fact might help you develop a rich story line that you can share with others in class.

Exercise 15.3

THE END   ***Practical Problem Solving***

Questions

The following are examples of questions that could be helpful in evaluating the severity of depression.

- Have you ever felt like this before?
- How long have you been down?
- What kinds of things are bothering you?
- Are you religious?
- What are you hopeful about?
- Are you physically healthy?
- Are you suicidal?
- Do you have a plan?

The list of questions is relatively easy to generate but depression and suicide are surprisingly difficult to discuss. Our reluctance to pursue these topics may be linked to the fear that we could implant a suggestion if a person has not considered suicide. This fear is probably unwarranted. Most depressed people feel a sense of relief when the topic is introduced and is followed by assistance in securing the services of a mental health professional.

Risk Analysis

Morgan is suicidal and you correctly identify his intentions.
Advantages: You can help him get treatment, and his depression may be alleviated.
Risks: He may initially be upset with you.
Morgan is not suicidal and you correctly identify his intentions.
Advantages: You will have avoided a confrontation that would have exposed your worrying nature.
Risks: You may lose the opportunity to show support for a friend who, although not suicidal, may be suffering.

If you confront Morgan and verify his suicidal intention, you are correct. This step can lead to professional intervention and the possibility that he can get treatment to keep him safe. If you fail to confront him and he is not suicidal, there is no loss. Both of these conditions represent "hits" in decision theory terminology.

Morgan is suicidal and you don't correctly identify his intentions.
Advantages: There is very little, if any, advantage in this situation.
Risks: You could lose your friend, and you could be left with a lifetime of regret for not acting on your impulse.
Morgan is not suicidal and you don't correctly identify his intentions.
Advantage: You demonstrate your support and concern for a friend.
Risk: You may appear foolish or overconcerned.

The "misses" have fairly serious consequences. If you confront Morgan and he intends not to harm himself, your risk lies in his interpretation of your confrontation. He may be touched by your concern, thereby deepening your friendship. Or he may be alienated by your overconcern, causing strain in your relationship.

Far worse, however, is the "miss" in which you ignore your accurate suspicions. If you do not act on your fears and Morgan commits suicide, you not only will have lost a friend but also may be saddled with regret about the path that you didn't take.

So what would you do in this situation? Reviewing these options may help you determine the safest course of action when confronted with the serious depression of a friend or a loved one. Perhaps the best way to reduce your own regret involves proposing the possibility of suicidal intentions to your friend when you feel worried about her state of mind. If you are wrong, the risk will be small. A friend with hurt or irritated feelings at least has the opportunity to get over feeling disturbed. On the other hand, a seriously depressed friend may not be around for too long if you overlook the opportunity to demonstrate your sincere concern and your support.

Exercise 15.4

I'M JUST NOT MYSELF TODAY — *Scientific Problem Solving*

Although the evidence from PET-scan activity on the brains of persons with multiple personality disorder is compelling, there is a flaw. The challenge involves the absence of appropriate control subjects in the original design. Apparently, when normal individuals are asked to complete an activity during a PET scan but also to try to do so pretending to be someone else, their brain patterns show differences that parallel those of individuals with multiple personality disorder undergoing the same task. At the very least this finding suggests that the capacity to manipulate different areas in the brain may be under voluntary control. We still don't have good evidence to suggest that different patterns of brain activation contribute to multiple personality disorder. It will be very interesting to monitor what happens in this controversial area as we apply emerging technologies to the problem of establishing the validity of multiple personality disorder.

Exercise 15.5

THE LABELING CONTROVERSY — *Psychological Reasoning*

The Rosenhan study is a valid test of the problems associated with labeling.

Supporting arguments:
- There are real cases of individuals who have been misdiagnosed and who have experienced difficulties getting out of institutions.
- The kind of symptoms reported by the pseudopatients were realistic for patients who ask for emergency treatment at in-patient settings.
- The pseudopatients acted normally after admission. How closely could the hospital staff have been watching them if they did not detect this normal pattern?
- The pseudopatients took notes about their experience. How can hospital staff justify not attending to this behavior as a possible source of treatment information?
- All pseudopatients reported that they were treated in similar ways, despite the fact that they were in different hospital settings.

Can you think of other arguments that support Rosenhan's conclusions?

The Rosenhan study is not a valid test of the problems associated with labeling.

Supporting arguments:
- Expectations of hospital staff members are based on their collective experiences. Clients who report auditory hallucinations are likely to fit the patterns associated with schizophrenia, a condition that usually warrants long-term, intensive care.
- The ethics of the research designer are questionable since the pseudopatients are presenting a pattern that is rarely seen.
- Can anyone verify that the pseudopatients actually acted normally while they were hospitalized?
- It may be wiser to err on the side of greater protection for individuals whose behavior is questionable than to take risks by denying treatment to those whose symptoms suggest that they need care.

Can you think of other arguments that could be used as criticisms of Rosenhan's conclusions?

Exercise 15.6

WHY Y2K? *Psychological Perspective Taking*

The Y2K dilemma offers us an opportunity to apply historical perspective taking to diagnostic practice.

a. Most diagnoses of excessive Y2K responsiveness would fall in the paranoid personality disorder or obsessive-compulsive personality disorder. You may want to review the characteristics of these problems in your text to see the relationship between stockpiling and these Axis III dysfunctions.

b. The nondisordered person probably found the predicted disasters laughable and took no steps to prepare for the predicted worldwide disruption. The mildly disturbed person thought the predictions would be wrong but probably put in a supply of water and may have celebrated the new year at home "just in case." The moderately disturbed person laid in sufficient supplies to recover from the disaster and probably tried to read about the nature of the predicted problems. The seriously disturbed person focused on Y2K when making business decisions; this person stockpiled supplies and probably shifted resources to safer places to avoid complications that computer malfunctions would produce. The extremely disturbed person demonstrated "monomania" as Y2K concerns became central to his or her waking life prior to the start of the new year. Significant energies were devoted to stockpiling, reading expert predictions, making plans for recovery, and telling friends.

Based on this continuum and the reality that none of the serious predictions came to pass, where would you draw the line of diagnosable disorder on the continuum?

c. Had the Y2K predictions come true, then those who would have ignored the "obvious" signs of impending doom could have been diagnosed as suffering from hysteria. Of course, this assumes that there would have been a viable social/medical structure left to do the diagnosing!

ANSWER KEY

Therapy

Exercise 16.1

HOW DOES THAT MAKE YOU FEEL? *Pattern Recognition*

Statement	Options
1. "Tell me about your earliest memories from childhood."	d. Freudian therapy
2. "What were the consequences that happened after you punched your boss?"	f. Behavior therapy
3. "Rank order the things that frighten you from 'least' to 'most'."	j. Systematic desensitization
4. "Let's explore how your role as a daughter, mother, and wife might influence the problem."	e. Feminist therapy
5. "Have you been having recurring dreams?"	i. Jungian therapy
6. "In what ways do you think you have fallen short of your ideals?"	h. Humanistic therapy
7. "Pretend that your grandmother is sitting in the chair over there and tell her how you feel."	c. Gestalt therapy
8. "You have developed a very powerful mental set that you are a loser."	b. Cognitive therapy
9. "If you can refrain from losing your temper, you'll get two red stars."	a. Token economy
10. Let's try to figure out how your feelings of inferiority might be linked to your family."	g. Adlerian therapy

Exercise 16.2

| EVEN DOMESTIC ENGINEERS GET THE BLUES | *Practical Problem Solving* |

Psychoanalysis

This framework would focus on the contributions of early childhood experiences and the way they shape adult behavior. The therapist would focus on revealing unconscious forces and reducing neurotic choices. The advantage of this framework is the benefit gained by focusing on patterns that have developed through life. The main disadvantages are probably the expense of such intensive therapy as well as the potential for antifemale bias in the treatment.

Ellen could find herself committed to long-term intervention to address the unconscious conflicts that influence her adult choices. Her current unhappiness in the family would be seen as an extension of early fixations and losses in her own development.

Person-Centered Therapy

This treatment approach would focus on the quality of self-concept and self-esteem. The therapist would try hard to listen and reflect the main issues, offering unconditional positive regard about the difficulties expressed by the client. For individuals whose distress is the result of diminished self-esteem, this approach is well tailored. For individuals who seek more direction from therapists, this approach will be frustrating.

Ellen's general distress may be linked to issues of low self-esteem. The therapeutic intervention would focus on her definition of what feels unsatisfying in life. The therapist would offer reassurance but minimal direction in designing a new path for Ellen.

Aversive Conditioning

Aversive conditioning addresses excesses in behavior by reconditioning pleasurable but undesirable activities to take on new aversive qualities. This approach is best implemented when individuals experience disturbing impulses as the source of their pain. The specific conditioning process is cost-effective, but it requires fairly well-defined symptoms to be effective.

Ellen's symptoms may not be specific enough to embark on a counterconditioning procedure. Her unhappiness feels diffused, so it may be difficult to implement this procedure with her.

Cognitive Behavior Therapy

The primary focus on this intervention is to examine the relationship between cognitive interpretations and behavior. The therapist examines the client's expectations and the learning experiences that encouraged the development of those expectations. The therapist may assign homework to help the client to rehearse different patterns of behavior. This approach has clear advantages for those with strong motivation; however, there may be some disadvantage if no distortion in perception or cognition can be identified.

Ellen's sense of self-defeat lends itself to this framework. The therapist would try to determine what her self-image is and how she arrived at such a low point.

Drug Therapy

As the name indicates, this type of therapy focuses on relieving symptoms by prescribing medication. It is used for a variety of conditions that present symptoms of anxiety or depression. When the client and medication are matched carefully, relief of symptoms can be quite rapid, even dramatic. However, there are some risks of long-term dependence and possible side effects. Medication can be expensive, but so can long-term therapy when undertaken without the benefit of medication that could be helpful.

Ellen would probably be a good candidate for medication to relieve her depressive symptoms.

Family Therapy

Family therapy focuses on the family as a system. Sometimes the symptoms of one family member can signify serious problems in the family system. Bringing the whole system into the therapy situation can uncover and heal problematic dynamics that are likely to affect more than just the target client. Families can be stabilized, thereby reaching new levels of understanding that prevent further damage to family members. However, some disadvantage lies in defining mental health concerns as a family systems issue when the origin of the problems may be much more individual.

It is unclear from the case description how much of Ellen's distress is the result of her role in her family. However, family dynamics are certainly influenced by the amount of strain manifested by one of the key caretakers in the family.

Electroconvulsive Shock Therapy

Shock treatments are still used in situations where depression is unrelenting and does not respond to less severe treatments. Relief from symptoms is not guaranteed, but if it occurs, it is rapid. The significant risks of memory loss accompanying this therapy have led to protests by many former patients who have felt damaged by this intervention.

Ellen's distress does not warrant such severe intervention at this time. If multiple interventions are unsuccessful, shock might be considered. However, it is usually reserved as a last resort.

Which framework would you select for Ellen?

Based on the information available in Ellen's case study, we can eliminate aversive conditioning, psychoanalysis, and electroconvulsive shock therapy. Each of the remaining therapies—person-centered, cognitive-behavior, drug, and family—could make meaningful contributions to relieving her depressive symptoms. Each therapy offers a unique approach to defining and treating her symptoms.

Exercise 16.3

THERE MUST BE 50 WAYS TO LEAVE YOUR SHRINK — *Creative Problem Solving*

Below are several possible indicators that might help you determine that it is time to fly solo. How do these compare with the five alternatives you generated?

- Other people recognize that "there is something *different* about you."
- Other people don't recognize that "there is something different about you."
- You find yourself scrambling for things to talk about in therapy.
- You run out of funding.
- You find yourself quoting your therapist too regularly in social gatherings.
- You develop greater patience for human frailty.
- You have a strong sense of *déjà vu* in the treatment room.

- You know everyone in the waiting room by name (including their diagnoses and prognoses).
- You don't wonder about what your therapist would want you to do when confronted with a personal problem.
- You no longer have the impulse to call your therapist and brag when something goes well.
- You can comfortably disagree with your therapist without fear of reprisal or rejection.
- Your therapist falls asleep in session.
- *You* fall asleep in session.

Exercise 16.4

OUT, DAMNED SPOT! — *Scientific Problem Solving*

What is your hypothesis?

Your new intervention produces faster and more effective relief than is obtained with other known interventions for compulsive hand-washing or with no treatment at all.

What is your independent variable?

Type of therapy (your new treatment versus one or more other treatments versus a no-treatment control group).

How will you assign subjects to treatment conditions?

Random assignment among the treatment and control conditions will help eliminate alternative explanations. Perhaps the subjects could also be matched for type and severity of problem.

How will you measure your dependent variable?

By the frequency and intensity of anxiety attacks, as indicated by the number of episodes of hand-washing.

What other elements will you need to control in order to rule out alternative hypotheses?

You will need to ensure that the participants receive no other treatment that might pose an alternative explanation for symptom reduction. Creating a standard environment for the duration of the study would also clarify the role of the independent variable.

If all proceeded as planned and you obtained the results you intended, would your study offer proof of the superiority of your treatment?

No. Psychologists generally avoid the notion of *proof* in connection with experiments about human behavior. The constraints of the experimental format limit the scope of our conclusions. In this case, your study *demonstrates* superiority over the other treatment conditions, but it does not prove it.

Exercise 16.5

NOT-SO-CLEVER HANS *Psychological Reasoning*

If you wanted to design an effective outcome study on treatment effectiveness, here are the variables that might be pertinent:

1. How similar were the clients' psychological disturbances?
2. What was the length of treatment for the problem?
3. How were therapy dropouts classified? (In Eysenck's original study, dropouts were assumed to be and counted as "unimproved.")
4. What was the therapeutic orientation of the therapists?
5. Who was paying for treatment?
6. How experienced were the therapists?
7. How motivated were the clients to pursue change?
8. How satisfied were the clients with their treatment?
9. At what point was the measurement of symptom reduction completed?
10. Who offered the report of symptom reduction—the client, the therapist, or a third party?

As you can see from the number of variables that can complicate good controlled observation, producing a definitive outcome study is a challenging research problem.

Exercise 16.6

WHO'S GOT THE CHECK? *Perspective Taking*

Arguments against equal access/improved funding:

1. Equal access in the form of a national health care plan would prove to be enormously expensive and taxpayers cannot afford this kind of burden.
2. If we provide increased mental health support, we undercut the will of the individual to solve his or her own problems.
3. This kind of system might be easy to abuse for malingerers (i.e., people who are not really ill but attempt to exploit circumstances by pretending to be ill).
4. The effectiveness of therapy hasn't been sufficiently proven.
5. We already provide sufficient access to mental health care through community centers.
6. Increased access may not motivate individuals who need help to find their way into good mental health care.
7. I've never needed therapy so I think it is wasteful to have to pay for coverage I am unlikely to use.
8. The effects of therapy may make people too soft to survive in a difficult world.

Arguments in support of equal access/improved funding:

1. Improved access to mental health care may not cost more because earlier attention may reduce the severity of disorders and the length of treatment required.
2. Nearly everyone suffers mental health strain at some point, so coverage is reasonable because it parallels other physical health problems covered by insurance.
3. There is sufficient scientific documentation of the effectiveness of therapy.

4. People do not have any control over the conditions that produce severe disorder; a humane society takes care of those who fall behind.
5. Equal access to mental health care might reduce the stigma attached to seeking care and encourage those who need it to take advantage.
6. Good therapists can identify malingerers and address the problems that might cause them to malinger.
7. Although there are services available to those without resources, the quality of care may be questionable because most services of this type are currently underfunded.
8. Therapy should instruct a client in how to become more self-sufficient, which should strengthen rather than weaken the client's character.

17

ANSWER KEY

Stress and Health

Exercise 17.1

BETWEEN A ROCK AND A HARD PLACE — *Pattern Recognition*

Going to the Dentist to Have an Aching Tooth Repaired

Type of conflict: Approach-avoidance

Your stress-intensity rating: This, of course, is unique to you. No attempt will be made here to predict this rating.

Choosing Between Chocolate-Chocolate Chip and Rocky Road Ice Cream

Type of conflict: Approach-approach

Discovering That Your New and Very Attractive Dating Partner Has Bad Breath

Type of conflict: Approach-avoidance

Choosing Between a 7 A.M. and 8 P.M. Class

Type of conflict: Avoidance-avoidance

Deciding Between a One-Week Vacation at DisneyWorld and a One-Week Camping Trip in the Mountains

Type of conflict: Approach-approach

Choosing Between Breast Removal and Chemotherapy After a Diagnosis of Breast Cancer

Type of conflict: Avoidance-avoidance

Selecting One of Two Highly Rated Colleges That Have Admitted You

Type of conflict: Approach-approach

As a Vegetarian, Being Asked Whether You Want Steak or Ribs

Type of conflict: Avoidance-avoidance

Deciding Whether to Buy a Low-Priced, Beautiful Used Car That Needs a Major Repair on Its Engine

Type of conflict: Approach-avoidance

Having Plastic Surgery to Correct a Bump on the Bridge of Your Nose

Type of conflict: Approach-avoidance

Exercise 17.2

HEALTHY LIVING   *Perspective Taking*

As a person who tends toward health, you see this as a challenge and opportunity for personal growth. With children going into college, you know the extra money will come in handy, and you have always thought you could do this job well. You discuss the pros and cons with your entire family, and many of your friends, and you, your children, and husband sit down to plan out exactly what it would take to get everyone where they are supposed to be and to make sure all the work around the house gets done. During the two weeks when you are thinking and discussing your options, you continue with your normal lifestyle. You still take your evening walk every night after dinner and you spend time on the weekends with friends.

On the other hand, you may see this promotion as a problem; a threat to your current comfortable lifestyle. You could use the extra money, of course, but the travel seems like an insurmountable obstacle. After all, the kids have after-school activities and events and there is no way your husband can manage everything while you are gone. You don't want to ask your family if they are willing to make this sacrifice, so you spend a lot of time by yourself, thinking about how you might make it work. You also spend time wondering what will happen if you can't do the job as well as you think you can. After all, you've never done it before, and maybe you don't have the skills you think you do. During this two-week contemplation period, you are more quiet than usual, forgoing your usual activities, and comforting yourself with home-cooked pies and desserts.

Exercise 17.3

ENHANCING IMMUNE FUNCTION   *Scientific Problem Solving*

There are a variety of extraneous variables which you could try to control. One of the primary concerns would be the individual's previous experience with medication. In order to test your hypothesis, individuals would have needed to have successful experiences taking oral medication in the past. This would establish the pairing between taking pills and increased immune function. Another concern would be making sure that the individuals taking the placebo in their coffee were as convinced that they were taking medication as the individuals taking pills. If they suspect that they are not receiving the medication being tested, then they will probably not follow through with the regimen, and you will lose your comparison group. You would also be interested in the more "normal" extraneous variables like age and the severity of the illness.

If the two placebo groups are different, then you might conclude that immune enhancement could be classically conditioned through the pairing of the biochemical effects of certain medications with the actions of taking the medication. However, you would not be able to draw any conclusions about other effects such pairing would have on the person's long-term health. That would require a different and more involved set of experiments and longitudinal studies.

Placebo groups—groups of people who think they are getting the treatment being tested, but who are given a neutral substance to compare their performance with those who do receive the real treatment—are frequently used to demonstrate the effectiveness of a given medication or treatment. Such methods are often the only way to determine the effectiveness of new medications and treatments or to compare their effectiveness with other, more established procedures. The use of such groups comes under debate, however, because it means that some of the participants do not receive treatments that are potentially helpful and may be denied an opportunity to overcome their barriers to a healthy life. Even when the placebo group receives the real medication once its effectiveness has been demonstrated, some people argue that this delay is unethical. They believe that any potentially helpful treatment should be offered to all. What do you think about this issue? Do you think the benefits of using a placebo group outweighs the potential harm or do you think that "proving" the effectiveness of a treatment should take second place to offering potential help to individuals who need it?

Exercise 17.4

HEALTHY EXECUTIVES *Practical Problem Solving*

A strong stress management program will include opportunities for aerobic exercise, relaxation, and development of social support networks. In this type of environment, on-site programs would probably be the most effective because the employees don't have the time to go elsewhere to participate. For the same reason, the exercise programs should be short (maybe 30 minutes) and offered frequently during the day and every day of the week. This would increase the likelihood that employees could find times that fit their schedules, even if those schedules changed from day to day or week to week. There should also be opportunities for the employees to learn simple relaxation techniques that could be performed at their desks or in their offices. Some of this information could be handed out in the form of brochures and pamphlets, and brief classes or in-office sessions could be used for quick demonstrations of the techniques. For those who have the time and interest, biofeedback might be an option, but in this fast-paced environment it is probably too time-intensive to be successful. There are multiple ways in which employees could be encouraged to develop support networks. Simply taking part in one of the classes may provide people with an opportunity to converse and form new friendships. Hosting lunchtime discussions on various topics might also provide people with a chance to get together and talk about common interests. One possibility that would allow people to talk about problems related to work is to set up a mentoring program that pairs new employees with more experienced individuals. There is a multitude of possibilities; the important thing is to recognize the need for all three components.

Working with teachers would be very different from working with investment executives. Teachers have a much more predictable schedule with larger blocks of time potentially available for programs or classes. It might make more sense to offer exercise classes after school, three days a week, for example. You could expect more people to attend each class, and the classes themselves could serve as social groups. Teachers often work in groups or teams and may already have social networks in place. Instead of working to help them develop new networks, you might spend more time helping them identify and use the networks they already have in place. Relaxation techniques would need to be more suited for the public setting of the classroom or teachers' lounge rather than the privacy of an office. Shrugging shoulders or turning one's head from side to side would probably be okay; lying on the floor and lifting one's legs over one's head would probably not be okay. It might be more reasonable to offer biofeedback to this group than to the executives; the equipment and space might be more readily available in a school setting than in an investment office. What other differences did you think of?

Exercise 17.5

STEP ON THE GAS — *Psychological Reasoning*

Your answer will depend on the particular stressful situation you describe. Regardless of the situation, however, you should be able to identify and articulate the three stages Selye proposed. The first is the alarm reaction, in which the sympathetic nervous system is suddenly activated by the detection of the stressor. You should be able to identify the point at which you first identified the stressor and your immediate physiological reaction. During the second phase you cope with the stressor, and the sympathetic nervous system remains aroused to provide energy and protection against illness. Perhaps you spent a couple of weeks without much sleep while you made arrangements for a funeral or stayed with a sick friend and worked a full-time job. The final stage, exhaustion, occurs when the body's energy is depleted. During this stage your resistance to illness is diminished and energy levels are low. Maybe you had the experience of getting sick during Christmas vacation after a week spent studying all night for finals.

In terms of minimizing the negative effects of such experiences, knowing about the final stage of lowered resistance might be the most helpful. By recognizing that you will be more susceptible to disease or depression during this time, you could arrange to get some extra sleep, take vitamins, or have friends stop by to encourage and support you. Eating healthy foods and getting sleep during the second stage might also help by reducing your body's need to draw upon reserves of strength and lessening the exhaustion that follows.

Exercise 17.6

THE GAME OF LIFE — *Creative Problem Solving*

Again, your answer will depend on how you perceive the events listed. No matter which events you selected, however, the impact of the catastrophic event will be different if it occurs when you are 8 years old instead of when you are an adult. Predicting exactly how the experience will be different is difficult because of the great variation among individuals. Although an adult has more responsibilities and more decisions to make, adults also have more coping skills and strategies. An 8 year old is old enough to understand what is happening but generally not experienced enough to have developed successful ways of dealing with the event in question. Because the child may not have the capacity to see the challenge instead of the threat, and because personal health habits are not fully developed, the 8 year old may be more likely to be ill. On the other hand, children are less aware of consequences of events and actions and may not recognize the seriousness of the event in the same way as the adult. In this case, the adult is more likely to be ill.

ANSWER KEY

Social Psychology

Exercise 18.1

PRIDE AND PREJUDICES *Pattern Recognition*

These answers are uniquely your own.

Exercise 18.2

DEAR ABBY *Practical Problem Solving*

Regardless of how clever or poignant your letter as Abby's substitute may be, your advice to the lovelorn is likely to have touched on the following principles:

Proximity

Research indicates that proximity breeds liking. Therefore, your advice should reflect stronger attempts to put Worried in closer proximity to his beloved. Since they attend different universities, he might consider transferring. Alternatively, he could increase his letter writing and phone calling to simulate his presence. Perhaps you can think of other ways to enhance his presence in her life—the more creative the better.

Physical Attractiveness

Anyone aspiring to a serious emotional relationship spends time attempting to be as attractive a stimulus as possible. Part of the challenge in this simple advice, however, is that people differ in what they find attractive. Therefore, it may be useful to advise Worried to do some research on the tastes and preferences of his beloved. She may be wild about beards or turned off by extra weight. If he knows her preferences, he could tailor his energies to enhance attraction.

Similarity

You might advise Worried to find out more about his beloved's interests and leisure pursuits. What does she like to do? What interests does this couple have in common? What shared interests might create stimulating times together in the future? What could they learn from each other?

Arousal

A date to a horror movie or participating in some other highly arousing activity could help Worried in his campaign. In the presence of such activities, he could come to symbolize both excitement, indicated by the stimulating choice, and safety, reinforced by hugs, reassurance, and encouragement.

Equity

The principle of equity suggests that we tend to express our liking in relationships in which power feels fairly distributed. This suggests that Worried needs to carefully gauge his campaign so that he will not overwhelm his beloved but will offer some mild incentives to increase her involvement.

Self-Disclosure

Self-disclosure also needs to feel equivalent if the relationship is to feel balanced. When one partner shares too much too soon, the act can frighten and overwhelm the other person. On the other hand, sharing too little may cause alienation if it projects a remote quality. Worried would be well advised to show some restraint in his feelings until he has greater confidence that his beloved's feelings are similar.

Evaluate your comfort level in serving as Abby's substitute.

This exercise concludes by asking you to consider the emotional consequence of using psychology to influence the behavior of others. Advising the lovelorn may have been easy for you. Or you may have felt uncomfortable about the degree of manipulation inherent in applying the principles of psychology to promote affection. Although control of behavior is often cited as a fundamental goal of psychology, many circumstances may prompt ethical concerns that limit psychology's applications.

Exercise 18.3

BUT MY TEACHER *MADE* ME DO IT! *Creative Problem Solving*

Regardless of the norm you and your partner choose to violate, your description of the behavior that you attempted should be free from interpretation. What exactly did you do? What was the consequence? What was the context?

Attribution theory suggests that you (as the actor) will blame *external* forces (this assignment or your teacher) as the reason you broke the social rules. In contrast, the observer is likely to blame your unexpected behavior of your undesirable traits (e.g., being crazy, rude, etc.), creating an *internal* attribution for action. This distinction between the tendencies of actors and observers in explaining action is called the *fundamental attribution error.*

Exercise 18.4

HOW CAN I HELP? *Scientific Problem Solving*

Variables that might influence the decision to loan class notes include:

- timing of request (e.g., immediately after class has taken place vs. later)
- evidence of requester's disability (e.g., arm cast, crutches)
- gender of person making request
- proximity to exam
- presence or absence of incentive (e.g., promise to return favor)

proximity in seating

depth of prior acquaintance

Select one variable and work with the following questions to develop an experimental design on altruistic behavior:

A possible hypothesis regarding "class note loaning behavior" is: Factor X (your selected dimension) increases agreement to loan class notes in college populations.

Participants in the study would be: College students

The dependent variable would be: The participant's decision to loan or refrain from loaning the requested class notes

A possible description of the procedure, including any elements that you would attempt to control, would address the following issues: This dimension depends on the variable you have selected to manipulate as the independent variable, but everything else must be standardized if you are able to state with confidence that any differences in results were caused by the independent variable.

What independent variable would you be testing and why does this variable appeal to you? Did you select an independent variable similar to the one in the brainstorming list above or another factor?

Do you think the experiment would confirm your hypothesis? Some independent variables simply may not produce a robust enough impact to create a difference in the behavior of your experimental and control groups. What supports your level of confidence about your selected experiment?

Exercise 18.5

FOR THE SAKE OF THE CHILDREN — *Psychological Reasoning*

In each of the examples below, we offer a few suggestions; you may have been able to generate many other ideas related to the problem of reducing violence in children's schools.

1. Metal detectors at the school entrances:
   a. Related psychological concepts: signal detection, conformity, obedience to authority
   b. Positive criticism: provides a sense of security for students who are not tempted to bring guns to school; challenges students who intend to bring guns to school to be more creative at smuggling them
   c. Negative criticism: expensive and oppressive
   d. Predicted success: what is your opinion?

2. The requirement to wear school uniforms:
   a. Related psychological concepts: social stigma, conformity, obedience to authority, physical attraction through similarity
   b. Positive criticism: reduces the sense of competition among students on the basis of looks; reduces financial pressures for parents to provide their children with the most popular clothing; reduces the grounds on which students can be harassed for failure to conform to popular standards
   c. Negative criticism: reduces individual expression; superficial approach to reducing harassment of individual students
   d. Predicted success: what is your opinion?

3. Sensitivity training built into the curriculum:
    a. Related psychological concepts: empathy training, interdependence, appreciation of diversity
    b. Positive criticism: provides for safer expression of individual differences; encourages students to understand the consequences of their actions
    c. Negative criticism: may appeal only to a selected portion of the population of students; may be too superficial to address profoundly disturbed individuals in the population
    d. Predicted success: what is your opinion?

4. Holding parents accountable for the violent actions of their children:
    a. Related psychological concepts: scapegoating, attribution
    b. Positive criticism: might encourage parents to pay more attention to children who are showing signs of difficult adjustment
    c. Negative criticism: parents are not the only influences on their children's choices of personal expression
    d. Predicted success: what is your opinion?

Exercise 18.6

PEOPLE WERE STUPID BACK THEN — *Perspective Taking*

The thoughts and feelings of the subjects in Milgram's original study are relatively easy to describe. With each successive step in Milgram's procedure, their anxiety and confusion mount. The participants begin the experience believing they are about to undergo a demonstration in learning; they complete the experience with, at the very least, some concern that they may have harmed the other participant. Even Milgram was surprised by the degree to which the intensity of the situation encouraged obedience to authority.

How did the setting contribute?

The laboratory in which Milgram's demonstration was conducted was organized to promote maximum credibility. The institution at which the demonstration was originally run was Yale University, one of the most prestigious universities in the United States.

How did the behavior of the learner contribute?

The learner, actually the experimenter's confederate, also enhanced credibility of the experimental manipulation. He gave no indication of being in league with the experimenter and convincingly acted the part of an unlucky volunteer with heart problems, compromised by his random assignment as the learner.

How did the emotional state of the true subject (the "teacher") contribute?

In most experiments, volunteers feel some nervousness at the outset of their participation. However, in this situation the anxiety didn't diminish; it continued to mount with each step of the demonstration. Milgram's original subjects demonstrated anxiety in their body language, hesitant speech, requests for clarification of the researcher's intent, and nervous laughter in response to the confederate's protests.

How did the teacher's experience of being shocked contribute?

The teachers were exposed to a mild form of shock during the preparation phase of the experiment. The mild level was distinctly uncomfortable but was not painful. Such exposure probably added to the sense of relief the subject had when assigned to the teaching role rather than to the learning role.

How did "luck" contribute?

The participant was assigned to be the teacher by a rigged flip of the coin, with the role of the learner left to the confederate. This assignment may have enhanced the teacher's obligation to follow through on the roles that fate had determined. Perhaps the teacher felt more justified in executing the orders since he believed he could just as easily have been assigned to the role of the learner, where he would have had to endure the discomfort of that condition.

How did the demeanor of the researcher contribute?

The demeanor and dress of the researcher were consistent with the command and power of an authority figure. The experimenter wore a lab coat and referred to himself as a "doctor." In addition, his approach to the experience was quite serious and businesslike. When teachers questioned the procedure, the researcher responded with assurance and authority that he "would take the responsibility" and that "the experiment must continue." His manner encouraged submission and dependence.

Were people more stupid back then?

Probably not. There is a strong likelihood that under conditions of anxiety and confusion we will to look to others for answers and guidance. Sometimes obedience to authority may be an adaptive and appropriate action. However, Milgram's study underscores how potentially damaging the absence of critical thinking can be when there is a possibility of doing harm to others.